Natural Enemies

Throughout the world wild animals raid crops, attack livestock, and threaten people. Wildlife pests are actively resisted by local communities while routinely 'controlled' by state authorities. Yet the background to many people–wildlife conflicts is human encroachment on wildlife territory, and some 'problem animals' may themselves become endangered and arouse conservationist concern.

Natural Enemies examines people–wildlife conflicts from a social anthropological perspective. The authors focus on the human dimension of these conflicts – an area often neglected by specialists in applied ecology and wildlife management – and on their social and political contexts. Case studies of specific conflicts are drawn from Africa, Asia, Europe and America, and feature an assortment of wild animals and birds, including chimpanzees, elephants, wild pigs, foxes, bears, wolves, pigeons and ducks.

Examining the symbolic, as well as material, dimensions of wildlife pestilence, anthropologists can reveal the cultural character of many of our 'natural enemies'. These reports from the 'front line' show that human conflict with wildlife is often an expression of conflict between people.

John Knight is Lecturer at the School of Anthropological Studies, Queen's University Belfast. He has carried out field research in Japanese mountain villages and has published widely on rural Japan.

European Association of Social Anthropologists
Series Facilitators: Jon P. Mitchell, *University of Sussex*
Sarah Pink, *University of Loughborough*

The European Association of Social Anthropologists (EASA) was inaugurated in January 1989, in response to a widely felt need for a professional association that would represent social anthropologists in Europe and foster co-operation and interchange in teaching and research. The series brings together the work of the Association's members in a series of edited volumes which originate from and expand upon the biennial EASA Conference.

Titles in the series are:

Conceptualizing Society
Adam Kuper (ed.)

Other Histories
Kirsten Hastrup (ed.)

Alcohol, Gender and Culture
Dimitra Gefou-Madianou (ed.)

Understanding Rituals
Daniel de Coppet (ed.)

Gendered Anthropology
Teresa del Valle (ed.)

Social Experience and Anthropological Knowledge
Kirsten Hastrup and Peter Hervik (eds)

Fieldwork and Footnotes
Han F. Vermeulen and Arturo Alvarez Roldan (eds)

Syncretism/Anti-syncretism
Charles Stewart and Rosalind Shaw (eds)

Grasping the Changing World
Václav Hubinger (ed.)

Civil Society
Chris Hann and Elizabeth Dunn (eds)

Nature and Society
Philippe Descola and Gisli Palsson (eds)

The Ethnography of Moralities
Signe Howell (ed.)

Inside and Outside the Law
Olivia Harris (ed.)

Anthropological Perspectives on Local Development
Simone Abram and Jacqueline Waldren (eds)

Recasting Ritual
Felicia Hughes-Freeland and Mary M. Crain (eds)

Locality and Belonging
Nadia Lovell (ed.)

Constructing the Field
Vered Amit (ed.)

Dividends of Kinship
Peter P. Schweitzer (ed.)

Audit Cultures
Marilyn Strathern (ed.)

Gender, Agency and Change
Victoria Ana Goddard (ed.)

Natural Enemies

People–wildlife conflicts in anthropological perspective

Edited by John Knight

London and New York

First published 2000
by Routledge
11 New Fetter Lane, London EC4P 4EE

Simultaneously published in the USA and Canada
by Routledge
29 West 35th Street, New York, NY 10001

Routledge is an imprint of the Taylor & Francis Group

Selection and editorial matter © 2000 John Knight; individual chapters © 2000 the contributors.

Typeset in Galliard by
M Rules
Printed and bound in Great Britain by
Biddles Ltd, Guildford and King's Lynn

All rights reserved. No part of this book may be reprinted or reproduced or utilised in any form or by any electronic, mechanical, or other means, now known or hereafter invented, including photocopying and recording, or in any information storage or retrieval system, without permission in writing from the publishers.

British Library Cataloguing in Publication Data
A catalogue record for this book is available from the British Library

Library of Congress Cataloging in Publication Data
Natural enemies: people–wildlife conflicts in anthropological perspective/edited by John Knight
  p. cm.
  Includes bibliographical references and index.
  1. Human–animal relationships. 2. Animals–Folklore.
  I. Knight, John, 1960–
  QL85 .N38 2000   00-056127
  304.2–dc21

ISBN 0-415-22441-1 (pbk)
ISBN 0-415-22440-3 (hbk)

Contents

List of contributors vii
Editor's preface ix

1 Introduction 1
JOHN KNIGHT

2 Wildlife depredations in Malawi: the historical
  dimension 36
  BRIAN MORRIS

3 Half-man, half-elephant: shapeshifting among the
  Baka of Congo 50
  AXEL KÖHLER

4 Chimpanzees as political animals in Sierra Leone 78
  PAUL RICHARDS

5 Wild pigs, 'pig-men' and transmigrants in the
  rainforest of Sumatra 104
  SIMON RYE

6 Animals behaving badly: indigenous perceptions of
  wildlife protection in Nepal 124
  BEN CAMPBELL

7 Culling demons: the problem of bears in Japan   145
   JOHN KNIGHT

8 The wolf, the Saami and the urban shaman:
   predator symbolism in Sweden   170
   GALINA LINDQUIST

9 The problem of foxes: legitimate and illegitimate
   killing in the English countryside   189
   GARRY MARVIN

10 The Great Pigeon Massacre in a deindustrializing
   American region   212
   S. HOON SONG

11 Ducks out of water: nature conservation as boundary
   maintenance   229
   KAY MILTON

   Index   249

Contributors

Ben Campbell lectures at the Department of Social Anthropology, University of Manchester and at the School of Social Relations, Keele University.

John Knight is Lecturer in Social Anthropology at Queen's University Belfast.

Axel Köhler holds a research post at the Centre for Mexican and Central American Studies in San Cristóbal de las Casas, Chiapas, Mexico.

Galina Lindquist is Research Fellow and part-time Lecturer in the Department of Social Anthropology, University of Stockholm.

Garry Marvin is Senior Lecturer in the Department of Sociology and Social Policy, University of Surrey Roehampton.

Kay Milton is Reader in Social Anthropology at Queen's University Belfast.

Brian Morris teaches anthropology at Goldsmiths College, University of London.

Paul Richards is Professor of Anthropology at University College London and Chair of the Technology and Agrarian Development (TAO) Group at Wageningen University, The Netherlands.

Simon Rye is a researcher at the Centre for Development and the Environment, University of Oslo.

S. Hoon Song is a PhD candidate in the Department of Anthropology at the University of Chicago. He is also Visiting Assistant Professor in the Department of Anthropology at George Washington University (Washington, DC).

Editor's preface

The origins of this book lie in the *Politics of Wildlife* workshop convened as part of the Fifth Conference of the European Association of Social Anthropology, held at the Johann Wolfgang Goethe University in Frankfurt in September 1998. The book chapters comprise a selection of the Frankfurt papers, along with additional papers prepared especially for this publication.

I would like to thank all of the participants in the *Politics of Wildlife* workshop, as well as the organizers of the EASA conference, especially Ms Jean Lydall, the Conference Co-ordinator. My own participation in the Frankfurt conference was supported and encouraged by the *International Institute for Asian Studies* (IIAS) in Leiden, The Netherlands, and especially its Director, Professor Wim Stokhof. Much of the editorial work that went into the preparation of this volume was done at this same institution. The final stage in the preparation of the manuscript took place in the School of Anthropological Studies at Queen's University Belfast. To both institutions and their staff I am grateful.

Encouragement, advice, suggestions and other forms of assistance which contributed to the emergence of this publication were received from Hastings Donnan, Manuel Haneveld, Cen Huang, Tim Ingold, Galina Lindquist, Kay Milton (who, among other things, suggested the title *Natural Enemies*), Shoma Munshi, Gerard Persoon, Paul Richards and Reed Wadley. I am grateful to Jon Mitchell for his valuable editorial advice in the course of preparing this book. I would also like to acknowledge the constructive criticisms and helpful suggestions made by the anonymous reader (appointed by EASA/Routledge) of this manuscript.

Finally, I would like to thank Fiona McKinley for help with the index.

Chapter 1

Introduction

John Knight

The problem

Conflict between people and wildlife is ubiquitous. Rats in Asia ruin the rice harvest, lay waste to grain stores and cause hunger and malnutrition, elephants in Africa plough up crops, bulldoze villages and cause human injury, and wild pigs everywhere feed on crops, trample fields and cause great economic loss. Jaguars in Central and South America attack cattle, tigers in India snatch village animals, and the reintroduction of wolves in Montana is opposed by ranchers fearful of livestock losses. Tigers, wolves, mountain lions, bears, dingoes and eagles all feature in occasional reports of attacks on people.[1] These are just a few examples of people–wildlife conflicts; a great many other wild animals (crows, cormorants, monkeys, hippos, crocodiles, seals, kangaroos etc.) find themselves similarly at odds with nearby human populations.

The wildlife threat elicits a variety of human responses. East African pastoralists ritually sacrifice cattle to protect sorghum and maize fields from monkeys and birds (Fukui 1996: 377), Spanish shepherds invoke Christian saints to protect their sheep from wolves (Cátedra 1992: 45), and Japanese farmers bury Buddhist amulets in their fields to ward off wild pigs, deer and monkeys (Kawaoka 1994: 720). In their struggle against rats southeast Asian villagers use traps and cages, employ rat-catching cats and dogs, and try to poison, drown and gas the hated rodents (McNeely and Sochaczewski 1994: 296). Cameroonian farmers 'sleep in the crop fields to guard them from elephants' and children 'lose many school days when they have to help their parents guard the farms or chase [away] the elephants' (Tchamba 1996: 38). American cattle ranchers, when they encounter protected wolves, simply 'shoot, shovel, and shut up' (Youngblood-Petersen 1995: 545).

Human conflicts with wildlife assume a variety of forms, take up much human time and energy, and are often multifaceted in character. People–wildlife conflict is universally found – on land and in rivers and seas, in the north and the south, in the city as well as the country – but tends to be especially marked in human settlements in forest-edge regions. As a threat to agricultural production and an impediment to rural development, wildlife depredations are an area of state concern and an object of expert intervention ('wildlife control' etc.), but also overlap with the issue of wildlife conservation (especially in the case of larger wild mammals).

A number of different kinds of people–wildlife conflict can be distinguished. These include:

- attacks on people (wild predators);
- attacks on livestock (wild predators);
- crop-raiding (wild herbivores and birds);
- forestry damage (wild herbivores);
- competition for wild forage with human gatherers, with livestock or with game animals (wild herbivores);
- competition for prey with human hunters (wild predators);
- house and other building infestations (roosting birds, rats, mice etc.); and
- threats to other natural species and to biodiversity – i.e. 'environmental pests'.

In addition, there are a number of other kinds of conflict.[2]

This book brings together ten social and cultural anthropologists to examine the phenomenon of people–wildlife conflict. Case studies of particular conflicts are drawn from Africa, Asia, Europe and America, and feature an assortment of wild animals, including predators such as lions, bears, wolves and foxes, and crop-raiders such as baboons, chimpanzees, elephants and wild pigs. In addition to these mammalian pests, two bird pests (ducks and pigeons) are examined in the final two chapters. As anthropologists, we are concerned not just with the material dimension of these examples of wildlife pestilence, but also with their social and cultural dimensions. In particular, we focus on the tensions and divisions in human society that affect conflicts with wild animals. One of the main contentions of this book is that many people–wildlife conflicts can be understood as people–people (or people–state) conflicts.

This Introduction identifies some of the main themes that emerge in this anthropological examination of people–wildlife conflicts. These themes include the socially constructed character of pestilence discourses, the relation between wildlife pestilence and conservationism, the symbolic dimension of the wildlife threat, the moral specification of dangerous animals, and the variety of ways in which conflicts with wildlife overlap with conflicts among people.

Specifying people–wildlife conflicts

There is an extensive English-language vocabulary for inconvenient, bothersome or damage-causing wild animals: 'nuisance animals', 'troublesome animals', 'problem species', 'pests', 'vermin', 'varmints', etc. As these terms suggest, the wildlife pest is defined in anthropocentric, utilitarian terms.

People–wildlife conflicts are relations of rivalry or antagonism between human beings and wild animals which typically arise from territorial proximity and involve reliance on the same resources or a threat to human wellbeing or safety. People–wildlife conflicts thus include both competition and predation: *competition* for food between humans and other animal species and wild animal *predation* on people. In the first case, the conflict is indirect in character (over a third [plant or animal] species) and between two species which (with respect to the object of competition) share the same trophic level. In the second case, the conflict takes the form of a direct antagonism between species at different levels of the food chain. This book examines both kinds of people–wildlife conflict – 'horizontal' competition and 'vertical' predation.

An important qualification must be entered here. As we are dealing with an anthropocentric phenomenon, important aspects of both kinds of conflict are not addressed in this book. Logically, competition works both ways: if wild animals are rivals for human (or human-claimed) foods or territory, human beings are also rivals for the food and territory of wild animals. Predation likewise works in both directions, involving not just wildlife attacks on people, but also human attacks on wildlife – that is, hunting. However, with respect to human livelihood, human hunting represents a different, inverse relation to wildlife in which the prey animal forms a part of (rather than a threat to) human subsistence. This book is principally concerned with the wildlife threat to people, rather than the human threat to wildlife.

A further qualification concerns the scope of the book. The people–wildlife conflicts examined in the following pages concern vertebrate pests, but clearly invertebrate pests would invite similar kinds of analysis. It is also the case that human conflict with other species extends beyond other animals to include plants – that is, weeds (see Knobloch

1996). The weed would be the vegetal counterpart of the animal pest. The farmer's crop is threatened 'horizontally' by weeds as it is 'vertically' by pests. Weeds compete with crops to grow; pests compete with the farmer for the crop. The farmer is involved in a twofold struggle – with weeds at the early stage of crop growth and with pests at later stages.

Sometimes horizontal and vertical people–wildlife relations overlap. In what is known as 'garden hunting', game animals are killed as they come to feed on (usually swidden) crops which serve, in effect, as a kind of hunting bait (Linares 1976; Wadley *et al.* 1997: 253–254). In other words, competition (between human and animal) leads to predation (human on animal). But there are other permutations: in the case of crop-raiders such as bears or livestock-predators such as tigers or wolves, 'horizontal' rivalry (over crops and livestock respectively) can lead to 'vertical' predation – that is, 'maneating'.

Anthropology and people–wildlife conflicts

There is a large and wide-ranging literature on the subject of people–wildlife conflicts. This is mainly from fields such as applied zoology, applied ecology and wildlife management, and is concerned with the measurement of wildlife damage, the assessment of wildlife pest numbers and population dynamics, the determination of the causes of pestilence, the development of technologies of damage limitation and pest control, and the application of such technologies. It is an interdisciplinary area of research which brings together many different specialists in search of practical responses and solutions to wildlife pestilence, ranging from more efficient techniques of obstruction and repulsion and more effective methods of culling and eradication, to habitat management, crop replacement, and fertility control.[3]

The topic of people–wildlife conflicts has not attracted much interest from anthropologists. Occasional references to people–wildlife conflicts are made in some of the classic works of anthropology. In *The Golden Bough* Frazer gives examples of exotic customs for controlling farm pests and other bothersome animals (Frazer 1996 [1922]: 637–638), in *Coral Gardens and Their Magic* Malinowski refers to the spells recited by Trobriander 'garden magicians' to ward off wild pigs (Malinowski 1935a: 117–119, 469n; 1935b: 48), and in *Nuer Religion* Evans-Pritchard points out the link between totemic ritual and problem animals among the Nuer ('lions should refrain from killing the cattle of those who respect them, crocodiles should not injure those who respect them, and ostriches should not eat the millet of those who respect them') (Evans-

Pritchard 1956: 79). In general, people–wildlife conflicts, if they appear in anthropological texts at all, do so in the margins and attract little, if any, analytical attention in their own right.

Yet a case can be made for anthropologists paying more attention to people–wildlife conflicts. First, conflict with wildlife is found in a great many societies. In fact, human conflict with wildlife tends to be at its sharpest in the remote, forest-edge locations where much anthropological fieldwork has been – and still is – carried out. Such conflict with wildlife is set to continue into the foreseeable future as small farmers from Brazil to Indonesia colonize frontier land in tropical forest regions (Rudel and Roper 1997).

Second, an anthropological input into the study of people–wildlife conflicts would also make a contribution to the field of wildlife management. The importance of the human aspect of wildlife management is becoming increasingly recognized among wildlife managers, especially those who deal with 'problem wildlife'.

> [A] wildlife damage manager is a professional 'buffer' between wildlife and humans, protecting humans from animals, while at the same time protecting wildlife from humans. The wildlife damage management professional needs to be able to understand humans as well as he or she understands wildlife. Ironically, this human element tends to be a weak link in our educational chain . . . [Damage managers] tend to be well-trained in their technologies and in wildlife biology, and not well-trained in sociology, anthropology, economics, history, psychology, or political science – the 'human dimension' fields.
>
> (Schmidt and Beach 1999: 2)

Anthropology is in a position to offset this deficit in understanding of the 'human dimension' of wildlife management, especially where this involves cultures different from that of the wildlife professional. One contribution anthropology can make is to document and highlight the existence of local or indigenous knowledge and practices in the area of wildlife management and control (for example, Parrish 1995).[4]

Another can be to help ensure that wildlife management strategies are culturally compatible with the local context in which they are applied. By ethnographically documenting local perspectives on wildlife, anthropology provides a cultural contextualization of wildlife that could help achieve a more locally sensitive wildlife management policy (Breitenmoser 1998: 288).

Anthropology can also contribute to wildlife management by taking it as an object of study in its own right, focusing critically on the cultural assumptions underlying it. Kay Milton has argued that 'anthropologists are well placed to become theorists of environmentalism' (1993a: 6), and the same point can be made with respect to the field of wildlife management and conservation.

People–wildlife interfaces

Many wild animals adapt to, and benefit from, humanized environments. This phenomenon of other species subsisting in human spaces is sometimes referred to as 'commensalism', the spaces involved as 'commensal habitats', and the animals in question as 'human commensals' (Southwick and Siddiqi 1994: 224). According to optimal foraging theory, wild animals 'tend to feed in a manner that maximizes their nutrient (energy, protein, minerals etc.) intake in the minimum possible time' (Sukumar 1994: 308), and anthropogenic sites can offer prime foraging opportunities. For wild predators, domestic livestock often makes for easier prey than wild herbivores; for wild herbivores, cultivated crops tend to be more appealing and digestible than wild forage. Other examples of wild animals which exploit humanized environments include house rodents, barn swallows, trawler- or tractor-following birds, garbage-raiding raccoons, and mammals and birds that feed on roadside vegetation (see Budiansky 1996: 219–221; 1999: 50–51).

In many cases, wild animals are indirectly beneficial to humans (in addition to the direct benefits wildlife brings through its contribution to livelihoods). This is most clearly the case with the natural predators of pests. Snakes keep down rat populations, birds control harmful insect populations, hedgehogs and frogs eat slugs, and wild predators such as tigers and wolves keep down the numbers of crop-raiding herbivores. But the benefits of wildlife are not confined to such 'regulatory predation' (Newsome 1991). The 'honey guide bird' (*Indicator indicator*) guides human gatherers of wild honey (Budiansky 1999: 47–49), crocodiles improve river ecosystems to the benefit of the people who depend on the river (McNeely and Sochaczewski 1994: 205), and elephants create useful inroads in the forest (Richards (1993: 151–152).[5]

Despite these human benefits of shared territoriality, wildlife proximity to human spaces often leads to conflict. The title of this book – *Natural Enemies* – refers to the rivalry between humans and animals with respect to their material conditions of existence. Much human settlement is predicated on the environmental displacement and territorial expulsion of other large mammals. This theme of an original conquest over wild animals is evident in many local rites and myths relating to land reclamation or pioneer settlement (Leach 1992: 79–80; Richards 1996: 307). Cultivators in the Trobriand Islands recite spells to expel wild pigs from the new swidden fields they cut from the forest (Malinowski 1935a: 100–101), founders of Japanese mountain villages are depicted as brave men who removed wild animals from the territory that became the village (Nebuka 1991: 52), and 'wolfers' in colonial America are remembered as 'the bulwark of western progress' because, by eradicating wolves, they made new frontier land safe for livestocking and settlement (Steinhart 1995: 41).

This people–wildlife rivalry may persist long after the human colonization of a territory because of the appeal of human spaces to many wild animals. People who live and cultivate in the forest zone must exercise constant vigilance towards the threat of wildlife forays into village space and must be prepared to violently resist invasive wildlife through regular trapping and hunting in and around the settlement. Indeed, forest-edge farming might be said to consist of two kinds of labour: the labour of production *and* the labour of protection necessary to secure the fruits of this production from the threat of wild animals.

Control of commensal and other wild pests has been routinized as civic duty in many societies. This takes the form of communal labour tasks directed to pest defences (field-guarding, patrolling, maintenance and repair of protective barriers, etc.), community pest hunts ('wolf chases', 'rattlesnake round-ups', 'pigeon-shoots', etc.), and even taxes and fines levied in pest carcasses.[6] Protection of the community from harmful animals may well be formally institutionalized as a social or political duty and publicly honoured as heroism. In Andean villages, in recognition of their efforts at protecting the communal potato crop, young male 'potato guards' are rewarded with an elevated social status (Urton 1985a: 265–266). The vanquishing of predators tends to assume a special importance. One of the roles of African kings was to defend their people from predators and other harmful animals (Simonse 1992: 265–269; see also Lienhardt 1961: 213–214, 240–241), jaguar-killing among Amerindians is 'a route to gaining and maintaining social prestige' (Saunders 1994: 107), and wolf-killers in many societies are fêted and rewarded by the wider community.[7]

Other forms in which this conflict with wildlife is culturally institutionalized include rituals, festivals and children's games. African harvest-time masquerades (in which elephant masks are worn) simulate 'elephant intrusions into human space' (Kasfir, in Ross 1992: 18), in rural Japan annual festivals (such as 'deer dances' and 'monkey-chasing festivals') ritually re-enact wildlife crop-raiding and village resistance to it (Moon 1989: 156–162; Nomoto 1995: 128), and in the livestock-based communities of northern Spain children play a wolf-hunt game in which they act out the roles of mounted hunters, horses and wolves (Fernandez 1986: 32–33). The human experience of people–wildlife conflict is therefore a twofold one: the conflict is both *directly* experienced through the confrontation itself and the protective labour entailed by it, and *indirectly* experienced through these assorted cultural practices and performances which refer to it.

Pestilence discourses

One theme running through this book is that of the distinction between wildlife pestilence and discourses of wildlife pestilence – between, as it were, objective and subjective pestilence. Many claims of wildlife pestilence are inaccurate, exaggerated or ill-founded.[8] Some claims of wildlife damage may even be 'illusory' (Putman 1989a: 9), with many supposed wildlife 'pests' serving as the 'scapegoats' of human society (Anderson *et al.* 1989: 252; Dunstone and Ireland 1989). There are a number of reasons for the exaggeration of wildlife pestilence: because inefficient farmers seek to save face, because of a desire to maximize compensation or because of inflated perceptions of risk among marginal peoples whose fears of what could happen (devastation of the whole crop by crop-raiders or lethal attacks by predators) outweigh their recognition of what generally does happen.[9]

A number of chapters in this book call into question local pestilence claims and, by extension, the 'pest control' operations which they justify. In Chapter 7 John Knight examines the bear's status as a pest in Japan and shows that, in general, the scale of concern over bears greatly exceeds the actual damage done by the animals. While bears are widely denounced as pests, there are also local voices which challenge the bear's pest status and suggest instead that, given the extent of human colonization of bear territory, it is really people who are the 'pests' in relation to bears, and not bears in relation to people.

At a time when a proposal to ban fox-hunting is being debated by the British parliament, Garry Marvin in Chapter 9 examines the well-known defence of fox-hunting in England in the name of pest control. Foxhunts are said to benefit the countryside by keeping in check a farm pest, but Marvin shows that this claim is highly questionable. First, the emergence of elite foxhunting in early modern Britain involved the rejection of the image of the fox as vermin in favour of an image of the fox as a worthy adversary. Second, foxhunting's claim to be a form of pest control begs the question of its efficiency, as opposed to other, more direct methods such as trapping.

In Chapter 10 S. Hoon Song reflects on the justification of a regional American pigeon-shoot in the name of pest control. Despite the claims of his informants that pigeons are 'rats with wings', Song concludes that local antipathy to the birds, as manifested so graphically in the pigeon-shoot, cannot be accounted for in terms of actual pigeon damage to farms or other human spaces. The shoot's claim to be a form of pest control is further undermined by the fact that most of the pigeons involved in the shoot are not local birds at all, but birds brought in from outside! Song argues that pigeon pestilence claims should be understood instead as a rationalization for a practice – pigeon-shooting – which is subject to a different set of (social and political) motivations.

These case studies challenge the self-evident status of pestilence discourses by setting them in their wider social context and analysing them alongside the cultural symbolism of the animal in question. They also recall the widely reported tendency for some animals to be selected for attention as pests, while others (though responsible for damage) receive little if any attention. In particular, the more conspicuous animals tend to receive an inordinately large share of the blame for damage – such as wild primates in East Africa (Hill 1997: 82), wolves in Indian Himalaya (Mishra 1997: 342) and bears in Arizona (Pavlik 1997: 481). Other animals, such as smaller mammals, domesticates and ferals, may, for one reason or another, be relatively ignored, despite being responsible for similar kinds of damage.[10]

Wildlife pestilence changes over time. Pest status changes according to changes in land-use. The extension of farming into the forest interior, the establishment of timber, rubber or oil palm plantations and the introduction of a livestock economy respectively make wild animals into farm pests (browsing and rooting herbivores), plantation pests (browsing and barkstripping herbivores) and livestock pests (carnivores). However, changing historical circumstances can lead to the disappearance, and not just the emergence, of wildlife pestilence. For example, the decline of swidden farming meant the end of the swidden pest; of course, farm pestilence might well continue, but permanent farms typically lack the peculiar vulnerability of swidden fields surrounded by forest (Mehta and Kellert 1998: 330).

The threshold of tolerance of damage also changes over time. Wildlife damage has often been treated as natural or axiomatic; many cultivators expect a certain amount of loss to wildlife. For example, in Chapter 2 Brian Morris points out that Malawian farmers have a saying that 'in planting maize you need to put three seeds in the hole – one for yourself, one for the guinea-fowl, and one for the bush pig', and similar sayings have been reported elsewhere (for example, Sutlive 1978: 75). However, in the modern era wildlife damage becomes the object of a new kind of social accounting. Pesticides and other new technological inputs, because of their promises of preventability, can have the effect of lowering a farmer's tolerance of damage, which is consequently denaturalized to become 'pestilence'.

In addition to the focus on particular pestilence discourses, we should recognize the dualistic character of pestilence discourse in general. Despite the reality of people–wildlife co-territoriality and co-existence outlined above, pestilence discourses are premised on a dichotomous view of people–wildlife relations, according to which wild animals in human space are deemed unnatural and something to be removed. Such dichotomies are of course familiar to anthropologists; the related dichotomies of nature–society and nature–culture have been the focus for much critical reflection within the discipline.[11]

More specifically, anthropology has helped to demonstrate the variation in cultural understandings to which wild animals are subject. Certainly, the idea of wilderness, as a category of environmental space beyond human control, is evident in many cultures (Descola and Pálsson 1996b: 9–10), and it would follow that the idea of wild animals as animals beyond human control (in contrast to tame animals) is also widely held. However, anthropologists have shown that in other cultures wild animals may not be viewed as beyond human control: many hunter-gatherer groups believe that they can influence the behaviour and reproduction of prey animals through ritual activity (Ellen 1996: 117; Howell 1996: 136). Nor is the opposition between wild and domestic animals universal: in some cases it is undermined by a belief that the realm of the wild is a kind of domesticated order in its own right and that the animals in question are herded by a spirit guardian with which human beings enter into a relationship (Reichel-Dolmatoff 1985: 119–120; Descola 1996: 257–258).

The anthropological critique of pestilence claims would therefore range from (ethnographically informed) 'reality checking' into particular local contexts of supposed pestilence to a (theoretically based) questioning of the assumptions underlying pestilence discourse in general. Moreover, the analysis of pestilence discourse extends, as we shall see, to the areas of symbolism and morality. But first, we should recognize that the dualistic categorization of wildlife is also found within conservationism. Indeed, pestilence discourses that exclude wildlife from the human realm recall conservationist discourses that exclude human beings from the natural realm.

Conservationism

Many of the animal pests discussed in this book are also objects of outside conservationist concern. The chapters that follow feature a number of what might be called *(inter)nationally protected local pests*. The notion of the *protected pest* is somewhat counterintuitive because pests tend to be associated with excess and proliferation and do not therefore self-evidently seem to be in need of protection. But the background to wildlife pestilence is often one of habitat depletion, the effect of which is *both* to endanger the reproduction of wild animal populations and to displace these animals on to human territories in a kind of compression effect. Larger mammals, because of their sizeable home ranges, tend to be particularly vulnerable to habitat loss.

Although wildlife pestilence arises in large part from the human colonization of animal territories, pestilence can also be exacerbated, even generated, by conservationism. Much wildlife conservationism is based on a dualistic view of nature and society, according to which nature is a sphere that should be free from human resource appropriation. According to this kind of conservationism, sometimes referred to as 'preservationism', the presence of local people tends to be viewed as the problem and their removal from protected areas in favour of wildlife populations the solution. Some critics even see modern wildlife conservationism as a new kind of authoritarianism which creates a *'lebensraum'* for protected animals that are free to invade vulnerable rural communities (Guha 1997: 16).

The clash between wildlife pestilence and conservationism is mentioned in a number of chapters. National parks and other wildlife reserves make up one much reported source of people–wildlife conflicts,[12] and in Chapter 6 of this book Ben Campbell describes one such site of conflict in Nepal. Tamang villagers living next to Langtang National Park have little share of the wealth generated from park tourism, but incur major costs in the form of restricted access to the natural resources of the park and increased vulnerability to park wildlife (which they are not allowed to control themselves). The local sense of inequity at this state of affairs disposes the villagers to try to get something back – by 'poaching' park animals or by collecting grasses inside the park – and thereby restore some degree of balance in the village–park relationship. But in the longer term, the effect of the de-linkage of park wildlife from village livelihoods, encouraged by the preservationist views of nature on which the national park as an institution is founded, is to make local people hostile to wildlife conservation.

Even in the absence of a wildlife reserve, crop-raiders or livestock-killers receive national legal protection or are the object of national conservation campaigns. In some cases, strong (inter)national concern for wildlife can lead to the alienation of local people from the wild animals in question, which come to be associated with outside interference. In Chapter 8 Galina Lindquist shows how, for the Saami reindeer-herders of northern Sweden, the wolf is a local pest, which, incongruously, enjoys national protection. The reindeer-herders feel powerless to challenge this national conservationism; in desperation, they attempt to shock the rest of Sweden into recognition of their problems by high profile protests such as that staged in the run-up to Christmas in 1995 when in a public square in Stockholm they dumped the dead bodies of reindeer killed by protected predators, to the horror of the Christmas shoppers passing-by.

Dualistic conservationism is also evident in the case study of the ruddy duck campaign presented by Kay Milton in Chapter 11. But in contrast to the usual scenario, whereby outside conservationist involvement is in defence of an animal deemed locally to be a pest, in the ruddy duck problem it is (inter)national level conservationism which specifies the duck as a pest to be culled, while local land-users generally tolerate its presence. Milton shows that one of the boundaries that the conservationists attempt to maintain, in addition to the species boundary (threatened by hybridization), is the nature–culture boundary, based on the idea of nature as a sphere which excludes all human agency and contact. Because of the human involvement in the spread of the North American ruddy duck in Britain and continental Europe, these new duck populations (in the words of one conservationist) have 'nothing to do with nature'.

The kind of exclusionary conservationism evident in these examples has attracted much criticism from anthropologists and other scholars. A new conservationist orthodoxy – variously known as 'community-based management', 'co-management' and 'participatory conservation' – has emerged in which emphasis is placed on the involvement and participation of the local population in conservation initiatives.[13] One of the main arguments for participatory conservation (in addition to that of equity) is in terms of efficacy – that local inclusion makes for more effective wildlife management because, in order to become committed to conservation initiatives, local people require 'incentives' or 'benefits'

(Jusoff and Majid 1995; Heinen 1996). In other words, where wildlife is useful to local people, they will conserve it.

Much local or participatory conservationism appears to be premised on such utilitarian logic. But this is the same utilitarian logic, *mutatis mutandis*, on which pestilence discourses tend to be based. This raises the following question: What about situations in which wildlife is use*less* rather than useful, or indeed harmful rather than beneficial? It follows from the utilitarian reasoning above that, where such a local stake in wildlife is absent or, *a fortiori*, where this or that wild animal is a source of disutility (as in the case of the pest), conservation would be locally ineffective. The only local 'incentives' offered by the pest would be to its eradication rather than conservation.

On narrow utilitarian grounds, the argument could be made that it is totally rational for livestock herders to remove wolves that threaten their livestock, for farmers to eliminate wild pigs that raid their crops or for fishermen to cull seals that deplete their fish stocks. To the extent that wild animal numbers are excessive, conservation arguments would not apply, but, as we have seen, many wildlife pests are in fact endangered and therefore do merit conservationist concern. The new utilitarianism would appear to offer little basis for the conservation of animals locally viewed as obnoxious and dispensable.[14]

The phenomenon of the *endangered pest* poses a challenge to the new conservationist orthodoxy because its utilitarian logic offers no obvious grounds for conservation. However, many anthropologists would point out that utility is not the sole basis of local evaluations of wildlife to begin with, and would argue that the symbolism of wild animals also needs to be taken into account. Utilitarianism is an important basis for the appraisal of wildlife, but it does not follow that local views of wildlife can be reduced to a simple utilitarian calculus. One main objection to applied utilitarianism – whether in the form of pestilence or conservationist discourse – is that, in assuming the existence of local utilitarian determinations independent of cultural context, it neglects the fact that much of the human experience of nature, including wildlife, is symbolically mediated.

Symbolism

Anthropologists have contributed to the understanding of human–animal relations through their emphasis on the symbolic aspect of these relations. In Lévi-Strauss's famous critique of the functionalist explanation of totemic animals (and plants), the particular species 'are chosen not because they are "good to eat" but because they are "good to think"' (Lévi-Strauss 1969: 162). Much of the subsequent anthropological work on animals has documented the human practice of thinking with or 'signifying' animals in different cultures (Willis 1990; see also Shanklin 1985; Urton 1985b). Central to this structuralist approach to animal symbolism has been an emphasis on the role of classification in fixing the meanings of animals.

Symbolic analyses of human–animal relations have spread beyond anthropology to the other human sciences. There are even examples where scientific specialists on wildlife pestilence have incorporated some of the insights of symbolic analysis. The following definition of pests was put forward in the Introduction to a book on mammalian pestilence:

> much as we may define a weed as a plant in the wrong place, or a pollutant as a perfectly respectable chemical in the wrong place or in inappropriate concentration, so some animal pests too are only pests when in inappropriate numbers or in the wrong context.
> (Putman 1989a: 2)

For anthropologists, such comments readily recall the work of Mary Douglas on pollution beliefs according to which 'dirt' is 'matter out of place' (Douglas 1966: 35) and therefore a product of social understandings of environmental order. Along similar lines, pests would become examples of *animals out of place* (and indeed of *dirty* animals *par excellence* – 'filthy vermin', 'dirty rats', and so on). In her examination in this book of the reaction against introduced ruddy ducks in Europe ('environmental pests'), Kay Milton draws on this insight (entitling her chapter, 'Ducks out of water').

The disorderly character of pests readily follows from structuralist models of animal symbolism. According to structuralist principles, culture consists of the dichotomous ordering of the world into so many discrete classes, but certain phenomena resist such classificatory schemes and are consequently viewed as anomalous. A wide variety of 'anomalous animals' have been identified in the anthropological literature, including the pig, the cassowary, the monkey and the whale.[15] These are all physically anomalous animals, but another common form of animal anomaly is in terms of space. Where space is culturally divided into different spheres, each of which carries a distinctive moral evaluation, it can serve as a basic classifier of animals. Among Lele animals, the pangolin, the wild pig, the baboon and the antelope are all anomalous because, despite being land mammals, they are also associated with a different sort of space – water (Douglas 1975: 282, 301–302).[16] Another kind of boundary-breaching arises with domestic animals: as animals that straddle the nature–culture boundary, livestock (and pets) have also been ascribed an anomalous status by anthropologists.[17]

Routine territorial boundary-crossing behaviour forms another basis of anomalous status. Where such mobility occurs, the spatially based taxonomic order is threatened, with the result that a particular moral significance attaches to the animal in question. In the well-known example from rural Thailand offered by Stanley Tambiah, the buffalo, civet cat, toad and otter are all marked as anomalous creatures because of their perceived spatial boundary-crossing behaviour (Tambiah 1969: 450–451; see also Condominas 1994: 116–117; Jackson 1975: 398–399). A number of scholars, including anthropologists, have applied this perspective to wildlife pests: rodents in Britain are disgusting and inedible because they are beasts of the field which invade the human domain of the house (Fiddes 1991: 142–143), hyenas are stigmatized because (in addition to their apparent sexual ambiguity) they cross culturally important spatial boundaries when disturbing gravesites (Glickman 1995: 527–528), and coyotes are tricksters because they inhabit 'liminal regions' (Meléndez 1987: 204).

A major influence in this style of analysis has been Edmund Leach, who, in a famous essay on animal symbolism, interpreted 'vermin' in terms of boundary-crossing – as an intermediate category of animals that breach symbolically marked spatial boundaries (Leach 1964: 45). One of the animals mentioned by Leach in his study of English conceptions of social space was the fox, and in Chapter 9 of this book Garry Marvin, in his examination of the symbolic logic of English foxhunting, critically engages with Leach's argument that foxes have a special anomalous or ambiguous status because they straddle the boundary between field animals and remote wild animals. In short, this anthropological perspective suggests that at least some wildlife pestilence is about boundary-crossing animal behaviour as such as much as its economic consequences.

Whether 'anomalous' or not, wildlife pests are frequently the object of negative symbolism and liable to be attributed an immoral character. Crop-raiding wild primates are 'thieves' in Uganda (Naughton-Treves 1997: 41), 'criminals' in Japan (Knight 1999: 628), and an evil omen among Costa Rican Amerindians (Gonzalez-Kirchner and Sainz de la Maza 1998: 17). Wild predators invite especially strong moral condemnation as violent deviants: in parts of Africa the leopard is an 'evil' animal (Douglas 1975: 301), in Spain wolves and bears are 'accursed animals'

(Cátedra 1992: 328–330), and in North America predators are 'natural born killers' (grizzly bears) (Kellert *et al.* 1996: 983), 'serial killers' (mountain lions) (Wolch *et al.* 1997: 109), and even 'the Saddam Hussein of the Animal World' (wolves) (Grooms 1993: 141).

In this volume too we encounter examples of negative anthropomorphic terminology applied to animal pests. Japanese newspapers refer to bears as 'criminals' which merit 'the death penalty' (Chapter 7); Saami reindeer-herders liken wolves to 'thieves' (Chapter 8); foxes in medieval England were 'assassins' and 'murderers' (Chapter 9); pigeons in rural Pennsylvania are seen as AIDS-carriers (Chapter 10); and ruddy ducks from Britain mating with native ducks in continental Europe are 'lager louts' (Chapter 11).[18]

If, as many of these examples suggest, pestilence is crime, pest control becomes a kind of law enforcement. In sixteenth-century France rats were accused by an ecclesiastical court of having 'feloniously eaten up and wantonly destroyed the barley-crop' of a certain province (Evans 1906: 18), in early modern England foxes were trapped and killed using a 'noose . . . as if they [were] human criminals' (Fissell 1999: 11), and on British shooting estates use is still made of 'gamekeepers' "gibbets" where the corpses of weasels, stoats, rats, crows and other vermin are displayed, ostensibly to serve as a warning to others' (Serpell 1996: 200). Predator control is especially prone to take on a 'moralizing' character: in the American mid-west, according to one widespread view, '[y]ou don't just kill a predator, you execute him' (in Steinhart 1995: 56).

The moral specification of wildlife does not always have this absolute character. Underlying many people–wildlife conflicts are ideas of balance and reciprocity, with respect to which the behaviour of this or that animal may be deemed to be problematical. In seventeenth-century England, '[b]ooks on vermin-killing often noted that vermin died because they ate "greedily"', this invocation of 'greed' serving to 'displace any anxieties about killing vermin . . . as though the vermin invited their own deaths because of their greedy behaviour' (Fissell 1999: 5). Predators too are condemned for 'greed', 'avarice' and 'blood lust' (Meléndez 1987: 204; Worster 1977: 277). This perception is reinforced by the phenomenon of surplus damage or surplus killing. In this book, Japanese farmers complain that bears cause wanton damage to crops (Chapter 7), Saami reindeer-herders complain of excessive wolf-predation (Chapter 8), and English farmers complain that foxes kill more hens or lambs than they eat and are 'vicious' animals guilty of 'senseless' killing (Chapter 9).

However, the logic of reciprocity can also work the other way round, such that destructive wildlife behaviour points not to animal immorality but to earlier morally questionable *human* conduct. According to Quechua mythology, pumas (mountain lions) 'eat the llamas of guilty people' (Zuidema 1985: 192); in the Trobriand islands wild pig damage to taro gardens is evidence of earlier illicit human behaviour (such as fornication) near the fields affected or of malevolent human sorcery (Malinowski 1935a: 119); and in southeast Asia tiger attacks can be interpreted as punishments of those who have sex outside marriage, those who usurp the rights of others, and, more generally, those who ignore the Prophet's teachings.[19] Wildlife damage or attacks become acts of judgement against the people who suffer them.

Shapeshifting

There is another respect in which wildlife dangers point to human immorality. The above specification of natural predation in human terms would seem to indicate an underlying concern with *human* predation. The connection is only reinforced when human violence and killing are denounced in the idiom of natural predation – when criminals and war enemies are branded 'jackals', 'wolves', 'mad dogs', etc. These idiomatic crossovers give expression to a pervasive human belief in (and fear of) human–animal continuity with respect to predation. Predatory animal behaviour disturbs not just because it is an outside threat, but also because it is potentially internal to the realm of human actions. The predator looms large in the pervasive human belief in 'the beast within', according to which human beings have inside them an animal core, and human morality is predicated on controlling and transcending this inner animal element (Midgley 1979; Salisbury 1994). One of the most striking expressions of this concern with the predatory potential of human beings is the belief in human-to-animal shapeshifting.

Shapeshifting beliefs have been widely documented, from werewolf lore in Europe to beliefs involving elephants, baboons and chimpanzees in West Africa, jaguars in Central and South America, tigers, crocodiles and wild pigs in Indonesia, and foxes in Japan.[20] In shapeshifting beliefs the behavioural overlap between wild predator and human being arises from temporary physical identity, and the human relation to predation moves from latent potential to occasional or periodic actualization. The were-animal is an outwardly, and not just inwardly, transformed person. Striking examples of such human-to-animal shapeshifting beliefs are presented by Axel Köhler (Chapter 3), Paul Richards (Chapter 4) and Simon Rye (Chapter 5) in relation to elephants, chimpanzees and wild pigs respectively.

All three animals are pests, but some are much more serious than others. Among Javanese rice farmers in Sumatra, crop-raiding wild pigs are a major livelihood threat, and call into question the viability of farming on the edge of the rainforest. For Baka hunter-gatherers, elephants are the prime game animal on which livelihood depends, but elephants can also actively interfere with Baka livelihood in certain ways. Although elephant crop-raiding is not a significant problem among Baka foragers (as it is for nearby Bantu farmers), elephants compete for the wild plants gathered by the Baka and destroy Baka campsites. Among the Mende villagers of Sierra Leone, chimpanzees are occasional raiders of cocoa and fruit crops. But unlike the Sumatran case, in neither of these African examples are the animals a serious livelihood threat. Both elephants and chimpanzees are capable of horrific acts of lethal violence against the human beings they encounter, and to this extent pose a physical threat to people living in or near the forest, but the full horror of such violent actions has to do with the suspicions of human involvement through shapeshifting that they arouse. Notwithstanding the physical dangers involved, the major threat posed by these animals would appear to be a *moral* one.

If, as noted above, wildlife crop-raiding threatens symbolically important spatial boundaries, shapeshifting threatens the very distinction between humans and animals. Because of their radical, boundary-breaching character, one would expect were-animals, even more than the anomalous animal mentioned above, to arouse a strong human reaction. Thus some historians account for the fear of werewolves in medieval Europe in terms of anxiety over boundary-breaching and interpret the violent punishment of werewolves as a means of boundary restoration on the part of society (Cohen 1994: 65). The fear generated by were-chimpanzees, were-elephants and were-pigs might be similarly understood in terms of an elemental concern over boundary-breaching, especially where this involves human beings taking on the aggressive and predatory nature of dangerous animals. But there are important differences in the way in which the Baka, the Mende and the Javanese migrants view the social distribution of this human predatory potential.

In the case of the 'human elephants' of Central Africa and the 'human chimpanzees' of West Africa, local people attribute the capacity for metamorphosis to themselves and to others. For the villagers of Sierra Leone, 'chimpanzee business' (attacks on people by human chimpanzees) is something of which everyone is capable, even though it is particularly associated with the 'mandingo' chiefs (of outside origin) of the past who sold local people into slavery. But in the were-pig beliefs of the Javanese transmigrants on Sumatra described by Rye, this power is exclusively attributed to *others* – the tribal peoples of the rainforest. This would suggest a suspicion among the new migrants that these forest-dwellers covet their rice, and recalls other documented shapeshifting beliefs involving farm-raiding wild pigs (Ruel 1970: 341; see also Reichel-Dolmatoff 1985: 133–134).

One reaction to beliefs in shapeshifting might be to treat them as cultural residues or 'survivals' from a traditional past, with little connection to recent history. But modern history, rather than simply erasing such beliefs, can sustain or even accentuate them. Richards relates the Mende belief in 'chimpanzee business' to the Atlantic slave trade, which left a profound legacy of distrust among villagers in their rulers. He also suggests that the recent civil war in Sierra Leone only exacerbates fears about the predatory character of people, lending credence to the idea that people can turn into violent chimpanzees, and that this situation only worsens the conservation prospects of an animal that locally epitomizes illicit violence. The were-pig beliefs reported by Rye are similarly infused by recent history: the 'pig-man' lurking in the forest can be understood as an animal idiom which expresses social tensions arising from the new ethnic interface created by the Indonesian policy of large-scale Javanese transmigration to outer islands.

Of course, this is only part of the story. Animal predators can attract human admiration just as they can (and, in part, *because* they can) arouse human fear. Well-documented examples of positive predator symbolism include the wolf in native North America (wolf warrior societies etc.) (Lopez 1995: Ch. 6), the tiger in Asia (Wessing 1986), and the jaguar in Central and South America (Saunders 1990; 1994). This book too offers examples of predators serving as legitimate natural symbols of social power. As Brian Morris shows (Chapter 2), Malawian farmers may fear lions, but their chiefs were associated with these arch-predators: the chief – that lion among men – would be reincarnated as a lion after his death. Among Japanese mountain villagers the bear is not just feared as a bloodthirsty 'demon', but is also admired for its great power, and among hunters is even an animal model of masculinity (Chapter 7).

In her chapter, Lindquist examines the contrast between the romantic appeal of wolves, lynxes and bears in urban Swedish society and the fear aroused by these predators among Saami reindeer-herders. A group of New Age 'neo-shamans' in Stockholm adopt and incorporate wild predators as guides or 'Power Animals' in their inner journeys of spiritual development. Lindquist gives examples of shamanic practitioners who draw on their inner wolf or bear to deal with difficult situations in their personal or professional lives, particularly where they need to overcome stress and anxiety when dealing with other people. The inner predator, by teaching the shaman how to summon up fierceness and other qualities of strength and power, facilitates human self-assertion and, ultimately, a transformed relation to the wider world. This New Age movement in effect *converts* the wolf from an object of (natural) fear to a remedy for (social) fear.

This belief in invisible 'Power Animals' can be seen as a kind of inversion of shapeshifting beliefs. In both cases human beings become animals or animal-like, but while in shapeshifting a physical transformation occurs, in the activation of a Power Animal what takes place is a behavioural transformation as the human form remains constant. The neo-shamans of Stockholm are not *shape*shifting (their appearance does not change) but *mind*shifting (they adopt the disposition of the animal).

Social determinations

Shapeshifting beliefs are not present in most people–wildlife conflicts. But such striking beliefs, exceptional as they may be, do serve to underline a more general point: that many apparent conflicts with wildlife have to do with tensions, divisions and antagonisms on the human side as much as actual animal depredations. The examples of 'natural enemies' presented in this book suggest that much wildlife pestilence is not reducible to an elemental conflict between people and wildlife, but is also the site of conflict with other people.

Three different relations between these two dimensions of wildlife conflicts – between natural and social enmities, as it were – can be distinguished. First, human social divisions are present in conflict *with* wildlife. One aspect of this concerns the differential exposure of people to wildlife damage. As Ben Campbell (Chapter 6) shows for Nepalese villagers, poorer, forest-edge farmers are often disproportionately affected, and in effect serve to buffer wealthier farmers from wildlife crop damage. In some cases, vulnerable farmers are immigrants forced by poverty to farm at the forest-edge, an instance of which is provided by the Sumatran case described by Simon Rye in Chapter 5 (see also Hill 1997; Naughton-Treves 1997: 37–38). Another way in which divisions among people inform conflict with wildlife is the anthropomorphic symbolism applied to wildlife pestilence noted above, whereby people–wildlife conflicts are represented in (and polarized by) idioms of human conflict such as crime and war.

Second, human divisions are evident in conflict *over* wildlife. People with different relations to wildlife have different interests in it. Insofar as wildlife pestilence is land-use-specific, where there are multiple human land-uses there will be multiple, and sometimes opposed, views of the animal in question. The wild herbivore may be a resource for the hunter but a pest for the farmer; the wild predator may be an enemy of the shepherd but an ally of the crop farmer (insofar as it helps control crop-raiding herbivores). Some of the conflicts over wildlife featured in this book involve an opposition between local farmers or livestockers and non-local conservationism – such as the conflicts over national park wildlife in Nepal (Chapter 6), bears in Japan (Chapter 7) and wolves in Sweden (Chapter 8).

Secondary conflict over wildlife can also be *generated by* the primary conflict with wildlife, especially where the latter involves lethal human violence against animals (Lee 1988; Einarsson 1993). A number of examples of such controversies are reported in this book. Bear-culling in rural Japan is condemned by urban public opinion (Chapter 7), Saami killing of wolves in defence of reindeer is denounced in the Swedish mass media and punished by the Swedish state (Chapter 8), English fox-hunts (which ostensibly remove fox pests) occasion vociferous protest from opponents (Chapter 9), animal rights protesters picket the annual pigeon-shoot (which ostensibly removes pigeon pests) in the Pennsylvanian town of Hegins and even get into fights with local people (Chapter 10), and the campaign to remove the North American ruddy duck from Europe is condemned as (and conservationists denounced for) 'ethnic cleansing', 'xenophobia' and 'genocide' (Chapter 11).

Yet the distinction between these two levels of antagonism often becomes blurred as national controversy over local people–wildlife conflicts in turn inflects such conflicts, altering their character. When urbanites condemn rural culling or champion predator conservation, this outside interference may further charge the rural conflict with wild animals, which come to be associated or identified with their urban defenders and even become highly charged symbols of outside domination (Moore 1994; Wilson 1997; Breitenmoser 1998: 287–288). At this point, crop-raiding herbivores or livestock-killing predators become a dual – material *and* symbolic – threat. Many of the wildlife conflicts presented in this book are overdetermined in this way.

Third, human conflicts are sometimes *projected on to* wildlife. In some cases, as noted above, the reality of the claimed animal damage or threat is questionable or at least exaggerated, and the salient conflict is actually a human one. The ostensive conflict with wildlife may in fact be a symbolic vehicle for the expression of a social conflict between people. This is suggested by Song's analysis of the pigeon issue in Pennsylvania in which he argues that the underlying conflict is a social one which has to do with the experience of marginality among the inhabitants of this part of deindustrializing America. The pigeons are the focus of this conflict because, through the animal welfare concern attracted by the pigeon-shoot, the birds come to be associated with aspects of urban American society (drug-addiction, abortion and moral decline generally) towards which feelings of anxiety and hostility *already* exist. The pigeons express a wider social division that does not derive from the pigeon-shoot but is activated by it.

People–wildlife conflicts are vehicles for social aggregation as well as sources of social division. In her analysis of 'natural dangers', Mary Douglas argued that natural threats to human wellbeing are important political and ideological instruments of social integration: the moral construction of natural dangers serves to 'uphold community values' (Douglas 1992: 4) and even to constitute a group (Douglas 1992: 77; Douglas and Wildavsky 1982: 138–139). As one category of 'natural danger', wildlife pestilence too would have a generative potential: by identifying social others with the wildlife threat, it can serve to constitute or reinforce in-group boundaries. Viewed in these dynamic terms, the 'people' of the people–wildlife conflict ceases to be a given or fixed category, but emerges in a complex *process* of conflict that may well span local, national and international levels. Many of the wildlife conflicts featured in this book can be understood in terms of such social galvanization.

An increasingly important factor in the social determination of people–wildlife conflict is the state. Many human conflicts with wildlife are informed by people–state conflict. When wild animals become the object of official protection measures, whether in the name of game management or wildlife conservation, local victims of wildlife damage may well attribute blame to, and seek political redress from, state authorities. Montana ranchers oppose not just the reintroduced wolf but also the national authorities that champion wolf conservation; one pamphlet they produced even portrayed 'a wolf dressed as a Washington bureaucrat' (Moulton and Sanderson 1997: 54). This association between problem wildlife and the state is also evident in the local demands sometimes made that the state take away 'its' animals to its own territory: in response to federal conservationist pressure, the Montana ranchers above had a resolution passed by the state legislature calling for wolves to be introduced to Washington DC (Primm and Clark 1996: 1037), while officials trying to explain the need to protect lions to Gujarati villagers near an Asiatic lion sanctuary were told 'to take all the lions with them to Delhi' (Sukumar 1994: 315).

In this book the state is implicated as a blameworthy antagonist in conflicts between Tamang villagers and national park wildlife (Chapter 6), between Japanese mountain villagers and bears (Chapter 7), and between Saami reindeer herders and wolves (Chapter 8). In this last case, the Saami herders associate the wolves which kill their reindeer with the wider Swedish society and state which accords the predator legal protection: 'Lapps and reindeer don't count in your Swedish society. When wolves rip off the flesh of our reindeer, the friends of animals and the bureaucrats say nothing.' For these remote Saami villagers, the reindeer's vulnerability to the wolf is readily suggestive of their own marginality in the modern Swedish nation-state.

Beyond natural enemies

Finally, the question might be raised as to the wider political implications of an anthropological knowledge of people–wildlife conflict. There is a tendency for anthropologists to highlight the existence of local level people–wildlife conflicts by way of challenging the national domination of the remote peoples they so often study. From this perspective, conservationism can appear an idiom of social domination. In a world where remote peoples are often unfairly exposed to assorted environmental risks and dangers, this advocacy role is of obvious importance. Yet, alongside the seeming absence of any symmetrical anthropological advocacy *vis-à-vis* the endangered wild animals involved in such conflicts, it might well appear to confirm the not uncommon view of anthropology as an incorrigibly anthropocentric discipline. 'Alas, there exists no anthropology of animals, only an (anthropocentric) anthropology of humans in relation to animals' (Noske 1997: 169).

On this reckoning, this book might well appear to fall squarely within the tradition of anthropocentric anthropology. The discourse of people–wildlife conflicts or wildlife pestilence is clearly an anthropocentric one; this book does not explicitly address the issue of how people interfere with the livelihoods of wild animals, even though the background to many of the conflicts examined is precisely that of human encroachment into animal territory and human obstruction of animal feeding behaviour. The effect of pestilence discourses is to make the wild animal the problem, and to obscure the circumstances in human society that have led to or exacerbated the conflict with wildlife. A book on *wildlife–people conflicts* would read very differently from this one.

Given that the intellectual practices of anthropology have often led to 'animal objectification' (Noske 1997: 168) and served to 'police' the human–animal boundary (Roebroeks 1995), it might seem to follow that a book by anthropologists on people–wildlife conflicts (especially one entitled *Natural Enemies*) would be doubly disposed to anthropocentrism. But to focus on the human perspectives on this relation is not in itself illegitimate; what matters is how such perspectives are analytically treated. The contributors to this book would oppose the implication that anthropology is condemned simply to reproduce the anthropocentrism (or indeed ecocentrism) of the people it studies.

The aim is rather to contextualize and render intelligible the phenomenon of human antagonism towards animals as a step towards reflexively engaging with it. This begins with the conventional anthropological procedure of culturally specifying, and thereby denaturalizing, the object of study – that is, showing the cultural character of 'natural enemies'. But it then advances this critique one stage further to that other, more elemental anthropological interface – with those animal 'others' which make us human (see Shepard 1996). A truly reflexive anthropology would be one able to transcend its anthropic insularity to the point where the liberal ideal of challenging xenophobia naturally extends to zoophobia. A discipline that routinely questions the objectification of other people can also contest the objectification of other animals.

Acknowledgements

I would like to thank Professor Hastings Donnan (Queen's University Belfast), Dr Kay Milton (Queen's University Belfast) and Dr Reed Wadley (International Institute for Asian Studies, Leiden) for their valuable comments on an earlier draft of this Introduction.

Notes

1   On rat damage, see McNeely and Sochaczewski (1994: 290–298) and Islam and Karim (1995). On elephant damage, see Barnes (1996) and Tchamba (1996). On wild pig damage, see Naughton-Treves (1998) for Africa; Merrigi and Saachi (1992) for Europe; and Brooks *et al.* (1989) and Gold and Gujar (1997) for Asia. On jaguar attacks on cattle, see Weber and Rabinowitz (1996); on tiger livestock predations in India, see Sukumar (1994); and on opposition to wolf reintroduction, see Fritts *et al.* (1997). On claims of wolves snatching children in India see Rangarajan (1996: 25); on mountain lion attacks on humans in North America, see Beier (1991); on claimed dingo child-snatching, see Marcus (1989); and on claims of bald eagles snatching children see Lawrence (1990: 66).

2 Other kinds of wildlife pestilence involve garden damage (to flowers etc.), traffic accidents (road collisions (deer, elk etc.), bird strikes on aircraft), and disease (wildlife as vectors of disease) – for overviews, see Hone (1994) and Trout (1997).
3 See the volumes by Putman (1989b), Hone (1994), and Berwick and Saharia (1995), and the many specialized journals such as *International Journal of Pest Management* and *Tropical Pest Management*.
4 For examples of ritual measures used against wildlife pests, such as ritual medicines and charms, see Melland (1923: 234), Gelfand (1967: 143–144), and Sunseri (1997: 242).
5 A further contribution claimed for commensal wild animals is that they may have been the forerunners of domesticates. According to this processual view of domestication, wild animals were drawn to areas of human settlement as scavengers, but gradually became domesticated as a result of this proximity (Zeuner 1963: 39–45; Budiansky 1999).
6 On communal labour tasks directed to maintaining villages defences (building and repairing protective walls, checking traps etc.) in Japan, see Sutô (1991: 156). On collective wolf hunts, see Rheinheimer (1995: 281) and Moore (1994); on annual 'rattlesnake round-ups' in Oklahoma, Texas and New Mexico, see DiSilvestro (1991: 170–176), Weir (1992), and Moulton and Sanderson (1997: 213–215); and on pigeon-shoots, see Song, this volume, Chapter 10. On wolf-skin taxes and fines in Europe and early colonial America, see Harting (1994: 12–13) and DiSilvestro (1991: 93–4); on rat levies (for example, twenty-five dead rats to be produced by would-be bridegrooms in Central Java), see McNeely and Sochaczewski (1994: 296).
7 See, for example, Behar (1986: 211, 368) for wolf-killing celebrations in Spain; Moore (1994: 82) for Greece; and Hiraiwa (1992: 132–133) for Japan.
8 See, for example, White (1995: 232–233) on claims of elephant damage in colonial Rhodesia; Gipson and Ballard (1998) on claims of wolf damage in the American West; and Siex and Struhsaker (1999) on claims of colobus monkey damage in Zanzibar.
9 On reasons for exaggeration, see Sutlive (1978: 80); Cozza *et al.* (1996: 335); and Naughton-Treves (1997: 35).
10 On small animals, such as rodents, as neglected pests (despite being responsible for more actual farm damage than larger animals), see Naughton-Treves (1998: 163) and Descola (1996: 166). Both authors point out that this has to do with the fact that, while frequent, the gravity of these attacks on crops are much lower than the larger animals. On livestock animals as crop-raiders, see Ivens (1927: 356) and dogs as predators of livestock (Dwyer 1990: 55–56). On feral animals as pests, see Cowan and Tyndale-Biscoe (1997: 33–34).
11 See the collections of MacCormack and Strathern (1980), Croll and Parkin (1992), Milton (1993b), and Descola and Pálsson (1996a).
12 See, for example, Naughton-Treves (1998), Parry and Campbell (1992), and Tisdell and Zhu (1998).
13 See, for example, Taylor (1994), Orlove and Brush (1996), and Vandergeest (1996).
14 The utilitarian response to this dilemma would be to call for novel forms of local exploitation of the wild animal in question that enable local human

populations to become 'stakeholders' in a valuable wildlife 'resource' rather than victims of wildlife pestilence (Thomas 1994; see also Barnes 1996: 72–73; Kiley-Worthington 1997: 466–469). However, many of the new forms of wildlife exploitation (such as tourism) involve some form of territorial confinement and even provisioning of wild animals, raising the obvious objection that they compromise the 'wild' status of the wildlife.

15 These references are to the pig of the Old Testament which is a cloven-hoofed non-ruminant (Douglas 1966: 55); the cassowary among the Karam of New Guinea which, being wingless and bipedal with human-like leg bones, is a human-like bird (Bulmer 1967: 17); the monkey in Japan which is an animal with a strong human resemblance (Ohnuki-Tierney 1987); and the whale which blurs the line between fish and mammal (Kalland and Moeran 1992: 6–7).

16 The pangolin might also be viewed as physically anomalous because it is a terrestrial animal 'with the scales of a fish'. In her analysis, however, Douglas argues that the significance of the physical appearance of the pangolin for the Lele has to do with the different spaces it represents and brings together.

17 For examples of anthropological analyses which view domestic animals as classificatory anomalies, see Gossen (1996: 96–98), Ortiz (1969: 179), and Cátedra (1992: 331).

18 It should be noted that people–wildlife conflicts may be the source, and not just the object, of analogy. A prime example is the term 'vermin' which is widely used as a stigmatizing animal analogy applied to people, such as the portrayal of Jews as rats in Nazi propaganda films (Serpell 1996: 229). The wild predator is another important animal vehicle for theriomorphic moral condemnation, as in nineteenth-century America where settler society likened the Indian to 'the howling wolf of the prairie' (Hampton 1996: 11). More generally, this phenomenon is illustrated by the currency of the word 'pest' as a (negative) term of social reference.

19 See Carey (1976: 97), Wessing (1986: 90–91), McNeely and Sochaczewski (1994: 190), and Howell (1996: 138).

20 On European lycanthropy, see Baring-Gould (1995) and Rheinheimer (1995), and on the contemporary werewolf motif in American popular culture, see Duclos (1998). On shapeshifting beliefs in Africa, see Brain (1970), Ruel (1970) and Richards (1993); on jaguar shapeshifting, see Saunders (1990: 163–164) and Overing (1996: 71–72); and on shapeshifting in Indonesia, see McNeely and Sochaczewski (1994: 137–142) and Wessing (1986). Fox shapeshifting beliefs in Japan are somewhat different from these other beliefs because the basic direction of transformation is from fox-to-human, rather than the other way around – people do become fox-like but this is through possession by foxes, and is one of a number of ways in which foxes manage to assume human form (see Eguchi 1991).

References

Anderson, S. S., Prime, J. H., Harwood, J. and Bonner, N. (1989) British seals – vermin or scapegoats?, in R. J. Putman (ed.) *Mammals as Pests*, London and New York: Chapman and Hall.

Baring-Gould, S. (1995 [1865]) *The Book of Werewolves*, London: Senate.
Barnes, R. F. W. (1996) The conflict between humans and elephants in the central African forests, *Mammal Review* 26(2–3): 67–80.
Behar, R. (1986) *The Presence of the Past in a Spanish Village: Santa Maria del Monte*, Princeton: Princeton University Press.
Beier, P. (1991) Cougar attacks on humans in the United States and Canada, *Wildlife Society Bulletin* 19: 403–412.
Berwick, S. H. and Saharia, V. B. (eds) (1995) *The Development of International Principles and Practices of Wildlife Research and Management: Asian and American Approaches*, Delhi: Oxford University Press.
Brain, R. (1970) Child witches, in M. Douglas (ed.) *Witchcraft Confessions and Accusations*, London: Tavistock.
Breitenmoser, U. (1998) Large predators in the Alps: the fall and rise of Man's competitors, *Biological Conservation* 83(3): 279–289.
Brooks, J. E., Ahmad, E., Hussain, I. and Khan, M. H. (1989) The agricultural importance of the wild boar (*Sus scrofa* L.) in Pakistan, *Tropical Pest Management* 35(3): 278–281.
Budiansky, S. (1996) *Nature's Keepers: The New Science of Nature Management*, London: Orion.
Budiansky, S. (1999 [1992]) *The Covenant of the Wild: Why Animals Chose Domestication*, New Haven: Yale University Press.
Bulmer, R. (1967) Why is the cassowary not a bird? A problem of zoological taxonomy among the Karam of the New Guinea Highlands, *Man* 2: 5–25.
Carey, I. (1976) *Orang Asli: The Aboriginal Tribes of Peninsular Malaysia*, Kuala Lumpur: Oxford University Press.
Cátedra, M. (1992) *This World, Other Worlds: Sickness, Suicide, Death, and the Afterlife among the Vaqueiros de Alzada of Spain*, Chicago: University of Chicago Press.
Cohen, E. (1994) Animals in medieval perceptions: the image of the ubiquitous other, in A. Manning and J. Serpell (eds) *Animals and Human Society: Changing Perspectives*, London: Routledge.
Condominas, G. (1994) *We Have Eaten the Forest*, New York: Kodansha.
Cowan, P. E. and Tyndale-Biscoe, C. H. (1997) Australian and New Zealand mammal species considered to be pests or problems, *Reproduction, Fertility and Development* 9(1): 27–36.
Cozza, K., Fico, R., Battistini, M. and Rogers, E. (1996) The damage–conservation interface illustrated by predation on domestic livestock in central Italy, *Biological Conservation* 78(3): 329–336.
Croll, E. and Parkin, D. (1992) Cultural understandings of the environment, in E. Croll and D. Parkin (eds) *Bush Base, Forest Farm: Culture, Environment and Development*, London: Routledge.
Descola, P. (1996) *In the Society of Nature: A Native Ecology in Amazonia*, Cambridge: Cambridge University Press.
Descola, P. and Pálsson, G. (eds) (1996a) *Nature and Society: Anthropological Perspectives*, London: Routledge.

Descola, P. and Pálsson, G. (1996b) Introduction, in P. Descola and G. Pálsson (eds) *Nature and Society: Anthropological Perspectives*, London: Routledge.
DiSilvestro, R. L. (1991) *The Endangered Kingdom: The Struggle to Save America's Wildlife*, New York: Wiley.
Douglas, M. (1966) *Purity and Danger: An Analysis of the Concepts of Pollution and Taboo*, London: Routledge and Kegan Paul.
Douglas, M. (1975) *Implicit Meanings: Essays in Anthropology*, London: Routledge.
Douglas, M. (1992) *Risk and Blame: Essays in Cultural Theory*, London and New York: Routledge.
Douglas, M. and Wildavsky, A. (1982) *Risk and Culture: An Essay on the Selection of Technological and Environmental Dangers*, Berkeley: University of California Press.
Duclos, D. (1998) *The Werewolf Complex: America's Fascination with Violence*, Oxford: Berg.
Dunstone, N. and Ireland, M. (1989) The mink menace? A reappraisal, in R. J. Putman (ed.) *Mammals as Pests*, London and New York: Chapman and Hall.
Dwyer, P. D. (1990) *The Pigs that Ate the Garden: A Human Ecology from Papua New Guinea*, Ann Arbor: University of Michigan Press.
Eguchi, S. (1991) Between folk concepts of illness and psychiatric diagnosis: kitsune-tsuki (fox possession) in a mountain village of western Japan, *Culture, Medicine and Psychiatry* 15(4): 421–451.
Einarsson, N. (1993) All animals are equal but some are cetaceans: conservation and culture conflict, in K. Milton (ed.) *Environmentalism: The View from Anthropology*, London and New York: Routledge.
Ekvall, R. B. (1968) *Fields on the Hoof: Nexus of Tibetan Nomadic Pastoralism*, New York: Holt, Rhine and Winston.
Ellen, R. F. (1996) The cognitive geometry of nature: a contextual approach, in P. Descola and G. Pálsson (eds) *Nature and Society: Anthropological Perspectives*, London: Routledge.
Evans, E. P. (1906) *The Criminal Prosecution and Capital Punishment of Animals: The Lost History of Europe's Animal Trials*, London: William Heinemann.
Evans-Pritchard, E. E. (1956) *Nuer Religion*, Oxford: Oxford University Press.
Fernandez, J. W. (1986) *Persuasions and Performances: The Play of Tropes in Culture*, Bloomington: Indiana University Press.
Fiddes, N. (1991) *Meat: A Natural Symbol*, London: Routledge.
Fissell, M. (1999) Imagining vermin in Early Modern England, *History Workshop Journal* 47: 1–29.
Frazer, J. (1996 [1922]) *The Golden Bough*, London and New York: Penguin.
Fritts, S. H., Bangs, E., Fontaine, J., Johnson, M., Phillips, M., Koch, E. and Gunson, J. (1997) Planning and implementing a reintroduction of wolves to Yellowstone National Park and central Idaho, *Restoration Ecology* 5(1): 7–27.
Fukui, K. (1996) Co-evolution between humans and domesticates: the cultural selection of animal coat-colour diversity among the Bodi, in R. Ellen and K.

Fukui (eds) *Redefining Nature: Ecology, Culture and Domestication*, Oxford: Berg.
Gelfand, M. (1967) *The African Witch*, Edinburgh: E. and S. Livingstone.
Gipson, P. S. and Ballard, W. B. (1998) Accounts of famous American wolves, *Canis lupus*, *The Canadian Field Naturalist* 112(4): 724–739.
Glickman, S. (1995) The spotted hyena from Aristotle to the Lion King: reputation is everything, *Social Research* 62(3): 501–537.
Gold, A. G. and Gujar, B. R. (1997) Wild pigs and kings: remembered landscapes in Rajasthan, *American Anthropologist* 99(1): 70–84.
Gonzalez-Kirchner, J. P. and Sainz de la Maza, M. (1998) Primates Hunting by Guaymi Amerindians in Costa Rica, *Human Evolution* 13(1): 15–19.
Gossen, G. H. (1996) Animal souls, co-essences, and human destiny in Mesoamerica, in A. J. Arnold (ed.) *Monsters, Trickster and Sacred Cows: Animal Tales and American Identities*, Charlottesville: University Press of Virginia.
Grooms, S. (1993) *The Return of the Wolf*, Minocqua, WI: North Word Press.
Guha, R. (1997) The authoritarian biologist and the arrogance of anti-humanism: wildlife conservation in the Third World, *The Ecologist* 27(1): 14–20.
Hampton, B. (1996) Shark of the plains: early Western encounters with wolves, *Montana: The Magazine of Western History* 46(1): 2–13.
Harris, D. R. (1996) Domesticatory relationships of people, plants and animals, in R. Ellen and K. Fukui (eds) *Redefining Nature: Ecology, Culture and Domestication*, Oxford: Berg.
Harting, J. E. (1994 [1880]) *A Short History of the Wolf in Britain*, Whitstable: Pryor Publications.
Heinen, J. T. (1996) Human behaviour, incentives, and protected area management, *Conservation Biology* 10(2): 681–684.
Hill, C. M. (1997) Crop-raiding by wild vertebrates: the farmer's perspective in an agricultural community in western Uganda, *International Journal of Pest Management* 43(1): 77–84.
Hiraiwa, Y. (1992) *Ōkami: sono seitai to rekishi (The Wolf: Its Ecology and History)*, Tokyo: Tsukuba Shokan.
Hone, J. (1994) *Analysis of Vertebrate Pest Control*, Cambridge: Cambridge University Press.
Horrocks, J. and Baulu, J. (1994) Food competition between vervets (*Cercopithecus aethiops sabaeus*) and farmers in Barbados: implications for management, *Revue d'Ecologie* 49: 281–294.
Howell, S. (1996) Nature in culture or culture in nature? Chewong ideas of 'humans' and other species, in P. Descola and G. Pálsson (eds) *Nature and Society: Anthropological Perspectives*, London: Routledge.
Ingold, T. (1994) From trust to domination: an alternative history of human–animal relations, in A. Manning and J. Serpell (eds) *Animals and Human Society: Changing Perspectives*, London: Routledge.
Islam, Z. and Karim, A. N. M. R. (1995) Rat control by trapping in deepwater rice, *International Journal of Pest Management* 41(4): 229–233.

Ivens, W. G. (1927) *Melanesians of the South-east Solomon Islands*, London: Kegan Paul, Trench, Trubner and Co.
Jackson, M. D. (1975) Structure and event: witchcraft confession among the Kuranko, *Man* (n.s.) 10: 387–403.
Jusoff, K. and Majid, N. M. (1995) Integrating the needs of the local community to conserve forest biodiversity in the state of Kelantan, *Biodiversity and Conservation* 4(1): 108–114.
Kalland, A. and Moeran, B. (1992) *Japanese Whaling: End of an Era?*, London: Curzon.
Kawaoka, T. (1994) Nôgyô (Agriculture), in K. Inada *et al.* (eds) *Nihon mukashibanashi jiten (Dictionary of Japanese Old Tales)*, Tokyo: Kobundo.
Kellert, S. R., Black, M., Rush, C. R. and Bath, A. (1996) Human culture and large carnivore conservation in North America, *Conservation Biology* 10(4): 977–990.
Kiley-Worthington, M. (1997) Wildlife conservation, food production and 'development': can they be integrated? Ecological agriculture and elephant conservation in Africa, *Environmental Values* 6(4): 455–470.
Knight, J. (1999) Monkeys on the move: the natural symbolism of people–macaque conflict in Japan, *Journal of Asian Studies* 58(3): 622–647.
Knobloch, F. (1996) *The Culture of Wilderness: Agriculture as Colonization in the American West*, Chapel Hill: University of North Carolina Press.
Lawrence, E. A. (1990) Symbol of a nation: the bald eagle in American culture, *Journal of American Culture* 13(1): 63–69.
Leach, E. R. (1964) Anthropological aspects of language: animal categories and verbal abuse, in E. H. Lenneberg (ed.) *New Directions in the Study of Language*, Cambridge, Mass.: MIT Press.
Leach, M. (1992) Women's crops in women's spaces: gender relations in Mende rice farming, in E. Croll and D. Parkin (eds) *Bush Base, Forest Farm: Culture, Environment and Development*, London and New York: Routledge.
Lee, J. A. (1988) Seals, wolves and words: loaded language in environmental controversy, *Alternatives* 15(4): 20–29.
Lévi-Strauss, C. (1969[1963]) *Totemism*, translated by R. Needham, Harmondsworth: Penguin.
Lewis, D. M. and Alpert, P. (1997) Trophy hunting and wildlife conservation in Zambia, *Conservation Biology* 11(1): 59–68.
Lienhardt, G. (1961) *Divinity and Experience: The Religion of the Dinka*, Oxford: Clarendon Press.
Linares, O. F. (1976) 'Garden hunting' in the American tropics, *Human Ecology* 4(4): 331–349.
Lopez, B. H. (1995) *Of Wolves and Men*, New York: Touchstone.
MacCormack, C. and Strathern, M. (eds) (1980) *Nature, Culture and Gender*, Cambridge: Cambridge University Press.
McNeely, J. and Sochaczewski, P. S. (1994) *Soul of the Tiger: Searching for Nature's Answers in Southeast Asia*, Honolulu: University of Hawaii Press.
Malinowski, B. (1935a) *Coral Gardens and Their Magic: Volume I, The Description of Gardening*, London: George Allen and Unwin.

Malinowski, B. (1935b) *Coral Gardens and Their Magic: Volume II, The Language of Magic and Gardening*, London: George Allen and Unwin.

Marcus, J. (1989) Prisoner of discourse: the dingo, the dog and the baby, *Anthropology Today* 5(3): 15–19.

Mehta, J. N. and Kellert, S. R. (1998) Local attitudes towards community-based conservation policy and programmes in Nepal: a case study of the Makalu-Barun Conservation Area, *Environmental Conservation* 25(4): 320–333.

Meléndez, T. (1987) The coyote, in A. K. Gillespie and J. Mechling (eds) *American Wildlife in Symbol and Story*, Knoxville: University of Tennessee Press.

Melland, F. H. (1923) *In Witch-bound Africa: An Account of the Primitive Kaonde Tribe and their Beliefs*, London: Seeley, Service and Co.

Merrigi, A. and Saachi, O. (1992) Factors affecting damage by wild boars to cereal fields in northern Italy, in F. Spitz, G. Janeau, G. Gonzalez and S. Aulagnier (eds) *Ongules/Ungulates 91: Proceedings of the International Symposium*, Paris/Toulouse: SFEPM – IRGM.

Midgley, M. (1979) *Beast and Man: The Roots of Human Nature*, Brighton: Harvester Press.

Milton, K. (1993a) Introduction: environmentalism and anthropology, in K. Milton (ed.) *Environmentalism: The View from Anthropology*, London and New York: Routledge.

Milton, K. (ed.) (1993b) *Environmentalism: The View from Anthropology*, London and New York: Routledge.

Mishra, C. (1997) Livestock depredation by large carnivores in the Indian trans-Himalaya: conflict perceptions and conservation prospects, *Environmental Conservation* 24(4): 338–343.

Moon, O. (1989) *From Paddyfield to Ski-slope: The Revitalization of Tradition in Japanese Village Life*, Manchester: Manchester University Press.

Moore, R. S. (1994) Metaphors of encroachment: hunting for wolves on a central Greek mountain, *Anthropological Quarterly* 67(2): 81–88.

Moulton, M. P. and Sanderson, J. (1997) *Wildlife Issues in a Changing World*, Delray Beach, FL: St. Lucie Press.

Naughton-Treves, L. (1997) Farming the forest edge: vulnerable places and people around Kibale National Park, Uganda, *The Geographical Review* 87(1): 27–46.

Naughton-Treves, L. (1998) Predicting patterns of crop damage by wildlife around Kibale National Park, Uganda, *Conservation Biology* 12(1): 156–168.

Nebuka, M. (1991) *Yama no jinsei: Matagi no mura kara (Mountain Life: From the Village of Matagi)*, Tokyo: NHK Books.

Newsome, A. E. (1991) Environmental facilitation of regulatory predation by carnivores on wildlife including vertebrate pests, in N. Maruyama *et al.* (eds) *Wildlife Conservation: Present Trends and Perspectives for the 21st Century*, Tokyo: Japan Wildlife Research Center.

Nomoto, K. (1995) *Nihonjin no dôbutsukan no hensen – shika o meguru kattô* (Changes in the Japanese view of animals: complications in the case of the deer), in M. Kawai and K. Hanihara (eds) *Dôbutsu to bunmei (Animals and Civilization)*, Tokyo: Asakura Shoten.

Noske, B. (1997) *Beyond Boundaries: Humans and Animals*, Montreal: Black Rose Books.

Ohnuki-Tierney, E. (1987) *The Monkey as Mirror: Symbolic Transformations in Japanese History and Ritual*, Princeton: Princeton University Press.

Orlove, B. S. and Brush, S. B. (1996) Anthropology and the conservation of biodiversity, *Annual Review of Anthropology* 25: 329–352.

Ortiz, A. (1969) *The Tewa World: Space, Time, Being, and Becoming in a Pueblo Society*, Chicago: University of Chicago Press.

Overing, J. (1996) Who is the mightiest of them all? Jaguar and conquistador in Piaroa images of alterity and identity, in A. J. Arnold (ed.) *Monsters, Tricksters and Sacred Cows: Animal Tales and American Identities*, Charlottesville and London: University Press of Virginia.

Parrish, A. M. (1995) 'There were no sus in the old days': post-harvest pest management in an Egyptian oasis village, *Human Organization* 54(2): 195–204.

Parry, D. and Campbell, B. (1992) Attitudes of rural communities to animal wildlife and its utilization in Chobe enclave and Mababe depression, Botswana, *Environmental Conservation* 19(3): 245–252.

Pavlik, S. (1997) The role of bears and bear ceremonialism in Navajo orthodox traditional lifeway, *The Social Science Journal* 34(4): 475–484.

Primm, S. A. and Clark, T. W. (1996) Making sense of the policy process for carnivore conservation, *Conservation Biology* 10(4): 1036–1045.

Putman, R. J. (1989a) Introduction: mammals as pests, in R. J. Putman (ed.) *Mammals as Pests*, London and New York: Chapman and Hall.

Putman, R. J. (ed.) (1989b) *Mammals as Pests*, London and New York: Chapman and Hall.

Rangarajan, M. (1996) *The Politics of Ecology: The Debate on Wildlife and People in India, 1970–95*, New Delhi: Centre for Contemporary Studies, Nehru Memorial Museum and Library.

Reichel-Dolmatoff, G. (1985) Tapir avoidance in the Colombian northwest Amazon, in G. Urton (ed.) *Animal Myths and Metaphors in South America*, Salt Lake City: University of Utah Press.

Rheinheimer, M. (1995) The belief in werewolves in the extermination of real wolves in Schleswig-Holstein, *Scandinavian Journal of History* 20(4): 281–294.

Richards, P. (1993) Natural symbols and natural history: chimpanzees, elephants and experiments in Mende thought, in K. Milton (ed.) *Environmentalism: The View from Anthropology*, London: Routledge.

Richards, P. (1996) Agrarian creolization: the ethnobiology, history, culture and politics of West African rice, in R. Ellen and K. Fukui (eds) *Redefining Nature: Ecology, Culture and Domestication*, Oxford: Berg.

Roebroeks, W. (1995) 'Policing the boundary'? Continuity of discussions in 19th and 20th century palaeoanthropology, in R. Corbey and B. Theunissen (eds) *Ape, Man, Apeman: Changing Views since 1600*, Leiden: Department of Prehistory, Leiden University.

Ross, D. H. (1992) Imagining elephants: an overview, in D. H. Ross (ed.) *Elephant: The Animal and its Ivory in African Culture*, Los Angeles: Fowler Museum of Cultural History, University of California.

Rudel, T. and Roper, J. (1997) The paths to rainforest destruction: cross-national patterns of tropical deforestation, 1975–90, *World Development* 25(1): 53–65.

Ruel, M. (1970) Were-animals and the introverted witch, in M. Douglas (ed.) *Witchcraft Confessions and Accusations*, London: Tavistock.

Salisbury, J. E. (1994) *The Beast Within: Animals in the Middle Ages*, London and New York: Routledge.

Saunders, N. (1994) Predators of culture: jaguar symbolism and Mesoamerican elites, *World Archaeology* 26(1): 104–117.

Saunders, N. J. (1990) Tezcatlipoca: jaguar metaphors and the Aztec mirror of nature, in R. Willis (ed.) *Signifying Animals: Human Meaning in the Natural World*, London: Routledge.

Schmidt, R. H. and Beach, R. (1999) What is 'wildlife damage management'?, from http://www.lincoln.ac.nz/ento/wild/wdamage.htm, 04/20/99. Originally published in *Wildlife Control Technology*, 1(1): 4–5, 1994.

Serpell, J. (1996) *In the Company of Animals: A Study of Human–Animal Relationships*, Cambridge: Cambridge University Press.

Shanklin, E. (1985) Sustenance and symbol: anthropological studies of domesticated animals, *Annual Review of Anthropology* 14: 375–403.

Shepard, P. (1996) *The Others: How Animals Made Us Human*, Washington, DC: Island Press.

Siex, K. S. and Struhsaker, T. T. (1999) Colobus monkeys and coconuts: a study of perceived human–wildlife conflicts, *Journal of Applied Ecology* 36(6): 1009–1020.

Simonse, S. (1992) *Kings of Disaster: Dualism, Centralism and the Scapegoat King in Southeastern Sudan*, Studies in Human Society, Volume 5, Leiden: E. J. Brill.

Southwick, C. H. and Siddiqi, M. F. (1994) Primate commensalism: the Rhesus monkey in India, *Revue d'Ecologie* 49(3): 223–231.

Steinhart, P. (1995) *The Company of Wolves*, New York: Vintage Books.

Sukumar, R. (1994) Wildlife–human conflict in india: an ecological and social perspective, in R. Guha (ed.) *Social Ecology*, Delhi: Oxford University Press.

Sunseri, T. (1997) Famine and wild pigs: gender struggles and the outbreak of the Majimaji War in Uzaramo (Tanzania), *Journal of African History* 38(2): 235–259.

Sutlive, Jr., V. H. (1978) *The Iban of Sarawak*, Arlington Heights: AHM Publishing Corporation.

Sutô, I. (1991) *Yama no hyôteki: inoshishi to yamabito no seikatsushi (The Mountain Landmark: A Record of the Way of Life of Wild Boars and Mountain People)*, Tokyo: Miraisha.

Tambiah, S. J. (1969) Animals are good to think and good to prohibit, *Ethnology* 8(4): 423–459.

Taylor, R. D. (1994) Elephant management in the Nyaminyami District, Zimbabwe: turning a liability into an asset, in M. M. R. Freeman and U. P. Kreuter (eds) *Elephants and Whales: Resources for Whom?*, Basel: Gordon and Breach.

Tchamba, M. N. (1996) History and present status of the human/elephant conflict in the Waza-Logone region, Cameroon, West Africa, *Biological Conservation* 75(1): 35–41.

Thomas, S. J. (1994) Seeking equity in common property wildlife in Zimbabwe, in M. M. R. Freeman and U. P. Kreuter (eds) *Elephants and Whales: Resources for Whom?*, Basel: Gordon and Breach.

Tisdell, C. and Xiang Zhu (1998) Protected areas, agricultural pests and economic damage: conflicts with elephants and pests in Yunnan, China, *The Environmentalist* 18: 109–118.

Trout, Jr., J. (1997) *Nuisance Animals: Backyard Pests to Free-Roaming Killers*, Tennyson, IN: Midwest Publishing.

Urton, G. (1985a) Animal metaphors and the life cycle in an Andean community, in G. Urton (ed.) *Animal Myths and Metaphors in South America*, Salt Lake City: University of Utah Press.

Urton, G. (ed.) (1985b) *Animal Myths and Metaphors in South America*, Salt Lake City: University of Utah Press.

Vandergeest, P. (1996) Property rights in protected areas: obstacles to community involvement as a solution in Thailand, *Environmental Conservation* 23(3): 259–268.

Wadley, R. L., Pierce Colfer, C. J. and Hood, I. G. (1997) Hunting primates and managing forests: the case of the Iban forest farmers in Indonesian Borneo, *Human Ecology* 25(2): 243–271.

Weber, W. and Rabinowitz, A. (1996) A global perspective on large carnivore conservation, *Conservation Biology* 10(4): 1046–1054.

Weir, J. (1992) The Sweetwater rattlesnake round-up: a case study in environmental ethics, *Conservation Biology* 6(1): 116–127.

Wessing, R. (1986) *The Soul of Ambiguity: The Tiger in Southeast Asia*, Urbana: Center for Southeast Asian Studies, Northern Illinois University.

White, L. (1995) Tsetse visions: narratives of blood and bugs in colonial Northern Rhodesia, 1931–9, *Journal of African History* 36: 219–245.

Willis, R. (ed.) (1990) *Signifying Animals: Human Meaning in the Natural World*, London: Routledge.

Wilson, M. A. (1997) The wolf in Yellowstone: science, symbol, or politics? Deconstructing the conflict between environmentalism and wise use, *Society and Natural Resources* 10: 453–468.

Wolch, J. R., Gullo, A. and Lassiter, U. (1997) Changing attitudes towards California's cougars, *Society and Animals* 5(2): 95–116.

Worster, D. (1977) *Nature's Economy: A History of Ecological Ideas*, Cambridge: Cambridge University Press.

Youngblood-Petersen, T. (1995) Speaking of wolves: a call to biophilia, *Transactions of the 60th North American Wildlife and Natural Resources Conference*, No. 60: 542–549.

Zeuner, F. E. (1963) *A History of Domesticated Animals*, London: Hutchinson.
Zuidema, R. T. (1985) The lions in the city: royal symbols of transition in Cuzco, in G. Urton (ed.) *Animal Myths and Metaphors in South America*, Salt Lake City: University of Utah Press.

Chapter 2

Wildlife depredations in Malawi

The historical dimension

Brian Morris

Introduction

It is difficult for people living in urban areas to realize how precarious life is for subsistence agriculturists, and it has to be remembered that historically the matrilineal peoples of Malawi were fundamentally subsistence hoe-cultivators. Not only is such agriculture highly dependent on rain, but the depredations of wild animals are a constant source of concern and anxiety. Thus although in hunting or in certain ritual contexts a close interdependent relationship is often expressed between humans and animals in Malawi,[1] in an agricultural context the larger mammals are seen as a constant source of threat to people's well-being and livelihood, as indeed they are. This chapter offers some reflections, from an historical perspective, on such wildlife depredations in Malawi.[2]

The depredations of wild animals in Malawi focused around two distinct groups of mammals: the carnivores (lion, leopard and hyena) who in certain circumstances were a serious menace to human life, and those mammals who raided village gardens for crops – and the most important of these were the elephant, baboon, monkey, hippo, porcupine, bush pig, and in certain situations some antelope species. We shall discuss each of these categories in turn.

Carnivores

In the past Malawi had a reputation for its man-eating lions. The memoirs of all the early missionaries and administrators in Malawi invariably contain a short section on the attacks inflicted on people by lions. Thus W. P. Livingstone in his biography of Robert Laws, and early missionary at Livingstonia, has a section entitled 'Nature's Cruelty'. He notes that

Christ's work and 'civilised conditions' entail the subjugation of the wilderness, making it less ruthless and cruel. And the lion is seen as the epitome of Nature's cruelty. Very many of the patients brought to the Livingstonia mission station, he noted, 'suffered from mauling by wild animals' and he recalls one night when five women and a child were attacked by a lion who sprang upon the roof and broke through the thatch of the hut. It killed two of the women and the child. Not long afterwards the same lion killed two other women and a girl, as well as killing another woman who had left her hut to find what the commotion in the night had been about. After failing to poison the lion with strychnine, it was later shot by one of the missionaries (Livingstone 1921: 288–289).

Laws himself noted in his memoirs that eight people were killed by lions in his first year at Livingstonia (1934: 224). An early administrator Hans Coudenhove, who lived in the Chikala Hills, also wrote of a man-eating lion near Lake Chilwa which for several months spread 'terror' among the villagers by its periodic appearance. The lion killed fourteen and wounded six people before its career was ended by Chief Chikewo and a group of men, armed with a rifle and spears (1925: 107–108).

When some decades later the well-known geographer Frank Debenham wrote his survey of Nyasaland for the colonial office, it was thus hardly surprising that one chapter was devoted to lions. It was entitled 'The Man eaters of Kasungu' and it reported that one administrative officer at Kasungu had shot a lion which 'had taken at least 60 Africans and was known far and wide'. Debenham noted the fact that local people tended not to report such man-eating lions, as it was widely believed that a lion may be a reincarnation of a former chief (1955: 186).

It would be tedious to recount all the reports of man-eating lions in Malawi during the past decades, but two particular incidents are worth noting. The first is the case of the man-eating lion which caused havoc in the Michinji district around 1929–1930. In May 1930 the Provincial Commissioner of the central province sent a telegram to the government chief secretary in Zomba which read:

> Man-eating lion causing serious trouble in Fort Manning (Mchinji) district. Stop. Five victims within the past two weeks. Stop. Owing the long grass unable to deal with the matter single-handed. Stop. Consider that the services of two Europeans needed urgently. Stop. Can you assist?

Apparently for some months a lion had been creating havoc and despair in the district and had caused at least thirty-six deaths in twenty-four villages. It attacked people during the daytime while they were working in the fields or fetching water and in one village it had been responsible for three deaths in one day. Many deaths, however, were not reported to the administration as people were always quick to remove the body of their dead relative. The majority of the lion's victims were women. The commissioner R. H. Murray, a month earlier, had toured the Mchinji area and had found it in a 'state of terror'. He reported that, because of lions, half the villages had planted no maize and the inhabitants of the others were afraid to sleep in their gardens (to guard crops). The result, he wrote, is that practically the whole of the crop has been destroyed by wild animals, especially by monkeys. Several villages had been abandoned. The lion, he continued, was operating over a wide area, as it never returned to its kill, and generally moved 15–20 miles before attacking another victim. The lion was thus covering a territory of around 400 square miles. To deal with the problem fifty police were brought in from Lilongwe, Dedza and Dowa – practically the whole police force from the central region. The only game warden for the territory, Rodney Wood, thought the local people themselves were largely to blame for the deaths – because the men were working away on tobacco estates and would not organize a communal hunt, because the women did not take full precautions and often worked or fetched water alone, and because the relatives removed the victims immediately after the killing, not allowing the administration to poison the body.

This was not a unique outbreak. In 1925 the Rev J. van Heerden of Mchinji mission had reported that people in ten villages in the district had not planted their gardens owing to the danger from lions, and wrote that during his eight years in the district, 'I do not remember a single year in which there were no man-eating lions'. One administrator estimated that in most districts throughout the country an average of fifty people were killed annually by lions. In the Ngara district all villages were stockaded as a protection against these beasts of prey. Eventually the Mchinji lion was killed in September 1930 by three well-armed Europeans, assisted by a host of trackers. One of the Europeans was the young E. C. Peterkins, who later became an important political figure in Malawi prior to independence (MNA 51/1721 A/23).

The second incident is the case of the 'Namwera man-eaters', the title of a chapter in the memoirs of the well-known game ranger Norman Carr. Born at Chinde in 1912, Carr spent his early years in Malawi, where his parents were tobacco farmers during the colonial period. Carr worked for the colonial government as a crop protection officer, and records in his memoirs how proud he was on shooting his fiftieth elephant near Liwonde in 1932 – on his twentieth birthday (1969: 20). During the war years he was stationed in the Namwera hills, near Mangoche. As the area was well-populated, game was scarce, apart from baboons and bush pig. As lions frequently crossed the border from Mozambique, and found it difficult to secure their normal prey, they sometimes turned, Carr wrote, 'to the only other available food: man'. Thus outbreaks of man-eating lions used to occur from time to time in the Namweras, 'spreading terror' among local people. While staying in the Namwera Carr received a message from Chief Kawinga about man-eating lions, two lions having been responsible for eleven victims in two weeks. His memoirs give a graphic account of the hunting of the two lions (1969: 84–99), both lions proving to be in prime condition. This, he felt, disproved the theory that only lions which are too old or too feeble to catch wild game will eat human flesh. The pioneer conservationist G. D. Hayes has more recently, in recalling his own experiences of 'man-eaters', suggested that a conservative estimate of deaths attributed to the Namwera lions was 'some fifty in a period of little over three months' (1979: 7).

Although at the present time lions are largely confined to conservation areas, occasional lions are still to be noted in the Zomba and Mulanje districts, and in other well-populated areas throughout Malawi – for lions appear to be great travellers. And deaths from lions are still occasionally recorded. George Welsh, who was a forest officer on the Vipya in the 1970s, reported the death of one forest worker, who was killed while riding his bicycle near the forestry compound. During the colonial period it was considered unsafe to travel on foot at night on the Liwonde road, as well as on the Zomba to Blantyre road. More recently, a game ranger was killed travelling by motorbike on the escarpment road through Nkhotakota Game Reserve.

Unlike lions, neither leopards and hyenas are widely known as 'man-eaters', but the records show that they too frequently take a toll of human life, particularly of young children. A missionary of Ekwendeni wrote to Alexander Hetherwick of a woman who put down her child at the edge of the field while she hoed, and on turning round found it gone. Only the footmarks of a leopard were there in evidence. Two man-eating leopards were noted in the Chikwawa district in the 1920s: one had killed four children and mauled many more; the other had killed at least nine youths between nine and thirteen years. Debenham (1955: 184) records a leopard in the Kasungu district which had killed thirty-seven people and was so renowned for its fury and cunning that the local chief was not allowed to participate in the final hunt. Although secretive, leopards are still plentiful in Malawi, many still taking their toll of young children, but their presence is usually known by the dogs and goats that regularly disappear from villages, or even from residences within towns. Hyenas, too, may kill or inflict serious injury to humans.

Throughout Malawi, the spotted hyena is widely feared, as it attacks people at night, especially during the hot season when people sleep outside on the veranda (*khonde*). Hector Duff at the beginning of the twentieth century wrote:

> Cowardly as it is, the hyena is a good deal feared by [people] owing to its unpleasant habit of sneaking up to them while they lie asleep, and biting their faces. I was assured in northern Angoniland (Mzimba district) that the hyenas there would often lie in wait outside the huts at dawn, and make a sudden rush at the inmates directly they put their heads out of doors.
>
> (1903: 107)

The Rev Charles Long at Chiddi recorded several cases of humans being attacked while sleeping out of doors on hot evenings (1973: 66).

The region best known in Malawi for hyena attacks on people is the Phalombe plain, to the north of Michesi Mountain. In the late 1950s a number of deaths of people were reported from this area. The first to be recorded was in September 1955, and was reported to Fred Balestra, a local planter, who farmed near Fort Lister. Balestra had lived in the area for over thirty years and was a keen hunter. He was called to a village in which a man, who was reputed to be mad (*misala*), had been killed and eaten by hyenas on a path near the village. Whether he was asleep at the time Balestra could not discover; all he found were patches of blood and a few shreds of cloth. Seven days later, and some eight miles away, an old lady was dragged from her hut, the flimsy grass door being broken down. She was dragged thirty yards, lost an arm and was badly mauled before her cries for help brought relief. Refusing to go to hospital, she died the next day. There was one more killing that year, a child of six. Thus that year there were three deaths. Then, Balestra records, the toll really began – five deaths in 1956, five in 1957, six in 1958. This pattern continued until 1961 when eight people were killed by hyenas. The killings always began in September, a time when people started sleeping outside on the veranda, and when bush fires are begun. The latter has the effect of making the normal hunting of game difficult for the hyenas. By January, when people began sleeping indoors again, the killings had ceased.

Balestra wrote his short article on 'The man-eating hyenas of Mulanje' in 1962. Some four decades later, the hyenas are still plentiful in the area, even moving through the middle of Migowi trading centre at night. But although there are still many reports of people being badly mauled by hyenas, actual deaths are now less frequent – despite the fact that many people still sleep outdoors during the dry season.[3]

Livestock losses

In the above paragraphs I have detailed the toll on human life exacted by three of the larger carnivores. But these same beasts of prey – as well as smaller carnivores like the zorilla, serval and mongoose – also prey on livestock. The matrilineal peoples of Malawi do not have a developed pastoral economy; nevertheless, the carnivores exact a heavy toll on the livestock that they do keep – cattle, goats, pigs and chickens. Records from the colonial period suggest the following depredations.

In a twelve-month period 102 goats, 22 sheep, 12 pigs and 20 cattle were taken by carnivores from fourteen villages in the Ntcheu district, and in the same district twenty-one pigs were taken by lions from just three villages in two days – lions being especially fond of pigs. In the same year (1926) it was recorded that twelve villages near Neno mission lost six pigs and fourteen cattle to lions, and thirty-two goats, five pigs and two dogs to leopards (MNA 51/1721A/23). Wherever leopards and hyenas are still to be found – and hyenas are still common on Sochi Mountain overlooking Blantyre township – they take an enormous toll of domestic livestock. A group of hyenas, who lived in a cave above my house in the Domasi valley, became so troublesome in the number of sheep and goats they took from the nearby villages that a group of men expended a great deal of effort over a number of days smoking out their cave.

The popular travel book *Leopards in the Night* (1955) by Guy Muldoon has six chapters devoted to lions and leopards. Muldoon in the 1940s was an agricultural officer stationed at Mwera Hill, and one of the main tasks he took upon himself was to shoot the leopards and lions that were molesting livestock. The Dowa hills at that period were 'infested' with these carnivores, and the lions, who followed a circular route in their travels between Dowa and Ntchisi Mountain in the north, had seemingly lost all fear of humans. They found the sheep and cattle in the villages far easier than wild game – and usually stampeded the animals from the kraal. Like Carr, he noted that the lions he shot, or which became 'man-eaters', were neither old nor decrepit, but rather young and virile and

Muldoon wrote that 'the most likely explanation for the [lions] acquiring a taste for human flesh is the contempt they developed for man after extensive raids on villages'. He noted that one notorious 'man-eater' of recent years was a lion that killed fourteen people in one month near Mzimba (1955: 38).

Given this background it is not surprising that Malawian attitudes towards the larger carnivores is one of apprehension and fear. They speak of being afraid of animals (*ku-opa*) and of expressing fear (*ku-chita mantha*). How deep such feelings may be, can be gleamed from the recent experience in Norway, where the presence of a single wild wolf near the vicinity of habitations apparently caused a near-hysterical 'frenzy' among the Norwegian public (Rowan 1991: 282). Some writers suggest that the fear of the wolf and its subsequent persecution is based primarily on 'misrepresentation' and inaccurate epithets and myths (see Serpell 1986: 159–160). But the fear and the hostility towards wolves and hyenas in Malawi are based on the substantive experiences of people living in rural environments.

Crop-raiders

The carnivores are not the only mammals that subsistence agriculturists have to contend with. Malawians also have to face the depredations to their crops caused by a variety of animal species. Historically the most important of these was the elephant. Nowadays elephants are largely confined to conservation areas and forest reserves, but in the past they were widely distributed throughout Malawi, and in many areas they created havoc during the harvest season. Apart from tsetse control, the main function of the Game Department throughout the colonial period was not the conservation of wild animals, but rather crop protection. Guy Muldoon, when he later became Game Control Officer at Nkhotakota, was nominally in charge of game reserve. But besides dealing with lions and leopards his main duties appear to have been the destruction of the baboons and wild pigs which raided local gardens and the control of the elephants that left the reserve (1955: 61).

The elephants of the Nkhotakota district were particularly troublesome, coming down to the lakeshore from the wooded escarpment and causing devastation in the local gardens. Other places in Malawi which were particularly known for their marauding elephants were the vicinity of the Tangadzi stream in the Lower Shire, the Kasungu district and the Southern lakeshore near Monkey Bay and Liwonde. As guns were strictly controlled during the colonial period – even though a few men owned old muzzle loaders (and this is still the situation) – local people had very little protection against the elephants. Herds of elephants seemed to be a rule unto themselves, not only raiding the gardens and destroying crops over a wide area, but also raiding maize granaries.

Even with a gun it was a brave man, as one administrator put it, who attempted to drive elephants away, knowing that about one in every three cartridges misfires. Elephants are described in government reports as 'wrecking' gardens, as reducing villages to 'famine', as becoming so bold as to ignore flares and drumming, and as 'terrorising' villages. The assistant resident at Ngara wrote 'complaints come in every week of elephants entering villages during the night, destroying grain stores, while the unfortunate owners are powerless to do anything to protect their stores or to drive away the elephants'.

There is the pathetic story of an old lady who went into the night with a lighted torch in an attempt to drive away an elephant raiding her granary (*nkhokwe*) – her whole livelihood – and who was trampled to death as a consequence. A. G. O. Hodgson estimated that in some parts of the Dowa district no less than 50 per cent of the maize crop was destroyed by elephants each year.

One of the most famous, or rather infamous, of the marauding herds was the Mpimbi herd which numbered about a hundred elephants. This herd wandered along the Shire River between Liwonde and Lirangwe during the 1920s and created havoc and despair wherever it went. It not only destroyed gardens, but the elephants helped themselves, and emptied people's grain bins. The herd took not the slightest notice of the flares and the beating of drums, and people were quite helpless to counter their maraudings. Those people who did, like the old lady, lost their lives. Many elephants were shot by local hunters working for the game department – as they still are – but this did not offset the damage done to crops by the elephants.

Many local European administrators wrote to the government in Zomba in exasperation, suggesting the best solution to the problem would be the extermination of the elephant population in such areas as Liwonde and Monkey Bay. But as some of the herds, like the Mpimibi herd, consisted mainly of females and carried few tuskers, European hunters were little interested in the herds. One administrator's answer to the problem was to suggest that elephants be used as field targets for machine gun practice by the army (MNA 51/1298/19).

It must be borne in mind of course that, prior to the development of muzzle-loading guns, humans and elephants vied with each other for territory. Ecologically, and in terms of social organization, humans and elephants are very similar. Elephants and many communities in east central Africa have social groupings that are essentially matricentric, and both humans – as shifting cultivators – and elephants are extremely destructive to the woodland habitat. Even the life cycles of human and elephants are similar, for both have protracted childhoods and are exceptionally long-lived species (Graham 1973: 97–98). Importantly, however, it has to be recognized that, as subsistence agriculturalists, for Malawians elephant were – and still are – a constant menace, a continual threat to their livelihood and well-being.

In many respects, the most serious depredations to cultivation were caused not by elephants – or even by the hippo along the Shire River or lakeshore (though these too can be a menace) – but rather by four mammals which are still ubiquitous in Malawi – baboons, porcupines, monkeys and bush pigs. All four species are widespread and common, found wherever there are rocky hillsides or woodlands giving them refuge. Essentially the baboons and monkeys raid the garden by day, the other two species by night. There is a saying in Malawi – which is common throughout Central Africa – that in planting maize you need to put three seeds in the hole – one for yourself, one for the guinea fowl, and one for the bush pig. The vast majority of damage to crops by wild animals in Malawi can be attributed to these four species.

During the 1920s when a new game ordinance was being implemented by the colonial government, missionaries, who felt themselves to be representing the interests of local people, strongly voiced their opposition to the ordinance. Their crucial argument was that the presence of game animals was contrary to the well-being of the Malawian people. Game animals, they suggested, meant not only the presence of carnivores (which took a considerable toll of human life in the country) but also the devastation of their crops. One missionary at Neno wrote:

> As for the losses suffered by the depredations of wild pigs and baboons they are very heavy indeed. We may say that there is not a single garden left intact in the whole district. At this season [March 1927] day and night the [people] stay in their gardens. In several villages we find not a soul; everybody is watching the maize.

Other missionaries stressed the enormous damage to cultivation caused by wild animals, particularly by baboons and wild pigs, noting that several villages were short of food on account of such depredations. This was the pattern found throughout Malawi: widespread depredations to gardens by monkeys, bush pigs, porcupines and baboons, and local people spending much of their time during the planting season protecting their crops. Although eland, kudu and bushbuck occasionally damaged crops (kudu were renowned for the damage they did to cotton), antelopes generally were not a serious problem (though many species were plentiful). The main culprits were the four species aforementioned.

Although these four species were not specifically protected by the game ordinance, the ordinance did in fact forbid traditional methods of hunting, viz., the game pit, spring traps, nets and communal hunting with fire and dogs. As firearms were also strictly controlled, all this seemed to many missionaries a great injustice: as one missionary put it, game animals prey upon people's crops, but the ordinance means that local people must simply content themselves with scaring the animals away. Another suggested that what was needed was not a game protection ordinance but a people's protection ordinance.

These adverse conditions for subsistence cultivation in Malawi were not only recognized by the missionaries in their polemics against the game ordinance; they were also transparent to the administration. Thus one administrative officer G. W. Kenyon-Slaney, who ironically was later to become a Nyau figure in Chewa rituals, when stationed in Nkhotakota, wrote to the Chief Secretary regarding a tour of the district in April 1927. He wrote of how amazed he was at the amount of foodstuffs that were lost by farmers to the depredations of baboons, bush pig and other wild animals. He speaks of the hardships they have to undergo to save their crops; in some villages men, women and children were living, both day and night, in the gardens (MNA 51/1721 A/23).

In a later decade Guy Muldoon continued to detail the crop depredations by wild animals and his memoirs significantly contain chapters entitled 'Baboon war' and 'Pigs, wild and tusky'. On the baboons he writes:

> Those who have never lived . . . in Central Africa . . . can have little conception of the tremendous damage that baboons cause year in year out in cultivated fields and gardens. In Nyasaland these creatures destroy thousands of pounds worth of foodstuffs annually and threaten the very survival of thousands of Africans.
>
> (1955: 145)

He speaks of villagers and baboons being in a 'state of war' during the planting season, and describes in detail the concentrated campaign he launched with the local people, who assisted with nets. Over a two year period in the Dowa and Nkhotakota districts Muldoon and his assistants destroyed 13,000 baboons. Similar net-drives were organized against bush pigs.

Wildlife 'control'

I have noted earlier that one of the main functions of the Game Department during the colonial period was crop protection – and the Department of National Parks and Wildlife still performs this function. It may therefore be useful to conclude this chapter with some reflections on the relation of the Game Department to wildlife depredations during this period (1930–1964).

When Rodney Wood resigned as game warden in 1931 he recommended to the government that the post of game warden be abolished, and that the maintenance of the three main game reserves, together with the duties of crop protection, be undertaken by the district administration. But by the 1930s, with much of the game population depleted in Malawi, there was a shift of opinion in the thinking of many Europeans, and a need was felt to preserve game mammals. Many of these new conservationists were 'penitent butchers' as Rodney Wood described himself. While in the early period the game laws essentially functioned to preserve game for ritualized sport hunting – focusing on the collecting of trophies which, to an important degree, served as a ritual of prestige and domination – the establishment of 'game reserves' had a different motivation. Even so, the motivation behind the establishment of 'reserves' in colonial Nyasaland were many and varied and largely geared to human problems and needs: with Lengwe, the need to protect declining numbers of nyala; with Kasungu, the need to protect people from the ravages of sleeping sickness; and with the later (1938) Nkhotakota game reserve, the need for a refuge for marauding elephants which were causing crop depredation along the lakeshore.

Whatever the motivations for the establishment of game reserves, the end of the colonial period went hand-in-hand with crop protection, and a determined effort to control, even to eradicate, all larger mammals outside of the reserves. This signified an implicit acknowledgement by the administration that larger animals and human populations whose subsistence was based on agriculture did not easily coexist. Such crop protection activities are still an important policy of the present government.

From 1931 until the end of the Second World War, game conservation was thus handled by the district administrations, and was to remain at a virtual standstill. Game guards were employed by these administrations mainly to protect crops, especially the ravages of hippopotamuses and elephants, often attempting to drive the latter back into the forest reserves or game sanctuaries. The game reserves themselves, like Kasungu and Nkhotakota, were largely a 'no-man's land'. They had few staff and there was no serious effort to enforce wildlife legislation. They were frequented only by the occasional subsistence hunter and people travelling across the country.

In June 1946, the report of a commission, especially appointed by the colonial government to look into the whole issue of forest and game reserves, recommended the formation of the Department of Game, Fish and Tsetse control. The department was finally established in 1949, and flourished (if that is the right word), even though it was under-staffed and under-funded until 1962. With regard to wildlife, it had essentially a dual function, being concerned with both game conservation and crop protection. Yet it is clear from the beginning that crop protection rather than wildlife conservation was the primary role of the department. As its 1949 report acknowledged: 'since the main reason for the formation of the game side of the organisation was the protection of crops, emphasis has to date been laid on game and vermin control rather than on game conservation'. Indeed, the game rangers were initially described as 'game control officers'.

During the fourteen years from 1948–1961, the following animals were killed in the protection of crops: elephant 852, hippopotamus 1,048, buffalo 562, waterbuck 489, roan, eland and kudu 554, other antelope 1,199 as well as more than 300,000 'vermin' (mainly bushpig and baboons). By 1955 buffalo, roan, eland and kudu and the other antelopes had ceased to be a problem, and hippopotamuses had been drastically reduced in number. They are now virtually extinct along with much of the lakeshore, and recent efforts (1995) to curb human–hippo conflict in the Lower Shire has led to their demise in this region as well.

During the past decades there has been a tremendous increase in the human population in Malawi. Less than 2 million in 1930, it now stands at nearly 9 million. As an inevitable consequence there has been a great reduction in the number of larger mammals over the past fifty years or so. Zebra, oribi and blue wildebeest, for example, are no longer to be found on the Phalombe plain (Dudley 1979). Nevertheless, wild mammals are still fairly plentiful: although Malawi is one of the most densely populated areas of Africa, 33 per cent of the country is under 'natural vegetation' and wildlife conservation areas and forest reserves constitute some 20 per cent of the total land area. Thus leopards and hyenas still roam at night in the Zomba and Blantyre townships, and in rural areas throughout

Malawi local people are still engaged during the agricultural season in a constant battle with hippos, porcupines, monkeys, baboons and wild pigs (not to mention the smaller rodents) in an effort to defend their crops.

We therefore find, as in the past, much time and energy devoted during the planting season to warding off crop-raiders. Wherever gardens border woodland areas special shelters (*chirindo*) are built, often on raised platforms, and people may eat and sleep in these shelters for several weeks – especially to guard against baboons. The importance and severity of what is now described as 'wildlife pest impacts' have been of special concern to the Department of National Parks and Wildlife, especially in relation to those village communities lying immediately outside wildlife conservation areas. An FAO-funded project in 1989 was specifically focused on 'Wildlife Management and Crop Protection' and one of its central aims was to seek ways in which to resolve the 'conflict' between wildlife and the local communities (Rogers and Jamusana 1989).

Conclusion

In this chapter I have outlined the serious conflicts that exist between wildlife and rural communities in Malawi, communities whose livelihood is centrally focused around subsistence agriculture. Such conflict inevitably gives rise to a pervasive cultural opposition between humans and animals, to an ethos of antagonism and opposition which, as Serpell writes (1986: 175), can be related specifically to animals and plant husbandry. This opposition in Malawi is expressed in ethnobiological classifications, in the symbolic demarcation between the woodland and the village domains, and in many rituals. But this ethos of fear and dread (*ku-opsya*, which is semantically akin to the verb *ku-psya*, to fire, or cook) and of opposition, though pervasive in Malawian social life and culture, reflects only one social attitude that exists between humans and animals. For, as in other cultures, Malawians express diverse and often contradictory attitudes towards animals. It has, however, been the 'ethic of antagonism' between humans and animals which it has been my purpose to highlight here, an ethic that is fundamentally linked to their life as subsistence horticulturists.

Notes

1 The complex, diverse and multifaceted relationships between humans and animals in Malawi is explored in my study *The Power of Animals: An Ethnography* (1998).
2 An earlier draft of this chapter was published in *Nyala* (The Journal of the Wildlife Society of Malawi) 18 (1995) 17–24.
3 There is a close association between witches (*afiti*) and hyenas in Malawi, for witches it is thought often take the form (*kusanduka*) of these and other animals.

References

Balcstra, F. (1962) The man-eating hyenas of Mulanje, *African Wildlife* 16: 25–27.
Carr, N. (1969) *The White Impala*, London: Collins.
Coudenhove, H. (1925) *My African Neighbours*, London: Cape.
Debenham, F. (1955) *Nyasaland: The Land of the Lake*, London: HMSO.
Dudley, C. (1979) History of the decline of the larger mammals of the Lake Chilwa Basin, *Society Malawi Journal* 32(2): 27–41.
Duff, H. C. (1903) *Nyasaland Under the Foreign Office*, London: Bell.
Graham, A. (1973) *The Gardeners of Eden*, London: Allen and Unwin.
Hayes, G. D. (1979) Lions – man-eaters and others, *Nyala* 5: 6–11.
Laws, R. (1934) *Reminiscences of Livingstonia*, Edinburgh: Oliver and Boyd.
Livingstone, W. P. (1921) *Laws of Livingstonia*, London: Hodder and Stoughton.
Long, R. C. (1973) A list with notes of the mammals of the Nsanje District, *Society Malawi Journal* 26(1): 60–77.
MNA (Malawi National Archives), Zomba.
Morris, B. (1998) *The Power of Animals: An Ethnography*, Oxford: Berg.
Muldoon, G. (1955) *Leopards in the Night*, London: Hart-Davies.
Rogers, P. and Jamusana, H. S. (1989) *Wildlife Pest Impacts and Wildlife Management in Malawi*, Lilongwe Department National Parks and Wildlife/FAO.
Rowan, A. N. (1991) The human-animal interface, in M. H. Robinson and L. Tiger (eds) *Man and Beast Revisited*, Washington: Smithsonian Institute Press.
Serpell, J. (1986) *In the Company of Animals*, Oxford: Blackwell.

Chapter 3

Half-man, half-elephant

Shapeshifting among the Baka of Congo

Axel Köhler

Introduction

Towards the end of my fieldwork among Baka (Pygmies)[1] in the Republic of Congo (Brazzaville), rumour suddenly spread that elephant footprints had been sighted close to a village near the Cameroonian border. The footprints indicated that the animals were passing nearby and were approaching the district centre.[2] This was highly unusual, and people became alarmed. Did these footprints belong to a group of *mòkìlà* elephant-men? Did this mean that the *mòkìlà* were on one of their expeditions to kill Baka men and to kidnap Baka women and children?

For the next few days, most Baka men stayed in the security of the village, and women and children went into the nearby forest only in small groups and accompanied by young men with guns. After a week, some hunters went out to check the vicinity of the village, and ten days after the *mòkìlà* scare had surfaced, life went back to normal. There were no more reports of approaching *mòkìlà* and this meant that they had either gone home or were looking for victims elsewhere. When I inquired about the *mòkìlà*, the following points emerged as conventional wisdom among the Baka on the subject of elephant-men and women.

Among the Baka, some people have the power to transform themselves into animals. They are called *mòkìlà*,[3] and it is especially among Baka living in Cameroon that people are known to possess the power to shapeshift into elephants. Although they are essentially human, *mòkìlà* are hybrid beings that can shift between the bodily appearances and behaviours of humans and elephants. They undergo metamorphosis only in the forest, either alone or in the company of fellow *mòkìlà*, but can change quickly back and forth whenever they like or need to.

There are some important features to note about *mòkìlà* physiology.

In their elephant shape, *mòkìlà* are said to be visually indistinguishable from real elephants, at least to the uninitiated. The body of a *mòkìlà* elephant harbours, however, the body and life-force of a human being. In the forest *mòkìlà* elephants browse like other elephants, but their faeces and body odour remained distinctly human. Furthermore, *mòkìlà* footprints may be less deep than real elephant footprints, and what is particularly revealing is a conspicuous lack of other elephant traces nearby. Apart from the footprints, there are neither the broken branches nor the typical odour of a real elephant – the normal signs indicating that an elephant has passed by.

No one wants to kill a *mòkìlà* elephant since this implies homicide and incurs revenge. The problem is therefore how to tell *mòkìlà* elephants apart from real ones during a sudden encounter in the forest. *Mòkìlà* get accidentally killed, since they do not change back from elephant into human shape in potentially dangerous situations. The dominant opinion has it that in this case the *mòkìlà* dies two deaths and leaves two corpses. At the moment of death, the human being 'jumps out' of the elephant body, together with his or her spirit, in order not to get trapped and die within. They are said to run for their home village to deliver (not unlike the Greek messenger from Marathon) the message of their own death, indicating with their last breath the place where they had been fatally wounded.

Heterodox Baka accounts suggest that a dead *mòkìlà* leaves a single human corpse, even when killed in its elephant shape. This interpretation is probably due to the fact that it is not uncommon for a hunter to shoot an elephant and then to lose track of the fleeing animal which then dies on its own somewhere else. Second, since shapeshifting is also associated with witchcraft, there is reason to argue that the appearance of a witch in animal shape can only be make-believe, a temporary means to achieve predatory aims.

Attacked elephants either flee or, so I was told, 'cleverly fake a flight' – that is, they only pretend to run off, but then return with cat-like stealth in a half-circle and come at their attacker from behind. Few hunters are known to have survived serious counterattacks, and accounts of how wounded and angry elephants retaliate all concur in their descriptions. The animal grabs the hunter with its trunk and lifts him up, squeezes his body and then smashes him against a tree or on the ground, before trampling on his extremities and crushing his bones. It then pierces his body with its tusks and rips it open, leaving a mess of blood, flesh and bones. But the body of a hunter who has been attacked and killed by a *mòkìlà* shows different types of wounds, which resemble the stab wounds from a knife or the cuts inflicted by a machete.

Mòkìlà only kill hunters, and their motive is clear: they want revenge for fellow *mòkìlà* that have been slain. But when they are on a raid and encounter women and children alone in the forest, they kidnap them and take them back to their village, where they adopt them and integrate them into *mòkìlà* society. After their initiation into the *mòkìlà* shapeshifting secrets, abducted Baka are said to remain voluntarily with their kidnappers.

When they are not out raiding, *mòkìlà* live a normal Baka life in villages in Cameroon, and an unsuspecting visitor would not be able to distinguish between *mòkìlà* and Baka villages, nor between their inhabitants. The main occasion on which *mòkìlà* change from human into elephant shape is when they leave their village for feuding or when travelling in the forest, but they quickly change back into human shape whenever they approach Baka forest camps or villages.

How to interpret shapeshifters

The transformation of human into animal form is a standard element in Baka *lìkànè* stories which recount God's creation of the animal kingdom. Human shapeshifting is a renowned Baka hunting technique used since mythical times. In the Tìbelà song-fable, the eponymous hero learns how to play the zither instrument in the heavenly village of Komba, the Creator-God. One day the hero leaves for the forest, where he discovers that his music attracts animals. Komba sends people out to find Tìbelà and to bring him back to his village. Tìbelà is caught in the middle of a huge herd of elephants, riding one of the animals while playing his zither. Forced to return, Tìbelà is transformed by Komba into the bird that henceforth indicates the presence of elephants to Baka hunters, and Tìbelà's hunting magic is then shared out to Baka women (Pepper 1955; Boursier 1994: 215). In contrast with *lìkànè* stories, *mòkìlà* stories make no reference to Komba, nor is there any claim that *mòkìlà* originate in mythical times.[4]

In the particular incident described above, the first signs of the *mòkìlà* were noticed near Ntam. This is a small commercial centre on the Congo–Cameroon border where Muslim traders notoriously engage in ivory trafficking and directly commission Baka for its production.[5] Until the collapse of the Congolese cocoa market in the mid-1980s, Ntam used to be a flourishing trading station for imports of consumer items from Cameroon. Now it mainly serves as an outlet for the Souanké production of gold and ivory. *Mòkìlà* stories could thus be interpreted in terms of political economy: as reflecting the conditions of the production and the flow of commodities, and in particular, the export of ivory to Cameroon in return for money and manufactured goods.

This equation certainly enters Baka *mòkìlà* discourse and it will be a significant part of my argument. However, to analyse the *mòkìlà* phenomenon as mainly a response to an expanding market sphere, and as a local interpretation (in graphic predatory imagery) of what Jean and John Comaroff have dubbed the 'malcontents of modernity' (1993), would be to bypass its underlying 'cultural logic' and simplify and reduce it to a commodity idiom. Commoditization and monetarization clearly represent an intrusion upon egalitarian Baka values, but they have been assimilated to a considerable extent to Baka cultural understandings and social purposes. Historically, Baka participation in the market economy has been linked strongly but not exclusively to the production of ivory, which has accounted for the most substantial individual profits to be made. But so far, these have been integrated into a largely subsistence-based economy in which sharing[6] is still the dominant practice. Indeed, ivory appears to be the most successful instance of the integration of a 'modern', money-driven economy into a 'traditional' economy based on sharing and socially motivated exchanges.

I challenge the kind of interpretation suggested by the Comaroffs, according to which ivory would have turned into a 'magical, impenetrable, inscrutable, uncontrollable, darkly dangerous' commodity illuminating the 'historical irony' and the 'cosmic oxymoron' of modernity (ibid.). Rather, I shall argue that commoditization and other aspects of 'modernity' have to be analysed in the local contexts in which they unfold. Although these are certainly connected and part of larger 'global' dynamics, as anthropologists we should take care not to succumb uncritically to metanarratives which prioritize market forces, political powers and a cultural logic 'centered elsewhere' (see Englund and Leach, forthcoming). This premise holds for an interpretation of apparently 'occult economies' as much as for an understanding of people–wildlife conflicts. For the current discourse on biodiversity, conservation and sustainable uses of natural resources, the indication is indeed, rather to the contrary, that the centres of innovative discourse and action are shifting towards the 'peripheries' or 'marginal sites' (see Escobar 1998).

So what can we make of *mòkìlà* from a distinctly Baka cultural perspective rather than a modernist one? Michael Jackson (1989) has provided an interesting approach to the subject of shapeshifting from a 'radical empiricist' perspective in his analysis of a Kuranko man who claimed that he 'could turn into an elephant'. Jackson traces the biography and personal experiences of the man and sets them within Kuranko colonial history to strive for an apt interpretation of the existential and psychological appeal of shapeshifting. In particular, Jackson reveals an ancestral connection – the totem animal of the shapeshifter's clan is the elephant – and charts the positive moral evaluation of the relations between humans and other agents of the natural world in Kuranko myths. In addition to a primordial attachment to his clan, the shapeshifter calls on culturally specific images of liminal life, thus following a Kuranko tendency to externalize interior states as ontological experiences in order to cope with personal crises.

My argument in this chapter focuses on the hybridity of *mòkìlà* and explores the relations between the hybrid's two constituent elements: people and elephants. Central to my analysis is a particular Baka perception of the forest as a shared lifeworld and a mode of socializing with non-human agents, drawing on Bird-David's (1992) notion of a 'cosmic economy of sharing'. Exploring the particular cultural meanings of Baka–elephant sharing relations, I will argue for an understanding of *mòkìlà* as an embodiment of these relations. If this argument holds, how can we then interpret the predatory plot and the terror evoked by *mòkìlà* threats? *Mòkìlà* stories point to the existence of a secret shapeshifting society that takes collective revenge for the killing of its members by Baka hunters. My hypothesis is that *mòkìlà* accounts represent a contentious moral discourse about human–elephant relations in which the motif of sharing is pitted against that of mutual predation. In short, these stories express an existential and moral dilemma from a sharing perspective.

In order to examine these dilemmas, I first sketch the complexities of Baka–elephant relations in a shared forest world. I then provide the socio-economic and historical context of Baka involvement in elephant hunting and ivory production, including their exchange relations with Bantu-speaking neighbours. Finally, I return to an analysis of *mòkìlà* stories. A comparison of shapeshifting and witchcraft reveals a common Baka preoccupation with the moral fabric of society and with sharing relations in particular. *Mòkìlà* imagery also evokes collective memories of ethnic strife in the nineteenth century and thus makes reference to wider social relations and conflictual Baka relations with other ethnic groups. My contention is that just as the elephant appears as the 'paradigm of all game' (Joiris 1993b: 54) in Baka thought, so Baka–elephant relations appear as the paradigm of forest sharing relations between humans, animals and plants more generally. This includes tensions arising from less egalitarian aspects of these relations. Examining the existential and moral dilemmas transparent in the *mòkìlà* threat, I extend the theoretical scope of the concept of sharing beyond the emphasis on egalitarianism. *Mòkìlà* stories problematize the inegalitarian aspects of social relations and express Baka concerns with sharing relations in the face of contradictory social realities.

Baka–elephant relations in a shared forest world

In Baka contexts, 'real' elephants are always forest elephants, *Loxodonta africana cyclotis*, which some biologists distinguish from another subspecies, *Loxodonta africana africana*, the savannah and bush elephant.

> [The] forest elephant is distinguished by its small size, up to 2.5 m tall at the shoulder in the bull and 2.1 m in the cow, with weights of 2.7 to 6 tonnes. It has characteristic rounded ears, unlike the 'map of Africa' shape of the bush elephant, and almost straight, downwardly pointing tusks.
>
> (Spinage 1994: 28)

Baka say that elephants are the biggest and strongest animals in the forest and that only man dares to attack them. Both predators like the leopard, and the 'hooligans' of the forest world, gorillas and chimpanzees (see Richards, Chapter 4), are known to keep out of the elephant's way. For Baka, elephants are the lords of the animal kingdom and powerful and mysterious ancestral figures of the forest. This status comes out particularly well in awe-inspiring stories about Njàbò, 'the biggest of all elephants'. Njàbò is a mythical being, a totem-like ancestor with enormous tusks. But there are also living incarnations of Njàbò, old bulls and cows of exceptional force which lead and guide actual herds. Njàbò leaders walk and feed mostly by themselves, but they are also said to have 'bodyguards like a president' who follow them at a respectful distance. A single signalling call from Njàbò suffices for a whole elephant 'battalion' to instantly rally around them.

An experienced elephant hunter knows how to tell Njàbò apart from other old and strong elephants. He has already seen Njàbò footprints – 'as big as a window' – and would not even imagine attacking such an elephant. He will just watch the animal and let it pass in awe knowing that were he to shoot, the moment he fires his gun he would be condemned to a terrible illness or instant death. It is said that the moment a bullet or *sàlà* enters the body of Njàbò, there will be thunder and lightning and a frightening storm will rage in the sky. One Baka man also related the claim – apparently made by 'great white hunters' – that each tusk of

Njàbò harboured another ten tusks inside it, and that the family of a successful hunter would find an enormous pair of tusks every five years on the spot where Njàbò had been killed.

Through this legendary figure we can glimpse the Baka perception of elephants and of the animals' status as giant masters of the forest. But elephants are also known as voracious eaters and forest 'bruisers' who regularly uproot trees to make a clearing or a path, or feed on tender top leaves and fruit. They leave scenes of destruction wherever they move. On their regular circuits, elephants create wide forest tracks. Baka appreciate them both for the walking comfort and the access they afford to wild forest resources. One of the 'modern' Baka metaphors to describe an elephant making a path is that it is a 'machine', while elephants on the move in the forest are also compared to 'lorries'.

Due to continued hunting pressure, elephants stay well away from major roads and tend to cluster in small groups in forest areas that provide refuge from humans (Fay *et al.* 1992: 26–28). Local people can thus largely avoid crop damage by clearing plots for cultivation away from well-worn elephant trails. However, small herds or rogue animals still raid outlying gardens, although not to the extent experienced by farmers in other areas where anti-poaching measures have been relatively effective. Fay (1993: 25), for instance, reports on how the success of elephant protection programmes in two conservation areas northeast of Souanké has introduced a 'classic paradox': extensive crop damage in the marginal zones of the conservation areas caused by increasingly fearless elephants (see also Lahm 1994, for similar problems experienced by forest dwelling cultivators in northeastern Gabon, an area directly bordering the Souanké District).

In 1989, the Convention for International Trade of Endangered Species (CITES) issued a world-wide ban on trade in ivory and other elephant products. This ban has had only limited effect in Souanké due to very limited border control, at least on the Congolese side. Also, the district administration does not include a wildlife management scheme. Elephant hunting thus continues both because there is a persistent demand for ivory on the Cameroonian black market and because local people lack much needed alternative opportunities to earn cash.

A core area of potential conflict and competition between Baka and the giant herbivores is over gathering fruit and tubers of the forest. Baka carry out gathering during the day, while elephants often 'gather' at night. Favourite Baka hunting-and-gathering grounds are abandoned village sites and surrounding gardens that have since reverted to secondary forest growth. Such sites are rich in wild-growing former cultigens and attract small game, but gorillas, wild boar and elephants also come to feed on the fruit and to dig for roots and tubers. Baka experience has been confirmed by research in northeastern Gabon which revealed a marked preference among these animals for secondary forest regrowth (Barnes *et al.* 1991; Lahm 1993). Baka greatly cherish wild yam tubers (*Dioscorea spp.*), which they appreciate both for their good taste and for their carbohydrates. Important plants in wild yam groves are semi-domesticated or 'paracultivated' as a staple forest foodstuff – that is, they are cared for and protected in their original environment, owned, managed over time and eventually inherited (Dounias 1993: 630). Baka paracultivation practices, however, do not make the plants safe from being 'harvested' by elephants.

Bà (*Dioscorea mangenotiana*) produces the largest of all forest tubers. In their later growth stages Baka compare these woody tubers, called *pàpè*, to elephants. This is a reference to shared size, colour and skin or peel texture,[7] but elephants are also known to dig the tubers up at this stage. Before turning woody, *bà* are considered a delicacy by Baka, and are also said to be the favourite food of the supreme forest spirit Jɛngì. This shared food preference plays an important part in Jɛngì rituals, in which the plant is symbolically highlighted as the nexus between the ancestral spirit world of both humans and elephants (Joiris 1993a: 633). In ceremonial 'dances',[8] the powerful tutelary spirit Jɛngì makes its appearance in Baka camps and villages in a plant mask that is a metaphorical representation of the yam. The various growth stages of *Dioscorea mangenotiana* are further designated with terms referring to spirits of the Jɛngì family, also called *mɛ na yà*, 'elephant spirits'. These are the spirits of deceased great hunters, who 'walk side by side with elephants' guarding the herds and guiding them in their search for yam. These anthropomorphic, dwarfish spirits are likewise the guides of Baka hunters in their search for game. *Bà* are taboo food for Jɛngì initiates, and great hunters will not carry this yam during the hunt in order to avoid being charged by elephants (Joiris 1993a: 636, 639).

Jɛngì rituals are full of symbolic references to a shared forest world, and exemplify a perception and an engagement with it. This would accord with Bird-David's (1992) concept of the 'cosmic economy of sharing'. This term implies a thoroughly social, undivided, and distinctive experience on the part of hunter-gatherer groups of their respective ecosystems, as well as the inclusion of non-human agents in social relations on an equal footing. Such sharing may hold from a Baka perspective, in which hunting – the main social interaction with animals – is experienced as a largely unconditional provisioning with game meat.

Actual elephants, however, may beg to differ. Defending their range and venting their anger on human intruders, elephants destroy Baka hunting camps. Focusing their anger on fireplaces and smoking racks, they kick the wooden constructions apart, trample on the ashes and disperse remaining pieces of firewood. For the Baka, fire is the essential distinguishing characteristic of a human way of life, and its destruction by the elephant is seen as an angry attempt to annihilate a human privilege. At issue too are competitive elephant attitudes to humans and aggressive territorial claims which suggest a disregard for sharing. One expression of this is the elephant crop-raiding mentioned above, something greatly feared by the Baka. They try to avoid elephant crop damage by establishing their gardens and fields away from known animal territories or in the vicinity of the village. However, they usually do not try and protect their crops by fencing in their fields, nor do they 'mine' them with traps – which the neighbouring Bantu do.

Analyses of Baka hunting rituals by Joiris (1993b; 1996) have emphasized the role of tutelary forest spirits as mediators or facilitators of successful big-game hunting. Human access to wild animal and plant resources, and notably to prestigious game like elephants, depends crucially on harmonious relations with the spirit world. This is the realm of the dead and the normally invisible agency of the ancestral spirits, and it is living human initiates, so-called *mo-mɛ*, 'spirit guardians' or 'keepers', who make contact with them to secure cosmic balance and social harmony. Great hunters enlist the support, protection and guidance of a number of spirits belonging to different families and classes, but the most important spirits are those of dead master hunters and of deceased initiates of ritual associations.[9]

The spirits of dead master hunters are called *ñabùlà*. Like access to other spirits, a personal and privileged relationship with a *ñabùlà* is often inherited, but it necessitates initiation and, in this particular case, the gift of a special visionary power. The *ñabùlà* ritual association is secret and normally does not organize public ceremonies or 'dances' in which the spirits of other associations make their appearance. *Ñabùlà* are invisible to the non-initiated, but show themselves to hunters, especially when a tusk elephant has been killed. Uttering elephant-like thundering sounds, the *ñabùlà* spirit then walks in front of the hunter as he walks back to the camp to announce the news of the game. At the site of the kill, the *ñabùlà* will later hold the tusks for a while before disappearing again (Joiris 1993b: 63–64).

Crucial connections between hunters and elephants thus exist in the spirit world. They are invoked in rituals of sharing that draw on personalized relationships between humans, animals and plants, and centre on a favourable 'giving environment'. The downside of this all-embracing nexus is that not all *mɛ* ('human spirits') walking the forest, are benevolent protectors of the living. The spirits of those who have met with a violent or witchcraft-induced death are likely to become malevolent or tricky trouble-makers, while witches themselves are unlikely candidates for a tutelary spirit existence. Their fate is rather reincarnation as small and medium-sized animals which become potential game for Baka hunters.

This outline of the mythical, spiritual and eco-cosmological ramifications of Baka–elephant relations has drawn attention to the particular cultural meanings of a Baka 'cosmic economy of sharing', and to what we might call its 'problematic' aspects like competition for shared resources, demand-sharing, territorial antagonism, and malevolence.[10] Concerning the intimate interaction within 'assertively egalitarian' societies like the Baka, Woodburn (1982) has argued that 'powerful levelling mechanisms', such as the imposition of sharing and a non-competitive value system, serve to counter the development of inequalities of wealth, power and prestige, and to maintain social harmony. The application of levelling mechanisms is, however, of limited appeal in relations with either non-egalitarian exchange partners or non-human agents (animals and plants) which have their own perspectives on such relations and interact accordingly. Their approach may be at variance with the Baka concern with sharing relations.

A Baka history of the ivory trade

Concerning the historical involvement of Pygmy groups in ivory trading, it has been argued that traditionally they neither hunted elephants nor ate elephant meat, and that they only began eating elephants when they developed big-game hunting techniques in response to rising market demands for ivory in the late nineteenth century (Bahuchet and Guillaume 1982: 200; Ichikawa 1991: 136). Early European sources, on the other hand, mention different Pygmy groups from the seventeenth century onwards both as producers and procurers of ivory and as consumers of elephant meat.[11] Historical linguistic research even suggests that already around 1000 AD, hunting-and-gathering peoples, among them Pygmies, had become specialist procurers of forest products, and that ivory was among the most valuable items that were traded through long-distance networks out of central African forests (Klieman 1999). Ivory continued to be an important trade item during the Atlantic era, when it was 'the most lucrative of all legitimate commodities and the mainstay of the trade throughout the whole period' (Vansina 1990: 209).

The Baka language has two words for ivory. The more common one is 'teeth of elephant' or *tɛ-yà*, an Ubangian term which is also used by their former neighbours living in the south-east of the Central African Republic. If Bahuchet's (1993a: 123–124) chronology is correct, Baka migrated out of this area into present-day Cameroon and Congo from 1765 AD onwards in order to escape the turmoil created by slave-raiders coming up the Ubangi River. According to Bahuchet (ibid.: 44–45), the shared vocabulary for ivory and other commodities indicates Baka involvement in trade with Ubangian exchange partners long before the colonial period. In his view, a Li-Baka synonym for ivory, *sɛmbò*, appears to be the 'original' term (ibid.: 44), a survival from a long-lost Pygmy *ur*-language. Alternatively, however, it could be derived through regular sound changes from an old Bantu term for ivory, *-ceba*, which was widely distributed in north-western Gabon, but also on important trade routes along the southern and southwestern border of the present-day Baka area (see Klieman 1999: 94, map 7). The adoption of a Bantu term would simply confirm Baka trading contacts with Bantu speakers[12] over the last two centuries and would fit a pattern of linguistic influences which is especially evident for terms relating to cultivated food and commodities.

By the 1880s, the Atlantic trading sphere had caught up with the forests of southern Cameroon and northwestern Congo, parts of which were, according to oral history, still 'full of elephants and full of Pygmies, just elephants and Pygmies' in the mid-nineteenth century (Laburthe-Tolra 1981: 156). Until then, ivory was traded through inter-ethnic networks connecting the hinterland with the coast. With colonial occupation, the agents of European concessionary companies sought to get forest products at their source in the interior rather than from coastal middlemen. But they experienced difficulties in trading directly with Baka and other Pygmy groups both because such groups were 'naturally' shy and because neighbouring groups had a vested commercial interest in preventing direct European access to them (Bruel 1910: 112; Regnault 1911: 264, 286). During this phase, European demand for ivory reached a peak.[13] The German colonial administration of the Ngoko area just north of Souanké, for instance, reported in 1905 that ivory, the second most important export item of this region after rubber, was already in serious decline. This was due to the 'mass murder' of elephants committed by the Baka, who were killing these animals as much for their meat as for their tusks (Archives Nationales de Yaoundé, FA 1/65: 214).

It was probably during the early days of colonial rule that expert Pygmy elephant hunters gained socio-economic and political salience in exchange relations with Bantu neighbours. Bantu consistently refer to what Baka call (*wà-*)*tuma* or 'great hunter' as a 'Pygmy chief'. Some informants pointed out that around the turn of this century important Pygmy 'chiefs' received Bantu wives (in some cases, a number of wives) from their patrons. Marriages between Pygmy men and Bantu women are rare today, but in the past Bantu wife-giving to Pygmies was clearly related to extraordinary services provided, particularly those rendered in elephant-hunting. One of the effects of the ivory trade was thus to reinforce the bases of authority and power among Pygmy 'masters of the great hunt' (Bahuchet and Guillaume 1982: 200).

With the decline of the ivory market due to overhunting and the gradual monetarization of the colonial economy, ivory began to lose part of its trading and prestige value among the Bantu. Especially from the late 1950s onwards, when the Bantu in Souanké moved very successfully into cocoa cash cropping, money and western consumer goods began to replace previous measures of value, notably ivory and regionally used African iron currencies (Vincent 1961; 1963). Ivory production remained, however, an important economic activity and money-earner for the Baka and was only partially eclipsed by wage labour and cash-cropping opportunities. Ivory rose to a more salient position again within the wider Souanké economy with the collapse of the cocoa market in the mid-1980s, when 'money', as locals comment, 'went back to its producers' or 'back home to the whites'. An otherwise favourable environmental report on Souanké thus came to state that 'only the elephant population has suffered relatively long term disturbance which has significantly altered densities and behaviour' (Fay *et al.* 1992: 30).

Like other Pygmy groups, Baka formerly exchanged ivory and other forest products for cultivated food, salt and iron, and nowadays also for money, clothing and other consumer items (old radios, household goods, machetes, etc.). In the second half of the nineteenth century, elephant tusks were not only important in Bantu bridewealth transactions but also in Baka ones, in combination with heavy metal objects[14] and, most likely, in addition to brideservice. The importance of ivory as an exchange item probably also encouraged Baka polygyny which is still significantly, though not exclusively, linked to great hunter status.

Despite Baka sedentarization and increased agricultural subsistence, elephant-hunting has remained both a culturally and an economically valuable activity. Elephant meat and fat are highly appreciated as a welcome change from the regular diet of small and medium-sized game, and constitute 'prestige' food. Elephant tusks were formerly used as tools, for instance, to beat bark into a fine cloth. They still occasionally serve to hammer smoked elephant meat to make it soft enough for consumption, but they are predominantly gifted and exchanged in Baka bridewealth transactions or find their way to Bantu exchange partners or traders. Ivory tusks thus combine the values of conceptually distinct economic modes and link different spheres of circulation. Depending on the situation, they are shared and given, gifted and exchanged, traded and sold.

Baka elephant terminology is more extensive than that for any other animal species. It is even more extensive than bee and termite terminology, even though bees produce the ultimate 'prestige' food, honey, and termites are a culinary delicacy after which Baka have named a whole season. Li-Baka elephant typology (Tables 1 and 2) shows the great concern with the gender, age, maturation and social behaviour of elephants, as well as, significantly, with the condition of elephant tusks (numbers 5, 6, 9, 11–14 and 16 in Tables 1 and 2, which represent almost half of all known 'types'). Otherwise, Baka hunters are very knowledgeable about elephant range, seasonal habitats and feeding patterns. All of these empirical observations make for good 'indigenous science', albeit one that is certainly not value-free and reveals a distinct preoccupation with ivory. This should come as no surprise considering the enduring appeal of ivory for Baka market and social exchanges.

Elephants are mainly hunted in the service of local Bantu patrons or immigrant Muslim merchants, who provide a commissioned hunter with a shotgun and ammunition and with food and tobacco. An elephant hunt can take up to a few weeks, and relatively few Baka hunters own a gun and/or are capable of saving up for the initial investment to embark independently on such an enterprise. This is due to an egalitarian ethos and 'demand-sharing', but also to Bantu control of the means of production and efforts to keep the Baka in dependent relations. Until the current 'economic crisis', elephants were often hunted with rifles, but rifle ammunition has become too expensive and hard to obtain. The most affordable and efficient technique today relies on a short, custom-made spear called a *sàlà*. The spear consists of a wooden shaft topped with a razor-sharp blade. It is inserted into the barrel of a shotgun and fired – usually from close range – at the side of an elephant to pierce its vital organs.

Success in big-game hunting depends upon a delicate state of harmonious and well-balanced relations among people, and between people and their environment. A Baka hunter and his family have to observe certain restrictions in sexual and dietary behaviour and undertake certain

Table 1 Classification of male and female elephants related to physical growth and tusk size

1.	(ʔè)pùsa	Newborn male
2.	(ʔè)pùnjɛ	Newborn female
3.	mòmbèngè	Juvenile male still 'walking with its mother'
4.	bèndùmù	Juvenile female still 'walking with its mother'
5.	(ʔè)sùʔbe	Pubescent male with very small tusks
6.	ʔaluma	Pubescent female with very small tusks
7.	mòsèmbi	Young adult bull
8.	mombongo	Adult bull at the height of his powers; leader of a bull herd who can assert his status by copulating with all the females in the area
9.	likòmbà	Adult cow with tusks
10.	kàmbà	Big, often solitary, bull; not a regular herd member or leader
11.	njàbò	(Mythical) ancestor figure of either sex, endowed with an enormous body and giant tusks

Table 2 Rogue males, solitary bulls and tusk-deficient exemplars

12.	(ʔè)mbutu	Either a bull or a cow without tusks
13.	(ʔè)selesele	Bull or cow with only one tusk
14.	(ʔè)sùpà	Cow with only one tusk or none
15.	(ʔè)koambe	The essential loner, *koambe* is said to prefer solitude to herd life from an early age onwards
16.	mòsàφòlà	Being a big, old and 'tired' solitary bull, *mòsàφòlà* is often suffering from molar tooth decay (caries), though he may still be in possession of his tusks. He is known for a limited walking range of approximately 10 km per day.
17.	sɛmɛ	Old, solitary bull known for a watery but strong-smelling secretion exuding from the temporal gland behind the eye, who also loses lots of water (probably old bull's incontinence) and is considered to be dangerous. 'The females refuse to copulate with *sɛmɛ*' (likewise with *mòsàφòlà*).
18.	séèmbìà	Elephant with a lame foot

ritual actions. Most importantly, great hunters abstain from consuming the meat of any of the big game animals they hunt. Their family and friends, however, make the most of a dead elephant, joining them in the forest to dry the meat and to rejoice in a feast. Professional Bantu elephant hunters, on the other hand, mainly go for the tusks; they cut off a few choice pieces of meat but leave the rest of the carcass to rot.

After this outline of the historical and socio-economic contexts of Baka elephant hunting and Baka participation in the ivory trade, let us return to the main subject, elephant-men, and their connections to both humans and elephants. It is predominantly Baka who kill and eat elephants, not the other way round. Baka hunters usually go for single, elderly tusk elephants, in part because they rarely have more than a couple of *sàlà* spears to hand. When a Baka hunter thus gets killed 'in combat' with an elephant, it commonly happens in a one-to-one encounter. *Mòkìlà* stories, on the other hand, talk of a lethal threat to Baka communities which takes the form of organized raiding and an all-embracing attack on Baka men, women and children irrespective of their age and involvement in elephant hunting. Clearly, the raiders are thought to be elephant-men and not real elephants. But this throws up two key questions. What does such concerted predation of *mòkìlà* hybrids on Baka communities mean in terms of Baka social relations? And what does it tell us about Baka perceptions of their relations with elephants?

Shapeshifting, witchcraft and ethnic violence

My interpretation of the *mòkìlà* is based on the premise that it embodies Baka–elephant sharing relations.[15] These people–elephant sharing relations in turn figure as the Baka paradigm of all sharing relations. I now attempt to show that the *mòkìlà* threat of predation highlights tensions and conflict that emerge in Baka social relations with others – be they elephants or Bantu – who do not possess the Baka sharing ethos. That *mòkìlà* are about a sharing problematic is suggested by the mutual association of shapeshifting and witchcraft, and the constitutive links between *mòkìlà* predation and the social organization and reproduction of *mòkìlà* society.

Concerning the association of the power and the practice of shapeshifting and witchcraft, we can note the following. In the hunting context, shapeshifting is said to be one of the techniques that Baka hunters employ to approach game or to avoid imminent danger by changing into the shape of an animal such as an antelope. Some hunters are also believed to use this technique to kill game by assuming the shape of predatory animals such as the leopard. The same technique may, however, be employed by witches or sorcerers (known as *wà-mbù*) to attack and prey on fellow humans by assuming an animal guise.[16] Here witchcraft is the source of shapeshifting powers.

The secret knowledge and power underlying the capacity to change from human into elephant form are thought to be passed on in one of two ways. Either they are inherited at birth like witchcraft, *mbù* (which also means *stomach*, the place where witchcraft substances are located), or they are transmitted like other forms of special knowledge through initiation into a kind of ritual association. Shapeshifting is thus a special, personal power, a skill, or both. The former is perceptually close to witchcraft or even directly associated with it; the latter is based on secret magical knowledge (*mà*, medicine, magic potion, or ritual substance) and can be acquired irrespective of age and gender. Again, there are forms of witchcraft based on initiation.

Both witchcraft and shapeshifting are ambivalent powers that can be used for good or bad purposes. A prime example is the Baka (as well as Bantu) healer. The possession of witchcraft is indispensable for healers, but they are considered to be benevolent witches who use their powers to cure, to detect evil forces, and to battle against malevolent witches. Nevertheless, there is always the danger that a healer turns 'bad'. A similar ambivalence surrounds great hunters. In addition to their hunting expertise, many are rumoured to possess special powers – including vision, privileged access to the spirit world, and shapeshifting – which help them to protect themselves and to find and kill game. But hunters also risk abusing such powers. After a series of unexpected deaths, great hunters with close kin ties to the dead easily attract suspicions that they have used witchcraft to 'eat' family members in order to enhance their own big-game hunting success.

A further indication of the proximity of shapeshifters and witches is their strange hybrid physiology. Witches in animal shape can be found out because they retain certain human characteristics, especially a hyper-aggressive and purposeful malevolence. Shapeshifters, on the other hand, maintain a distinctly human odour and faeces despite an otherwise perfect animal appearance and behaviour. The shared physiological characteristics and moral ambivalence make a clear-cut conceptual distinction between witches and shapeshifters rather difficult.

What *mòkìlà* and witches have in common is that they spill human blood instead of animal blood. But there are some crucial distinctions. *Mòkìlà* do not seek to harm or kill for individual gain, which is the underlying charge in witchcraft accusations; they are not the originators of malice; and they are not carnivorous. *Mòkìlà* raids are organized by their community. They strictly follow feuding rules and do not operate according to the logic of sorcerers' associations, for which members take turns in providing a victim for communally held blood feasts. Although the effect for Baka victims may be the same, *mòkìlà* do not act out of malicious self-interest. They kill in collective revenge and they kidnap in order to reconstruct their community. Baka are thus literally turned into game animals, a fate that normally only awaits witches at death. This appears to be the moral twist of the *mòkìlà* stories: an inversion of the role of hunter and hunted, and of the moral statuses of killer and killed. Killing animals and witches-turned-animals is not only acceptable, but is indeed a highly valued, life-sustaining human activity. But the Baka sharing ethos has a moral threshold, that of spilling human blood.

Picking up the recurrent theme of feuding and the 'war' *mòkìlà* are said to wage on Baka communities, there are some striking parallels to the nineteenth-century wars fought between Bantu groups in the wider region. Historical slave-raiding for the Atlantic slave trade only ever reached the border regions of the present-day Baka area, but in its aftermath most Bantu groups were engaged in territorial warfare against each other. Due to their basic segmentary pattern, relations within ethnic groups, that is, between 'Houses'[17] and villages, remained in a constant state of hostility. Both inter- and intra-ethnic violence commonly took the form of raids which produced another kind of 'slave'. Some enemies were killed, others were made prisoners or became refugees. Among the Njem and Bakwele, prisoners of war were only killed when they tried to flee or proved to be recalcitrant; although they were called *kuom* (*slave* or *prisoner*), they were not 'enslaved' in the sense of becoming a commodity. They were forcefully integrated into the social system of the victorious group, initially as members of an inferior status – women usually through marriage, and men and children through adoption (Siroto 1969: 108–109).[18] Refugees often depended on similar forms of social re-integration.

Baka witnessed those raids, became mediators between warring factions, and probably assisted Bantu patrons and 'war'-leaders as guides, scouts and possibly as spies. Joiris (1998) has recently suggested that contemporary inter-ethnic links between Baka and Bantu actually arose from long-standing 'razzia alliances' in pre-colonial times. Baka siding with Bantu warring factions may indeed have taken the form of raiding associations that drew their imagery from the purported shapeshifting powers of Baka hunters. The alleged *mòkìlà* practice of raiding to recoup previous losses, and the subsequent integration of raid victims into *mòkìlà* communities, reverberate with memories of a violent past and extraordinary forms of social relations.

The theme of enslavement also recurs in the current idiom of zombification, a belief that Baka share with Bantu neighbours. Zombification may itself be a twisted reflection of the history of slaving in the wider region and therefore represent a folk memory of violent and predatory social relations in the past (Shaw 1997). Beliefs in zombification certainly received new inspiration from the traumatizing experiences of colonial *corvée* labour and forced military recruitment in the early twentieth century, in which many local Bantu men had to leave their homes never to return.[19] The *mòkìlà* discourse shares a set of ideas with other tales of zombification, particularly the sinister allegations of an organized *mòkìlà* theft of human beings and their productive and reproductive capacities.[20]

The element of inter- and intra-ethnic strife, which we encounter in the assertion that *mòkìlà* are really Cameroonian Baka, is very explicit in surprisingly similar stories told among Mbendjelle Yaka Pygmies (Hauser 1951: 15; Lewis, forthcoming). Here we also find a direct and unequivocal association of shapeshifting with witchcraft. According to the Mbendjelle, who live across the Sangha River in north-eastern Congo, their Bangombe (Baka) neighbours to the west have been in conflict with them for around 250 years. Bangombe sorcerers are renowned masters of the art of shapeshifting or *mokidwa*, and are said to travel into Mbendjelle forests in elephant shape to kill men and to steal women and children.[21] Mbendjelle sorcerers claim to have their own mystical powers (invisibility and metamorphosis into dry leaves, whirlwinds, flying squirrels or birds) to counter such attacks and to combat Bangombe *mokidwa*.[22]

The motive for continued feuding is said to be competition for forest resources and the possession of (secret) knowledge and mystic powers (Lewis, forthcoming).[23] According to the Mbendjelle, a peace treaty was negotiated about a hundred years ago. During the meeting convened to establish lasting peace, the chief Mbendjelle negotiator managed to persuade Amata, his Bangombe counterpart, into giving away too many powerful secrets. Returning home, the other members of the Bangombe delegation killed Amata for having initiated the Mbendjelle into the secret powers of *niabula* or 'elephant hunting spirits' and vowed to get the *niabula* back. They thus declared the peace agreement null and void (ibid.). These events are said to have taken place about a decade before the ivory craze began to turn into an ivory crisis due to overhunting. A likely possible interpretation, therefore, is that they actually marked an intensification of the conflict between the two groups over spoils in the ivory market, or at least that they have come to represent such conflict in Mbendjelle oral history. Regnault (1911: 287–288), for instance, mentions 'palavers' and fighting between Pygmy groups over contested claims to ivory. An interpretation of market competition also agrees with other, rather enigmatic references to *mòkìlà/mokidwa* in the early colonial period, which speak of 'Pygmy warfare' while praising the Pygmy's 'gentle manners [and] a fear of spilling human blood' (Cottes 1911: 105).

People–elephant sharing?

My argument has been that *mòkìlà* elephant-men are the embodied image of a particular Baka perception and experience of sharing. I have outlined how vital the connections between humans, plants and animals inhabiting the forest are for Baka people embedded in the social relations of sharing. This implies a continuity of being and a mutual social involvement which extends beyond purely 'ecological' relations. The being-in-the-world of plants and animals is not understood reductively in terms of their utility for humans. In the Baka cultural perspective, they are clearly more than mere 'resources'; they share the relations and exhanges intrinsic to existence. Relations among people, and between people and the forest, are thus experienced as personal, intimate and shared. Baka are, to draw on Bird-David's model (1990: 192, 194), 'engaged with each other through giving and requests to be given that do not obligate them on the morrow ... they make demands on people [and, we should add, on non-human agencies] to share more but not to produce more'.

Forest hunting and gathering by humans and animals are an indispensable part of the ongoing process of life, and although they involve 'killing', there is felt to be nothing intrinsically bad about these activities. This point about the non-human constituents in hunter-gatherer sharing relations has been made by Tim Ingold:

> So long as they are treated with respect and consideration, they may be expected to act benevolently. But by the same token, they have the power to withhold if any attempt is made to coerce more than they are prepared to provide. Coercion, the attempt to extract by force, represents a betrayal of the trust that underwrites the willingness to give.
>
> (Ingold 1992: 42)

As we have seen, elephants can also react violently and get their own back. Their behaviour suggests a rather different perception of mutual relations; the territorial claims they make clearly oppose a sharing ethos. Baka maintain that the forest belongs to no one in particular, that it belongs to all its inhabitants; but such claims appear at odds with the fact that ivory hunting accelerated towards the end of the nineteenth century. Their active participation in the trade brought an element of coercion and strain into sharing relations with elephants.

What comes out from the Baka ethnography is a basic empathy with elephant communities. This empathy is not grounded in sentimentality or irrationality but in detailed observation of the sociality of elephants and an experience of a shared forest world.[24] Mixed with empathy, however, is a real fear of revenge. This fear of revenge derives both from the logic of personalized relationships and from the perceived intelligence and force of elephants. It is not so much that *mòkìlà* stories are driven by a 'nature-strikes-back' plot, but rather that they derive their cross-species dynamic from an existential dilemma and the conflicts inherent in sharing relations with another species.

Elephants are herbivores and as such not a natural Baka symbol of predation like the leopard. But they are a symbol of the paramount might and power of the forest. Furthermore, as ancestral figures, whose spirits share the realm of the dead with human spirits, elephants integrate aspects of the 'giving environment' and the cosmic sharing relations in a way that appears to be much more ambivalent than Bird-David (1990; 1992) has suggested in her writings on other hunter-gatherers. In her rather ideal-typical contrast of 'local economic models', she mentions the hunter-gatherer root metaphor of the forest as an unconditionally giving parent. But this metaphor of the forest-as-*parent* stands in opposition to the conditionally reciprocating *ancestor* upon whose blessings the subsistence of cultivators depends. I suggest that the Baka forest is literally – and not only metaphorically (Ingold 1992: 42) – both giving parent and reciprocating ancestor (Kenrick 1996), and that elephants, the prime natural providers for the Baka, integrate different economic models. Success in hunting elephants is related to a number of factors that combine conditional *and* unconditional provisions depending on social and cosmic harmony, hunting magic, spiritual protection and guidance, ancestral reciprocity, and personal knowledge and expertise. The fortuitous combination of 'local economic' factors in the context of production has its equivalent in the spheres of distribution and consumption. As I have shown, elephant meat and ivory are shared and given, gifted and exchanged, traded and sold. After all, Baka live in a 'modern' world and this is reflected in their mixed economy. However, there is a continuing Baka commitment to sharing, part of which is a deep moral concern with contradictory economic practices.

The above analysis of *mòkìlà* stories suggests that a broader understanding of sharing relations is required. This is necessary if we want to account for the continued emphasis on egalitarianism on the part of people who engage in important exchange relations with practitioners of very different kinds of sociality and economy. Sharing and an egalitarian ethos are not easily maintained in a world of unequal ethnic relations, disadvantageous market exchanges and hierarchical national and international politics. *Mòkìlà* tales express the potential to continue, *but also to fail*, at sharing.

In the nineteenth century, human sharing relations were severely put to the test in quarrelsome inter-ethnic competition for ivory spoils. At the same time, there was warfare and widespread social unrest in the region. The ruthless exploitation of both human and natural resources by European concessionaires at the turn of the twentieth century only added to the predicament. *Mòkìlà* stories, containing the elements outlined above, emerged at this conjunction of historical events which pitted violence, coercion and market competition against a prevailing Baka ethos of sharing.

At first, Baka *mòkìlà* discourse appears to reflect the relatively recent western anxiety about wildlife commoditization and conservation. I reject, however, the suggestive hypothesis that *mòkìlà* tales are about 'the malcontents of modernity' and, in particular, the concern with the commoditization of sharing relations and the attendant threat to endangered species of wildlife, since this would forcefully integrate Baka into a discourse that is not theirs. Indirectly, Baka discourse touches upon a problem with elephant conservation, but this is from a different perspective. This perspective has certainly been shaped by Baka participation in a world economy, but its foremost concerns remain embedded in a local sharing problematic rather than focusing on international capitalist relations or wildlife conservation. *Mòkìlà* tales represent a contentious moral discourse, in the idiom of shapeshifting elephant-warriors, concerned with the underpinnings of a shared lifeworld.

Conclusion

Interconnectedness and sharing have become key concepts in the current 'planetary consciousness' and a globalized discourse on ecosystems and their protection. One of the paradoxes of this discourse, and of biodiversity conservation in particular, lies in the projected image of a world that is shared by all organisms, but in which the decisions about a hierarchy of values, the right to be and to be different, and acceptable forms of species survival and 'resource' exploitation are made by humans and ultimately motivated by human interest. Current biodiversity conservation discourse and practice are still largely based on conventional paradigms of metropolitan science and are dominated by Northern capitalist interests, despite an increasing recognition of 'the impossibility of harmonizing the needs of economy and environment within the existing frameworks and institutions of the economy' (Escobar 1998: 58). This also became evident in the controversy over the conservation of the African elephant (see Freeman and Kreuter 1994). The decisive campaigns to implement a world-wide ban on ivory were all run outside the African continent, mainly by western conservation agencies in the USA and the UK. These agencies greatly profited from their campaigns in terms of increased membership and funding, but when it came to pay for anti-poaching programmes, the promises of the United States and the European Community to make good lost ivory revenues were not fulfilled, and the burden to sponsor the conservation of this 'part of the world heritage' was placed on Africans (Bonner 1994: 67–68). The sound conservation efforts by southern African countries were played down for almost a decade with reference to 'global interests', even though these efforts were backed by sufficient infrastructure to closely monitor elephant numbers and to control the use and marketing of elephant products in order to finance conservation projects.[25]

Baka tales of an organized elephant–man 'insurgency' reveal a particular cultural perception of people–wildlife, as well as people–people, conflicts. These culturally situated understandings of local ecology, economy, society, and their interrelations can be understood as a practical endorsement of participatory conservation statements.[26] If Northern conservation and sustainable development efforts are to be successful, they must move away from single species conservation, come to terms with local perceptions and practices, and encourage local participation on the basis of specific socio-economic and ecosystemic contexts.

Notes

1 Since colonial times, Baka – along with other central African 'hunter-gatherer' groups of similar phenotype and culture – have been subsumed under the racial category of 'Pygmies', an often derogatively used term referring back to ancient Greek myths about dwarfish African forest dwellers. In a highly contentious fashion, the relatively short stature of these peoples and their forest-based subsistence have been interpreted as indicators of aboriginal status and an age-old adaptation to the tropical rainforest environment. For a review of the historical 'invention of the Pygmies', see Bahuchet (1993b), and for a 'revisionist' critique of an assumed 'Pygmy' aboriginality, Blench (1999).
2 Souanké District lies in the Sangha Region of northwestern Congo and borders with Cameroon and Gabon.
3 *Mòkìlà* is a commonly used synonym of *mòkèlàkèlà*, to which I stick throughout this text.
4 Pöli, a middle-aged Cameroonian Baka woman, says: 'I think that our ancestors didn't know the *mòkìlà*, otherwise I would have heard them speak about them' (Boursier 1996: 124).

5   Much of the legal and illegal trade in and out of Souanké is organized by immigrants from countries to the north (Cameroon, C.A.R., Niger) who are locally referred to as Hauossa, although many are ethnic Fulbe.
6   I adhere to Ingold's (1986: 113–117) definition of the concept of sharing which includes all economic activities from production to distribution and consumption, and characteristically encompasses the totality of economic and social involvement with the world. As an unbounded extension of egalitarian exchange, sharing is an 'experience' rather than a behavioural code or a rule of prescriptive altruism.
7   This is a more mundane example of a Baka perception of shared human, animal and plant life. Metaphorical extensions linking the physical appearance or size of plants and their nutritional value in ambiguous references to certain animals are a common feature in Li-Baka terminology. One of the biggest domesticated members of the genus yam is called *elephant yam*, *kù?bè-à-yà*, and the Giant French plantain *mba-yà* or 'elephant plantain'.
8   The term *bè* designates a ceremonial complex including dancing, singing and sometimes feasting.
9   There are a number of ways (songs, dances, ritual substances, dreams and trance) in which grand living initiates can enter into contact with these spirits and procure their assistance.
10 According to Bird-David (1992: 30), 'human-to-human and nature-to-human sharing' are the principal constituents of a 'cosmic economy of sharing'. In the Baka context, nature-to-nature sharing is also evident. The forest shares, for instance, yam with elephants and other animals, just as it does with Baka. The sharing between Baka and elephants of wild food includes an accepted element of competition. When it comes to planted food, however, Baka try to avoid sharing by 'hiding' their gardens from elephants. The voracious appetite and the destructiveness of elephants introduce an element of excessive sharing and dangerous competition which make the 'visiting' of Baka gardens by elephants, otherwise an integral part of human-to-human and human-to-nature sharing relationships, highly undesirable.
11 The Dutch geographer Dapper (1686: 358, cited in Bahuchet 1993b: 162), for instance, refers to a small people known as 'Mimos' and 'Bakke-Bakke' along the central African Loango coast. These 'dwarfs' from the interior were reputedly capable of rendering themselves invisible and thus excellent elephant hunters, eating the meat and selling the tusks.
12 In order of their demographic importance, the contemporary 'non-Pygmy' neighbours of the Baka in Souanké District are Bakwele, Njem and Fang, all of them Bantu language speakers. To distinguish them as a group from the Baka, who speak an Ubangian language, I am referring to them throughout as their 'Bantu' neighbours.
13 From 1899 to 1910, the whole of French Equatorial Africa exported more than 100 tons of ivory per year. For German Kamerun, Stoecker notes that '[t]he amount of ivory shipped abroad increased rapidly up to 1905 but then declined abruptly because elephants had been hunted to extinction in large parts of the country' (1986: 72).
14 These were called *mendjokɵ* or *betumu*, and a Bangombe (Baka) elder near Ouesso mentioned an exchange rate with the Bantu of around 20 *mendjokɵ* for one 'head', i.e. a pair of elephant tusks, 'in earlier colonial times'.

Bridewealth for a Pygmy woman was then equally either a 'head' of ivory or around 20 *mendjoko* (Regnault 1911: 281).

15 Csordas has proposed embodiment as a non-dualistic paradigm for the study of culture positing the 'socially informed body' (Bourdieu 1977: 124) as 'the existential ground of culture' (Csordas 1990: 5, 40), which mediates fundamental distinctions and dualities such as mind/body, subject/object, perception/objectification and cognition/emotion. As a concept, embodiment thus allows an analysis of people's perception of their cultural world in existential and bodily terms. I am stretching the concept here to grasp Baka cultural experience and the existential meanings of a shared lifeworld in the bodily objectification of elephant-men who, I submit, integrate specific cultural 'selves' and 'others'.

16 The distinction between witchcraft and sorcery is somewhat fluid (and certainly not of much relevance to the victim). The main difference appears to reside in the intentionality and organization of harmful acts. Witches act individually, and while some are aware of their nocturnal activities, others are not. Sorcerers, on the other hand, are organized in secret ritual associations, and their acts are purposefully malicious. See Joiris's distinction between 'unwilling witches', 'willing witches', and 'real sorcerers' (1993b: 56–57).

17 In the sense that Vansina uses this term. 'House' is the gloss of a widespread central African terminology for 'a large household establishment' (1990: 73) and denotes a residential unit encompassing what anthropologists have conceptualized as 'lineage' as well as other indigenous forms of socio-economic organization.

18 For the treatment of prisoners of war among other Bantu groups in southern Cameroon, see Laburthe-Tolra (1981: 340–341, 343–344) concerning the southern Fang and the Beti, and Geschiere (1982: 31) concerning the Maka.

19 In the 1920s, many colonial subjects from the Sangha Region were recruited for the construction of the Congo–Océan railway and made to join work camps in which mortality rates reached up to 30 per cent (Robineau 1967: 325; Sautter 1967: 271).

20 For an extended discussion of zombification, see Geschiere (1991), who offers a number of interpretive leads and aims to show that diverging discourses on zombification in various regions of Cameroon are transformations of a 'similar set of ideas'. Depending on cultural and historical particularities, they can reflect pre-colonial slavery and forced labour regimes during the colonial period as well as current, more ambiguous associations with inequalities of political power and the accumulation of wealth.

21 The term *mokidwa* also designates the specific Bangombe sorcerer associations practising elephant shapeshifting. According to Mbendjelle, Bangombe sorcerers use elephant shape for important practical advantages. They can thus travel swiftly and safely through the forest, easily cross marshland and rivers, and raid relatively risk-free, remaining invulnerable to all but experienced elephant hunters.

22 Interestingly, the Mbendjelle – speakers of a largely unrelated Bantu language – also have the term *mòkìlà* in their lexicon. Jerome Lewis (forthcoming) points out that in the Mbendjelle language *ekila*, the commonly used plural form of *mòkìlà*, designates a complex polysemic concept. *Ekila* can refer to menstruation, nose-bleeding, hunter's meat, blood, taboo,

animals' power to harm humans, dangers to human reproduction, health, sanity and the food quest. Animals and certain plants have *ekila*, and humans develop their own, personal *ekila* as they grow up. It remains with them throughout life and must be carefully guarded to ensure success in daily activities.

23 Lewis's Bangombe informants asserted that feuding continues because Mbendjelle forests are richer in wild yams and because Mbendjelle women are irresistibly beautiful.

24 This empathy is based on a sharing experience and has to be distinguished from the sentimental anthropomorphization and the imputation of human feelings to 'totem animals' – such as elephants and whales – which has been a common feature in western conservation and animal rights discourses and campaigns (Kalland 1994).

25 After years of unsuccessful lobbying for a review of the trade ban, Namibia, Botswana and Zimbabwe's proposal to downlist the elephant to Appendix 2 in their countries was overwhelmingly accepted at the 10th CITES conference in Zimbabwe in 1997. These three countries have since been allowed to resume ivory trading under restricted conditions and tight international supervision (Crace 1997: 10).

26 At the fourth Conference of the Parties to the Convention of Biological Diversity (CBD) in 1998, 'indigenous representatives reached a consensus on the implementation of Article 8j of the CBD, which calls for the respect and maintenance of local knowledge practices. This consensus calls for the creation of a permanent working group with full participation of indigenous peoples' (Escobar 1998: 58).

References

Archives Nationales de Yaoundé. Jahresbericht der Verwaltung am Ngoko, Lomie, für die Zeit vom 1.4.1904 – 31.3.1905. FA 1/65: 202–219, Yaoundé, Cameroon.

Bahuchet, S. (1993a) *La Rencontre des Agriculteurs: Les Pygmées parmi les Peuples d'Afrique Centrale. Histoire d'une Civilisation Forestière*, Tome 2. Ethnoscience 9, Paris: Peeters-Louvain.

—— (1993b) L'invention des Pygmées, *Cahiers d'Études Africaines* 129, XXXIII(1): 153–181.

Bahuchet, S. and Guillaume, H. (1982) Aka-farmer relations in the northwest Congo Basin, in E. Leacock and R. B. Lee (eds), *Politics and History in Band Societies*. Cambridge and New York: Cambridge University Press.

Barnes, R. F. W., Barnes, K. L., Alers, M. P. T. and Blom, A. (1991) Man determines the distribution of elephants in the rain forests of northeastern Gabon, *African Journal of Ecology* 29: 54–63.

Bird-David, N. H. (1990) The giving environment: another perspective on the economic system of gatherer-hunters, *Current Anthropology* 31(2): 189–196.

—— (1992) Beyond 'the original affluent society': a culturalist reformulation, *Current Anthropology* 33(1): 25–47.

Blench, R. (1999) Are the African Pygmies an ethnographic fiction?, in K. Biesbrouck, S. Elders and G. Rossel (eds), *Central African Hunter-gatherers in a Multidisciplinary Perspective: Challenging Elusiveness*, Leiden: CNWS.

Bonner, R. (1994) Western conservation groups and the ivory ban wagon, in M. M. R. Freeman and U. P. Kreuter (eds), *Elephants and Whales: Resources For Whom?*, Basel: Gordon and Breach Science Publishers.

Bourdieu, P. (1977) *Outline of a Theory of Practice*, trans. R. Nice, Cambridge: Cambridge University Press.

Boursier, D. (1994) *'Depuis ce jour-là . . .': Contes des Pygmées Baka du Sud-Est Cameroun*, Paris: L'Harmattan.

—— (1996) *Pöli. Mémoire d'une femme Pygmée. Récit de Pöli traduit par Daniel Boursier. Témoignage auto-biographique d'une femme Pygmée-Baka (Sud-Est Cameroun)*, Paris: L'Harmattan.

Bruel, G. (1910) Les populations de la Moyenne Sanga: les Babinga, *Revue d'Ethnographie et de Sociologie* (Paris) 5–7: 111–118.

Comaroff, J. and Comaroff, J. (1993) Introduction, in J. Comaroff and J. Comaroff (eds), *Modernity and its Malcontents: Ritual and Power in Postcolonial Africa*, Chicago: The University of Chicago Press.

Cottes, A. (Capitaine) (1911) *La Mission Cottes au Sud Cameroun (1905–1908)*, Paris: Leroux.

Crace, J. 1997. Tinkering with the ivories, *Guardian Education*, 24 June.

Csordas, T. J. (1990) Embodiment as a paradigm for anthropology, *Ethos* 18: 5–47.

Dounias, E. (1993) Perception and use of wild yams by the Baka hunter-gatherers in south Cameroon, in C. M. Hladik, A. Hladik, O. F. Linares, H. Pagezy and M. Hadley (eds), *Tropical Forests, People and Food: Biocultural Interactions and Applications to Development*, Paris: Unesco and The Parthenon Publishing Group.

Englund, H. and Leach, J. (forthcoming) Ethnography and the meta-narratives of modernity, *Current Anthropology* 41.

Escobar, A. (1998) Whose knowledge, whose nature? Biodiversity, conservation and the political ecology of social movements, *Journal of Political Ecology* 5: 53–82.

Fay, M. J. (1993) *Ecological and Conservation Implications of Development Options for the Dzanga-Sangha Special Reserve and the Dzanga-Ndoki National Park*, Yobe-Sangha, Central African Republic, report to GTZ, Mission Forestière Allemande, Coopération Technique Allemande.

Fay, M. J., Agnagna, M., Wilkinson, A., Gereau, R. E., Harris, D. J., Moutsambote, J.-M., Thomas, D. W. and Sita, P. (1992) *A Survey of the Proposed Garabinzam – Mt Nabemba Conservation Area, Northern Congo*, report to Global Environment Facility, Republic of Congo.

Freeman, M. M. R. and Kreuter, U. P. (eds) (1994) *Elephants and Whales: Resources for Whom?*, Basel: Gordon and Breach Science Publishers.

Geschiere, P. (1982) *Village Communities and the State: Changing Relations among the Maka of South-Eastern Cameroon since the Colonial Conquest*, transl. J. J. Ravell, London, Boston and Melbourne: Kegan Paul.

—— (1991) Sorcery, witchcraft and accumulation: regional variations in south and west Cameroon, *Critique of Anthropology* 11(3): 251–278.

Hauser, A. 1951. *Les Babinga*, Brazzaville: O.R.S.T.O.M., Institut d'Études Centrafricaines.

Ichikawa, M. (1991) The impact of commoditisation on the Mbuti of eastern Zaire, in N. Peterson and T. Matsuyama (eds), *Cash, Commoditisation and Changing Foragers*, Osaka (National Museum of Ethnology): Senri Ethnological Studies 30.

Ingold, T. (1986) *The Appropriation of Nature: Essays on Human Ecology and Social Relations*, Manchester: Manchester University Press.

—— (1992) Comment, in N. H. Bird-David, Beyond 'the original affluent society': a culturalist reformulation, *Current Anthropology* 33(1): 25–47.

Jackson, M. (1989) The man who could turn into an elephant, in M. Jackson *Paths Toward a Clearing: Radical Empiricism and Ethnographic Enquiry*, Bloomington and Indianapolis: Indiana University Press.

Joiris, D. V. (1993a) The mask that is hungry for yams: ethno-ecology of *Dioscorea Mangenotiana* among the Baka, Cameroon, in C. M. Hladik, A. Hladik, O. F. Linares, H. Pagezy and M. Hadley (eds), *Tropical Forests, People and Food: Biocultural Interactions and Applications to Development*, Paris: Unesco and The Parthenon Publishing Group.

—— (1993b) Baka Pygmy hunting rituals in southern Cameroon: how to walk side by side with the elephant, in G. Thoveron and H. Legros (eds), *Mélanges Pierre Salmon II. Histoire et Ethnologie Africaines. Civilisations* 16, 1–2: 51–81.

—— (1996) A comparative approach to hunting rituals among Baka Pygmies (southeastern Cameroon), in S. Kent (ed.), *Cultural Diversity Among Twentieth-Century Foragers: An African Perspective*, Cambridge: Cambridge University Press.

—— (1998) Warring and Hunting in Eastern Cameroon: Interethnic Ritual and Symbolic Relationships amongst Baka Pygmies and their Neighbours, paper presented at the Eighth International Conference on Hunting and Gathering Societies in Osaka, October.

Kalland, A. (1994) Seals, whales and elephants: totem animals and the anti-use campaigns, in N. D. Christoffersen and C. Lippai (eds) *Responsible Wildlife Resource Management: Balancing Biological, Economic, Cultural and Moral Considerations*. Proceeding of the Conference held in the European Parliament, Brussels, November 1993, Brussels: European Bureau for Conservation and Development.

Kenrick, J. (1996) Trust and Fear in the Ituri Forest, paper presented at the Colloquium on Hunter-Gatherers of Equatorial Africa, held at Leiden, The Netherlands, October.

Klieman, K. (1999) Hunter-gatherer participation in rainforest trade systems: a comparative history of forest versus ecotone societies in Gabon and Congo, *c.* 1000–1800 AD, in K. Biesbrouck, S. Elders and G. Rossel (eds), *Central African Hunter-Gatherers in a Multidisciplinary Perspective: Challenging Elusiveness*, Leiden: CNWS.

Laburthe-Tolra, P. (1981) *Mínlaaba I. Les Seigneurs de la Forêt: Essai sur le Passée Historique, l'Organisation Sociale et les Normes Éthiques des Anciens Beti du Cameroun*, Paris: Publications de la Sorbonne.

Lahm, S. A. (1993) Utilization of forest resources and local variation of wildlife populations in northeastern Gabon, in C. M. Hladik, A. Hladik, O. F. Linares, H. Pagezy and M. Hadley (eds), *Tropical Forests, People and Food: Biocultural Interactions and Applications to Development*, Paris: Unesco and The Parthenon Publishing Group.

——— (1994) *The Impact of Elephants on Agriculture in Gabon*, Libreville: WWF Programme for Gabon.

Lewis, J. (forthcoming) PhD Thesis *Mbendjelle Yaka Pygmies in northeastern Congo*, London School of Economics.

Pepper, H. (1955) Un spécimen de la langue des Pygmées Bangombe (Moyen Congo), *Bulletin de la Société de Linguistique de Paris* 51(1): 106–120.

Regnault, M. (1911) Les Babenga (Négrilles de la Sanga), *L'Anthropologie* (Paris) 22(3): 261–288.

Robineau, C. (1967) Contribution à l'histoire du Congo: la domination Européenne et l'exemple de Souanké (1900–1960), *Cahiers d'Études Africaines*, VII, 26(2): 300–344.

Sautter, G. (1967) Notes sur la construction du chemin de fer Congo–Océan (1921–1934), *Cahiers d'Études Africaines*, VII, 26(2): 219–299.

Shaw, R. (1997) The production of witchcraft/witchcraft as production: memory, modernity and the slave trade in Sierra Leone, *American Ethnologist* 24(4): 856–876.

Siroto, L. (1969) Masks and social organization among the Bakwele people of Western Equatorial Africa, unpublished PhD thesis: Columbia University.

Spinage, C. A. (1994) *Elephants*, London: T. and A.D. Poyser.

Stoecker, H. (1986) The conquest of colonies: the establishment and extension of German colonial rule. Cameroon 1885–1906, in H. Stoecker (ed.), *German Imperialism in Africa: From the Beginnings until the Second World War*, Berlin: Akademie-Verlag.

Vansina, J. (1990) *Paths in the Rainforest: Toward a History of Political Tradition in Equatorial Africa*, London: James Currey.

Vincent, J.-F. (1961) *La Culture du Cacao et son Retentissement Social dans la Région de Souanké*, Brazzaville: O.R.S.T.O.M.

——— (1963) Dot et monnaie de fer chez les Bakwele et les Djem, *Objets et Mondes* III(4): 273–292, Paris: Musée de l'Homme.

Woodburn, J. (1982) Egalitarian societies, *Man* (n.s.) 17: 431–451.

Chapter 4

Chimpanzees as political animals in Sierra Leone

Paul Richards

Introduction

Interviewed about attitudes to conservation, some young people in forested districts of Sierra Leone expressed alarm that protection for chimpanzees provided 'cover' for 'chimpanzee business' (*ngolo hinda*). *Ngolo hinda* belongs to a more general class of beliefs, known to Mende-speakers as *bôni hinda* (somewhat misleadingly translated as 'cannibalism'), in which it is thought that power-seekers murder young people to obtain body parts for the manufacture of *hale nyamui* ('bad medicine') conferring special political or economic powers. It is understood that practitioners disguise themselves as leopards, crocodiles or chimpanzees (the only large animals in the Upper Guinean forest that kill humans other than in self-defence). Special knives are used to simulate the damage caused by a real animal. A variant belief is that the *bôni bla* – 'cannibal people' – appear as real animals through shape-shifting magic.

Fear of 'cannibals' operates as a 'weapon of the weak' (Scott 1985). The accusation is directed at those suspected of undermining society through excessive individualism. The leopard (*Panthera pardus*) and Nile Crocodile (*Crocodylus niloticus*) are virtually extinct in Sierra Leone. But the common chimpanzee (*Pan troglodytes*) – a mobile animal still frequently encountered, though total numbers are not very high – remains a viable model for concerns about the erosion of modes of social solidarity vital to the poor. Informants agitated by the moral hazard implicit in chimpanzee conservation were invariably clear that *bôni hinda* is political in character (Barrows 1976; MacCormack 1983).[1]

This chapter explains the cross that the chimpanzee continues to bear for inequities associated with rampant commerce. Primate conservationists need to take into account that they are dealing with a stigmatized animal (Goldman and Walsh 1997).

Animals as boundary markers and political tools

Anthropologists have long been fascinated by the way in which human groups regularly use their knowledge of non-human animals to help think through problems of human social cohesion. The early work of Mary Douglas was seminal (Douglas 1966; Fardon 1999). Douglas argued that 'unclean' animals are not inherently dirty, but find themselves stigmatized in the service of group and boundary maintenance. Gridding the animal kingdom according to a classificatory scheme may serve to sustain key social distinctions between stranger and community member.[2]

At first sight, a potential drawback to the use of animals as instruments in moral calculus is that they manifestly have a life of their own. Under environmental pressure, phenotype or behaviour may change. Genetically bottlenecked, the leopard might lose its spots. Pressed for habitat, it becomes a man-eater. Habituation may 'switch on' hitherto undetected behavioural possibilities. What kind of challenge does this plasticity pose to the social uses to which humans put their knowledge of animals?

Below, it will be argued that if the classification of animals has value for human group maintenance, humans may seize upon animal *behaviour* (including *changes* in animal behaviour) to model social conflict, or pursue political projects. 'Chimpanzee business' may be a form of moral panic, but a 'moral panic', it will be suggested, that is no 'mindless fear', but a carefully calibrated tool of protest directed towards distinctive egalitarian and youth-oriented political ends.

Human–chimpanzee interaction in the forest

Hanno the Carthaginian encountered apes along the West African coast some 2,500 years ago, returned to Carthage with three female specimens, and posted an account in the temple of Moloch. Local people named the apes 'gorillas'. McDermott (1938) comments that 'the savage resistance of the creatures [as recorded by Hanno] . . . does not agree with the [chimpanzee's] disposition', concluding the animals were in fact gorillas. But there is no evidence that the gorilla was ever present in the western forests of West Africa (Hanno's likely landfall). Recent primatological research suggests the chimpanzee is much more prone to violence than the gorilla (Wrangham and Peterson 1997). If indeed Hanno captured three female specimens on the coast of Sierra Leone (as one scholar has suggested) then it would be more reasonable to presume they were chimpanzees.

Even at this early date farming may have already reached coastal Sierra Leone, from the inland river basins where African Rice (*Oryza glaberrima*) was domesticated c. 3000 BP, before it spread coastwards via the Gambia and Senegal River basins. Certainly, European explorers in the fifteenth and sixteenth centuries met a well-established forest agriculture based on rice. Humans and chimpanzees are perhaps long habituated to each other's presence in this particular portion of the African forest. Today, the chimpanzee impinges upon forest farming communities as a noisy fruit tree-raiding pest.

Professional hunters (Mende *kamajôi*, pl. *kamajôisia*), typically found one or two to a village throughout the southern and eastern forests of Sierra Leone, know the chimpanzee very well indeed. During fieldwork in the Gola Forest 1988–1990 I collected several hunters' accounts of chimpanzee behaviour. On various occasions I was told how the animal hunts, uses leaves to treat skin complaints,[3] and teaches its young to crack nuts with stones and anvil.[4] Informants often commented on the animal's high social intelligence. 'Drumming' in the forest was one such manifestation.[5] A hunter opined that the chimpanzees made drumming noises 'for display' (i.e. to claim rank). Another informant told me he had witnessed a female chimpanzee cracking and piling nuts and then provisioning her young charges 'just like a [human] mother dishing food'.

At the time I was inclined to treat this material as fanciful, but later discovered it was consistent with accounts in the primatological literature (Kortlandt and Holzhaus 1987; Boesch and Boesch 1989; Boesch *et al.* 1994; Joulian 1995). For example, regarding the female chimpanzee 'mothering' young apprentices during stone-cracking sessions, it has been suggested that chimpanzees only master nut-cracking with difficulty and need substantial provisioning in order to acquire the skill (Mithen 1996).

The chimpanzee's propensity for violence is another aspect of the animal's behaviour upon which local ideas and modern primatological studies tend to converge. Villagers know the animal is exceptionally strong, and a hazard to young people in particular. There are well-attested reports of babies being snatched from the edge of forest clearings when adults have been preoccupied with farm work, or children being mugged while running errands through the forest from farm to village. Where the primatological literature once portrayed chimpanzees as largely pacific, if playful and destructive (as if the animal did not know its own strength), more recent work has changed the picture. Well-documented cases of chimpanzee murder, infanticide and sexual violence are now seen by some sociobiologists as illuminating the evolutionary origins of human conflict (Wrangham and Peterson 1997; but see Power 1991).

Capacity for deception and group-disruptive violence is the negative side of the chimpanzee's great social intelligence. Wrangham and Peterson (1997: 144–145) state that attacks on females are 'a consistent and regular . . . aspect of chimpanzee life' in which 'competition among males often becomes overwhelming, especially if the community's Alpha male is not supremely powerful'. Infanticide, cannibalism and genital mutilation (Suzuki 1971; Norikoshi 1982; Wrangham and Peterson 1997) are linked to coercion of sexual partners in conditions where leadership is weak.[6]

Seemingly, these kinds of attacks are also inter-specific, with human children falling victim to chimpanzee muggings. No such case occurred that I was able to examine directly during my own fieldwork but several incidents are reliably attested to in the colonial records for Sierra Leone. Migeod (1926) cites an instance in which a four-year-old girl was killed by a large female chimpanzee on a farm at Faama, headquarters of a remote chiefdom in the Gola Forest on the Liberian border, in September 1920. The animal did not run away after the attack, but gathering up its infant 'went up a tree and viewed the rest of the proceedings culminating in its own death [it was shot by a hunter] with complete mental detachment' (Migeod 1926: 167).[7]

Chimpanzee attacks on humans are a big challenge for the village elite. As we shall see below, 'big men' (including *kamajôi* hunters) – alpha males with slightly uneasy consciences – have a vested interest in coming up with convincing naturalistic explanations in this field! Some connect the social intelligence and capacity for violence of the chimpanzee with an 'evolutionary' hypothesis that primatologists might well applaud. Chimpanzees and humans once shared the same forest origins (a hunter once suggested), but whereas humans left the forest to become civilized, the chimpanzees remained behind. The morality of the untransformed chimpanzee remains 'low', while the morality of transformed humans is (or should be) 'high'.[8] Ordinary villagers, however, tend to have a more jaundiced and sceptical view of why there seem to be so many reports of chimpanzee attacks on young women. The answer is simple – it is because of 'cannibalism'.

Subsistence and witches

So we now need to try and fathom the 'cannibalism' belief. We should begin by noting that a special significance attaches to the fact that chimpanzee attacks are associated with periods when villagers are especially preoccupied with urgent tasks to do with their main forest subsistence crop, Upland Rice. As a short-season crop (cultivated over three to five months) Upland Rice requires intensely concentrated labour inputs, especially at planting, weeding and harvest (Richards 1986). Over the centuries, local communities, settled at low population densities, have adapted to these peak labour requirements by developing elaborate schemes for spreading rice cultivation activities up and down slopes, and for sharing labour on a household and inter-household level. The key to the subsistence success of forest rice farmers is not intensive land-shaping (as in many parts of rice-dependent lowland southeast Asia) but a repertoire of early, medium and late planting seed types. By varying the seed type used, farmers can stagger planting, and thus share labour, their most limited resource (Richards 1986; 1996).

Commerce has threaded its way through the Upper Guinean forest from the earliest days of the Atlantic slave trade (in the fifteenth and sixteenth centuries). The individualism associated with commerce is a threat to the collectivist values upon which labour pooling in subsistence rice farming depends. How can the weak protect themselves from an erosion of values vital to their food security and survival? The African ethnographic literature makes it clear that in such circumstances one weapon is the witchcraft accusation. It will be shown that to level the charge of chimpanzee 'cannibalism' is in effect to make a kind of witchcraft accusation.

An incident reported from the Sherbro coast in the 1780s (Fyfe 1964) makes the connection clear. The English merchant, botanist and reformer Henry Smeathman asked Sherbro chiefs why they rejected the sickle, an innovation he proposed to improve the efficiency of local rice farming. They told him any adopter would risk being charged with being a witch. The impatient English merchant dismissed this as African barbarism. But the innovation was more complicated than Smeathman had realized. The problem is that bunch harvesting tends to erode the varietal distinctiveness of rice (Jusu 1999), readily maintained (in an in-breeding crop) by the established practice, still current in the forest today, of harvesting by panicle (i.e. selecting and cutting individual heads with a knife). 'More efficient' bunch harvesting with a sickle might be effective in the short term, but would put at risk one of the basic cooperative techniques on which local food security depended – scope to share labour by spreading activities up and down slopes.[9]

The earliest outside accounts of political institutions in the forests behind the Guinea coast suggest a society of fairly autonomous family-based village republics, networked by male and female initiation societies comparable to the Poro and Sande Societies of today (d'Azevedo 1962). Slavery was certainly known in the Upper Guinean forests at this time, but initiation may have acted as a brake on the appearance of its more intense forms (Rodney 1970), even though forest communities remained vulnerable to kidnapping (see below). Self-provisioning, labour sharing in rice cultivation, 'secret' institutions, and a degree of political autonomy went hand in hand.

But the seeds of a social revolution were already planted. At the time of the arrival of Portuguese and other European traders on the West African coast, interior groups were becoming more involved in forest affairs, attracted by Atlantic commerce (dominated by the slave trade). A period sometimes referred to as the 'Mane invasion' (in the fifteenth and early sixteenth centuries) led to the emergence of a new but delicately poised accommodation between regionally networked Mane mercantile rulers and the local initiation associations in which the older families were prominent (Rodney 1970; see also d'Azevedo 1962).

According to Jones (1981) the 'Mane' were in fact the Vai, a group speaking a Northern Mande language, related to Kono, Koranko, Maninka, Bambara etc., and today concentrated on the coast in the vicinity of Cape Mount (in Liberia). Since the time of the Mane political upheavals the forests of southern and eastern Sierra Leone have been regularly subject to commercial and political influence from groups like the Vai tracing linguistic connections to, and cultural inspiration from, the peoples of the former Mali empire.

Today, forest-dwelling villagers sometimes use the ethnonym 'Mandingo' (in a very loose sense) to refer to all members of such groups (i.e. traders speaking Northern Mande languages and tracing historical connections to the savanna axis of the Upper Niger valley). This lack of precision should be underlined. In some respects 'Mandingo' signifies little more than a relatively rich person who lives (in a forest village) by commerce, probably Muslim, hostile to local initiation associations to some extent, and perhaps possessing some northern ancestry. It is more or less interchangeable in village usage with the Muslim honorific 'al-haji', a term often applied to merchants in general, rather than only those who have made a pilgrimage to Mecca. Throughout, I use the term 'Mandingo' in this broad local sense, and not as an exact ethnic category.

It will be contended below that witchcraft-style 'weapons of the weak' such as 'chimpanzee business' have been forged by rice-farming commoners in reaction to the political claims of commercially oriented elites of 'Mandingo' orientation.[10] The accusation of 'cannibalism', it is suggested, emerged as a resource with which to challenge political interests reflecting the elaboration of regional commerce.

Chiefs in league with traders who kidnap young people and sell them into slavery are no different from chimpanzees mugging young people on forest paths. Kidnapping and muggings occur when the community's attention is otherwise engaged. By stealing young people kidnappers undermine community capacity for labour sharing. Parents are left to scratch their plots unaided. The social order based on subsistence agriculture comes under threat. The morality of the big person (*numu wa*) who is a merchant at heart resembles that of a male chimpanzee attacking where leadership is weak. As categories, a 'big man' beefing up his depleted powers in the heart of the forest and the excluded but aggressive male chimpanzee bent on violence as a way of detaching sexual partners from a settled group begin to merge.

Today, the accusation of 'cannibalism' remains in use as a 'weapon of the weak', but to express unease at rampant commercialism in a country where a political elite with access to diamonds exports wealth overseas without re-investing in basic institutions (education, health, rural roads and markets) that support the poor. While 'chimpanzee business' still has some currency in rural areas, the 'modern' urban replacement tends to be a straightforward accusation that a 'big man' abetted by a 'Mandingo' sorcerer has kidnapped and murdered a child for body parts. Animals are a prop to the imagination but not in fact essential to the continuation of a belief that is rooted in the political, not environmental, situation in the country.

Chimpanzee muggers and kidnappers of slaves

Much of the slaving done in this portion of the West African forest was through kidnapping. The Mende word *pani mô* is listed in the dictionary as 'Spanish [person]'. Forest kidnappers were still supplying a slave trade from the forests of southern and eastern Sierra Leone to Cuba (a Spanish colony) as late as mid-nineteenth century. But Christopher Fyfe (personal communication) suggests *pani* might as well derive from Portuguese-derived 'panyarry', a word in West Coast trade English that referred to the activity of supplying slaves through kidnapping.

Trade slaves from this portion of the African forest were shipped to the Americas through outlets at Cape Mount, Gallinas and Bunce Island. Such slaves were especially valued in South Carolina for their knowledge of rice agriculture and ability to work hard, in gangs, in fever-ridden rice swamp conditions (Littlefield 1979; Opala 1986). Here was a double irony. Being busy with co-operative farm work meant that children running errands were vulnerable to kidnapping, while adolescents were honing the very skills that made them so valuable a target for the kidnappers of slaves supplying the needs of New World agriculture (Richards 1986).

The forest-supplied Gallinas and Cape Mount slave trades lingered in the eastern forests of Sierra Leone until the mid-nineteenth century. In 1989, an elderly Gola-speaking villager recalled what he had been told by his grandparents about the impact of the kidnappers. Traders (he told me) first penetrated the Gola Forest in the hope of exploiting local wild animal resources. They came from Bopolu, a town now in Liberia, described by the traveller Sims in 1858 as a mixed community of local and Mandingo 'roguish, kidnapping knaves'. The Bopolu traders plied the village chiefs with strong drink, in return for which they required the 'big men' to hunt for ivory and skins. When the consignment was ready for collection the traders prevailed upon the chiefs to order the young men to headload the items to the coast. On arrival, the weary youngsters were enticed on board a slaver to rest and relax, at which point the ship set sail and the young men were never seen again. Realizing they had been tricked, the chiefs went to war to drive off their erstwhile business partners, but the grief of the households at their loss of children sounds down the century (Richards 1998).

Domestic slavery survived in rural Sierra Leone until 1927. In parts of the north special arrangements (including the introduction of work oxen) had to be made by the British administration to compensate 'Mandingo' landlords for the loss of agricultural labour. In 1955 serious riots broke out in northern Sierra Leone in protest at the way chiefs still demanded communal labour from young people.

It is not surprising that when an unsupervised child running an urgent errand on a lonely forest path is 'mugged' by a chimpanzee the event evokes a strong folk memory of the process through which farm children disappeared into slavery in the Americas at the busiest moments in the subsistence farm cycle, leaving the parents hungry and bereft. The lonely and irascible chimpanzee – maybe a deposed alpha male (see p. 81) – readily assumes the mantle of the dread *pani mô*.

The forest and commerce

After the slave trade ended, the building of a railway line from Freetown during the first decade of the twentieth century facilitated new commercial developments in the forest belt. The railway terminated in Pendembu, a town adjacent to the northern tip of the Gola Forest, which today comprises a series of three boundary reserves stretching along the Liberian border for about 150 km. They are the single largest surviving portions of Upper Guinean high forest in Sierra Leone.[11]

The railway opened up the eastern forests to plantation agriculture. But it also brought a wide range of outsiders into the forest as well, seeking their fortunes as buyers of plantation produce, or in logging, alluvial diamond mining and other extractive activities. These extractive activities included commercial hunting. Professional hunters encountered during the course of fieldwork in the Gola Forest during 1988–1990 were mostly from Koranko country (northern Sierra Leone) or the Republic of Guinea. The main targets of the commercial hunters were monkeys and chimpanzees. Sierra Leone was a major supplier of chimpanzees to the world market for medical research in the 1970s. When the chimpanzee trade was halted a decade later, commercial hunters focused instead on larger species of monkey such as the Red Colobus. Monkey meat is in especially high demand in Monrovia, Liberia.

My central argument, therefore, is that to understand *bôni hinda* we must understand the penetration of forest environments by commerce shaped by centuries of slave trade. More generally, the emergence of global commerce in the Atlantic era is inextricably bound up with the history of the slave trade. But global commerce had profoundly different impacts on slave-raided and slave-receiving regions. In Europe and the New World, slavery liberated agrarian wealth foundational to the emergence of new individualized notions of property and persons.[12] In West Africa commerce built upon slaving weakened agrarian formations and clashed directly with collectivist notions of persons and property.

Conditions in the Upper Guinean forests were particularly conducive to the fostering of extremely negative popular attitudes to commerce, seen as a threat to social cohesion. Slave raiding in the savanna was often massively dislocative but necessarily short-term and episodic (as whole areas were emptied of populations by war). In the Upper Guinea forests, by contrast, slave raiding was a low-intensity activity based more on kidnapping than war, and co-existed with other modes of commerce for several centuries. This slow drip of a commerce poisoned by kidnapping – and the increasing involvement of chiefs in commerce as a precondition for amassing the material resources through which their authority was maintained – laid the foundations for popular fantasy about 'demonic big men' that has outlasted the ending of slavery itself. In part, the durability of these fantasies depends on the fact that many of those who now tap the new forms of 'legitimate' commercial wealth in the forests are some way linked to and descended from the commercial classes from the days of slavery.

'Cannibalism'

Documentary sources

I shall now seek to demonstrate this argument through examining a set of colonial documents on *bôni hinda* assembled by a Czech scholar, Milan Kalous (1974). Kalous lectured in history at the Fourah Bay College of the University of Sierra Leone in the 1960s. He scrutinized more than 1,000 colonial and missionary records of 'cannibalism' in the national archives, printing the more important ones. The collection was offered with little or no editorial apparatus, but in the expressed hope that an anthropologist would one day pay it some attention.[13]

Kalous' collection, examined for various patterns after entering into a text-oriented database, suggests that there is no distinction to be drawn in terms of purpose between the variant forms of *bôni hinda* – whether the animal disguise is that of chimpanzee, leopard or crocodile. In every case, the aim is to make *hale nyamui* ('bad medicine') through the murder of a child or youth.[14] The sources also agree that the key connection is the *combined* pursuit of political power and commercial wealth, and that 'cannibal' power seekers are in some way advised and abetted by migrant commercial 'strangers' (i.e. 'Mandingo').

A Prince Landy Luseni wrote to the British colonial government from the Gallinas country in 1914 to warn that the founder of the 'barboo' [i.e. chimpanzee][15] society 'is . . . an uncle of mine and he got great power [sic.], unlimited in the Country, he is a Merchant *and* paramount chief . . .' (Kalous 1974: 91, my emphasis). The statement of one Sehree to the police at Bonthe in 1890 was that '. . . poor people are not accused . . . it is only rich people with property' (ibid.: 196). In 1892 an accuser addressed the bludgeoned corpse of one Imperri 'cannibal' thus: 'you say you . . . are the richest man in Imperri . . . not you then . . . I shall burn you today' (ibid.: 207). The 'Mandingo'/stranger connections were pointed out by Governor Probyn in 1910. Probyn noted that 'cannibalism' cases involved 'nominal Mohammedans' he described as living one to a town and dependent 'for their livelihood to a considerable extent on the sale of charms' (ibid.: 47). A further minute the same year suggested that '[l]eopard murders are at times if not generally carried out by persons who come from a considerable distance' (ibid.: 292).

'Chimpanzee business' and its disguises

Whether such killing really occurs is impossible for independent observers to decide. This is because, as Mende villagers today are quick to point out, the behaviour of real animals provides plausible cover for the alleged activity. In one attack of *ngolo hinda* at Molokko in 1913, the victim reported thus:

> something fell over me and threw me to the ground with face downward . . . the thing hit me on the face, and scratched my face and eyes. I tried to get away and it bit my left thumb and foot [i.e. leg] near the knee. It also cut off the second and third fingers of my right hand and then left me lying on the ground . . . I saw a black thing like a baboon [i.e. chimpanzee] going towards the bush . . . it was about my height.
>
> (Kalous 1974: 90)

After personally examining a twelve-year-old boy in Pujehun hospital 'badly torn by a chimpanzee', Migeod comments that 'this species of ape runs to a large size in Sierra Leone' and 'noted for its ferocity . . . will without hesitation when it gets the chance attack children and run off with them with the intent to kill them' (1926: 162). He records that several attacks resulted in damage to the genitalia, something most likely to attract symbolic interpretation by human observers.

There seems little doubt, therefore, that a child caught walking alone in the forest and mugged and mutilated by real chimpanzees could suffer the kind of damage alleged in *ngolo hinda*. This complication makes the charge of 'cannibalism' hard to refute without recourse to special methods such as divination or trial by ordeal. In this respect, then, *bôni hinda* is equivalent to a witchcraft accusation, except there is no putative 'witchcraft substance' to act at a distance. The attack is real. Whether *ngolo hinda* is the morally culpable 'malice' of a disguised or shape-shifted human, or an animal behavioural response invoked by human–chimpanzee habitat competition, depends entirely on point of view.

The distribution of 'cannibalism'

Some anthropologists view culture as a 'thing in itself' (perhaps especially in North America, where culture has been erected as the idealized subject of the discipline, see Kuper 1999). Others see culture as a word empty of content except in the context of social interaction (Douglas 1999). Culture is often most densely manifested at the point of contestation between differently configured social worlds. On the idealist or 'essentialist' view of culture, *bôni hinda* is a cultural primitivism that might be expected to cluster in the remotest recesses of the Upper Guinean forests. But the actual pattern (as apparent through searching the database deriving from the Kalous collection) fits in better with the notion of 'cannibalism' as an epiphenomenon of a clash of social arrangements.

Analysis shows that outbreaks were common (and perhaps especially frequent, though due allowance should be made for the geographical selectivity of the colonial sources) in those parts of the forest zone most thoroughly transformed by commercial contacts – i.e. in coastal communities, or settlements associated with major long-distance trade-routes. One such region was coastal Sherbro, an area dominated by fissiparous and quarrelsome Anglo-African and interior ruling elites congregating at the coast to participate in the Atlantic trade from the sixteenth century onwards.[16]

Nor was the belief in 'cannibals', envisaged by the Mende as *bôni hinda*, tied to any specific ethnic group. Shape-shifted 'cannibals' freely crossed ethnic and linguistic boundaries in southern and eastern Sierra Leone through Liberia as far as the western Cote d'Ivoire. Killings attributed to leopard cults recur in the broad band of equatorial forest stretching from eastern Nigeria into the Congo basin (Joset 1955; Nwaka 1986).[17] 'Leopardism' was notorious in regions adjacent to the numerous small trading states shaped by early and intense involvement in the slave trade on the eastern flank of the Niger Delta (Nwaka 1986).

Along the Sierra Leone coast 'cannibalism' charges were frequently levelled at well-placed traders and modernizing chiefs. 'Cannibal' killings are always illegitimate, but popular opinion in communities with strong egalitarian leanings always suspected chiefly involvement. 'How else can chiefs become chiefs?' is the common sentiment (for example, as reported among Sherbro villagers by MacCormack 1983).

The detection of 'cannibalism'

The Imperri chiefdom of in the Sherbro district experienced several outbreaks of *bôni hinda* in the 1890s, with the culprits tracked down through the divinatory practices of specialists known as Tongo Players (Mende *tôngô mô* – 'a person who detects witches').[18] Mass immolation of the accused resulted on several occasions, ultimately provoking colonial intervention.

Close examination of material in Kalous (1974) suggests that the *tôngô mô* filled a gap created some years earlier by the decision of the Freetown colonial authorities to ban the sasswood ordeal as a means of detecting witches. Drinking sasswood poison tends to kill, or promote a vomiting reaction, according to levels of nervous agitation.[19] It might reasonably be described as trial by lottery.

Douglas and Ney (1998) remark that lottery is a much under-studied means to arrive at decisions in egalitarian communities, where the judgement of superiors will always be suspect. It is better to appeal to the divine will directly, than through any human judge or interlocutor. As an impersonal process through which those accused of cannibalism or witchcraft could clear their names, the sasswood ordeal confirmed immunity from any further such accusations for life (according to evidence cited in Kalous 1974).

It appears that the *tôngô* diviners, 'the great detective society among the Mendis and Sherbro' (Kalous 1974: 228) may have adapted skills perhaps originally deployed in healing and finding thieves. For diviners to be called, chiefs had to be willing to hire them. This meant they were open to being 'bought', sometimes by the very chiefs popularly suspected of involvement in anti-social practices such as *bôni hinda*.[20]

Even so, the *tôngô mô* enjoyed legitimacy through using lottery-like divinatory practices, and if unlike sasswood, a biological agent, the *tôngô* game could more readily be fixed, it was still directed at the same ends – defending agrarian egalitarians from political power rooted in commercial individualism.

The following account is from Imperri in 1890:

> medicine men came originally . . . to discover thieves, [and] after they finished they came . . . to discover the 'human leopards' . . . [Then] they and the chiefs went into the Porro bush . . . we are informed that the bargain made . . . is that they were to accuse any person who is wealthy and charge him with being a 'human leopard' . . . [and] without going through the old practice of giving him

sarse wood and getting him to confess his guilt or establish his innocence they were to seize him as soon as he is accused, tie him and burn him to death . . . There are many young people who follow the Tungoh people.

(Kalous 1974: 194)

The role of the consultation in Poro is a significant detail, reminding us of an old cleavage between communalistic and commercial political classes in the region. The principal victim of the next day's *tôngô* play was Chief Gbannah Bungay. According to other sources, the grievance against Gbannah Bungay was that he had been planning to sell extensive areas of land to a Freetown Creole merchant and planter, S. B. McFoy. 'The inhabitants of his own town discovered that he was about to hand the place over to Mr Mcfoy for a money consideration and . . . made arrangements with the Tongohs to have him killed under pretext of being a cannibal' (ibid.: 181).

The legacy of distrust of 'Mane' hegemony surfaces once more. Modern commerce could not hide the legacy of slave dealing of some of the Imperri chiefs. Far from being trusted arbiters of agrarian subsistence, they were widely suspected as double-dealing commodity-oriented business entrepreneurs 'bleeding' the people to tap new sources of late nineteenth-century wealth.

The British educated and supported a new generation of chiefs. Today, it is often said that the Mende 'respect' their chiefs. But commerce and community leadership remains a tricky brew, even for the highly educated. The fate of an American-educated Sierra Leonean missionary, Daniel Flickinger Wilberforce, offers a case in point. Wilberforce had become a local chief in the Imperri district in 1899 'because he thought it would give him a larger opportunity to introduce civilization among his people' (US vice-consul in Freetown, in Kalous 1974). Wilberforce had earlier been 'an active supporter of the Colonial Government in stamping out cannibalism' (ibid.). But in 1906 this paragon of Christian good governance and commerce stood accused of *bôni hinda* himself.

The evidence suggests that it was his mixed social loyalties that were at the root of his downfall (Abraham 1975; Winans 1992). As missionary and colonial chief, Wilberforce was accountable less to his cooperatively-minded farming subjects than to organizations with highly divergent institutional values (the nascent colonial bureaucracy and a mission hierarchy). Perhaps fearing he would one day sell agrarian cooperation down the river his subjects struck first. Incapable of forensic disproof, in a region of killer crocodiles and apes, the charge of 'cannibalism' readily stuck.

Wilberforce was no more a 'cannibal' than a witch. But attempting the difficult balancing act of loyalty to colonial hierarchy and the new gospel of commerce and free markets he was evidently not the man to help maintain the fabric of cooperative values upon which the ordinary people depended for their agricultural survival. It was his failure to encompass contradictory institutional values that made him a predator upon, rather than leader of, youth.

'Cannibalism' and colonial justice

The British colonial authorities banned Tongo Players as they had earlier banned the sasswood ordeal. But the moral hazard remained. Chiefs and big men continued to be suspected of 'cannibalism'. One option was to admit cases for trial in colonial courts. To understand why the normally hard-headed British inherited the mantle of the *tôngô mô* as detector of *bôni hinda* to agrarian communities in uproar, in a region undergoing far-reaching and socially dislocative economic change, we need to see that 'cannibalism' posed a more complex challenge to the administration of colonial justice than witchcraft cases.

British colonial law either ignored witchcraft and left witchfinders free to operate at the local level (Gittins 1987) provided public order was maintained, or made the assumption that since witches did not exist witchcraft accusations were the work of trouble-makers (Winans 1992). It was vexatious to cause such accusations to be brought, or to seek to detect witches. Such cases were decided not on the basis of evidence of the existence of witches but in terms of threats to public order.

From the colonial legal perspective, *bôni hinda* differed from witchcraft in that it alleged a concrete and detectable offence of murder (as distinct from unexplained death or death by misadventure – instances likely to excite witchcraft suspicions). In colonial Sierra Leone, although Tongo Players were quickly proscribed, on the grounds that they were a threat to public order, alleged practitioners of *bôni hinda* could be, and frequently continued to be, arrested and tried on the suspicion of murder. These cases were hard to disprove. There was a dead and mutilated body, a body of belief to suggest 'cannibals' were at work, and the possibility that revenge killings might be carried out in the confusion.

A man I knew well in the course of fieldwork had faced criminal charges of being a 'human chimpanzee' four times during his life (most recently in 1987), though he was always acquitted. I once enquired about why he faced this charge repeatedly. Apparently he had once revenged himself upon a wife by killing her love child, blaming the death on chimpanzee attack. Thereafter he was the first suspect whenever a young person was found dead in the bush (perhaps as the result of some accident). He was a skilled and wealthy blacksmith with a migrant background, much feared for his command of sorcery.[21] It was widely understood that he had the skill to furnish himself with the necessary implements to undertake 'chimpanzee business', and that he was motivated by the kind of anti-social 'selfishness' the village rank-and-file regularly presumed to find in wealth-seeking outsiders. Thus 'cannibalism' exists in a forensically unbreakable circle, while animal attacks provide occasional 'cover' for murder, and social tensions resulting in fear of child abuse remain unassuaged (La Fontaine 1998).

For a time British colonial officers continued to accept 'cannibalism' cases on the assumption that cannibal secret societies might actually exist, and that 'cannibals' had perpetrated real crimes. Later colonial officials became more circumspect about confessions beaten out of suspects in custody.[22] But it also began to be recognized that in trying *bôni hinda* cases allowance had to be made for animal behaviour as well as elements of agrarian moral panic. Officers with an interest in hunting and natural history re-assessed evidence of leopard, crocodile and chimpanzee attacks on humans (Stanley 1919), concluding that in some cases real animals were responsible.

Ironically, the chimpanzee was itself a factor in this re-assessment, because when, on the rare occasions it attacked humans, it was as likely to cause damage as death. A 1912 colonial ordinance made it automatically a crime to be found guilty of membership of the 'Alligator' and Leopard Societies, but failed to mention the chimpanzee. The first records of 'chimpanzee business' in Kalous' documentary collection date from 1913. These accusations caused colonial legal officers some puzzlement, since there is 'no case yet before the court in which proof had been forthcoming of murder by members of the Baboon Society – many of the victims (from whom pieces of flesh were torn or cut) being still alive' (Kalous 1974: 87).

It was accepted that the Leopard and Crocodile 'cannibals' had murder in mind. But what was the purpose of the putative Chimpanzee Society, since victims were more often maimed than killed? One inquiry even concluded that indeed the society existed *only* 'to maim and wound small children' (ibid.: 87). This was so implausible that, taken in conjunction with the evidence of Stanley, Migeod and others concerning actual chimpanzee 'muggings', colonial authority began to ponder whether it was right to believe in the existence of 'cannibal' secret societies at all. Maybe the damage was the result of occasional wild animal attack all along, which became inflated into a witchcraft-like 'moral panic'.[23]

Taming the beast: the legacy of the slave trade

I once asked a hunter about the relationship between the smaller and less dangerous broad-nosed crocodile found in the upland forest streams and the man-eating Nile Crocodile of the larger rivers of the coastal zone. The broad-nosed crocodile, I was told, was 'mother's brother' to the Nile crocodile.

The choice of kinship terminology was not accidental. 'Mandingo' traders passing through the forest historically dealt in slaves; today many deal in troublesome or dangerous commodities such as diamonds and guns. But 'Mandingo' merchants are also long settled in forest-zone villages where they are valued as commodity merchants and money lenders. Frequently, the settled 'Mandingo' is related by marriage to the chief. In seeking to manage any political fall-out from expansion of trade in the forest, the chief has positioned himself as 'mother's brother' to the children of the trader.

A village loan shark locked into the community by marriage has had his teeth pulled.[24] But unattached and foot-loose long-distance traders remain a threat. These potential rip-off merchants include *tamaboro* – men equipped with formidable hunting skills and special powers who roam far into the uncharted forest, protected by the special medicines that make their movements undetectable by animals and ordinary mortals.

In the stores of the Smithsonian Institution in Washington there is a collection of magical paraphernalia made from chimpanzee skulls and bones and tersely labelled 'Mandingo'. Surely an embarrassment to the modern curator, this little jumble of artefacts serves as a reminder of the activities of the long-distance traders and *tamaboro* who violently call into question the social assumptions and values of the subsistence farming community at the forest-edge. Commerce connects together far-flung social worlds with different and perhaps opposed value systems. Hunter magic invokes new riches. But when disturbed, the forest reacts.

The lonely leopard hunted to the edge of extinction and pressed for habitat turns to stalk human prey. Even more profoundly suggestive, young people struggling to survive in the forest are forced into the company of a wantonly-destructive deep-forest animal, the chimpanzee. The resulting cross-species habituation of two social groups with different moralities has unpredictable and at times disastrous consequences, as irascible animals maliciously attack the most vulnerable members of the human community. Humans are reminded by their 'low-life' shadows of how low humans can sink – even to the point of destroying their own children's futures for the sake of wealth and external contacts.

Civil war

This chapter has argued that the phenomenon of 'human chimpanzees' (and 'cannibalism' more generally) can be understood as an expression of the disquiet of forest youth at leaders' attempts to break egalitarian social contracts in favour of long-distance multicultural commercial interests. 'Chimpanzee business' (and its cognate forms) attacks, it is suggested, the moral relativism of the slave trade, and the trades which have succeeded it. Fear of being thought a 'cannibal' may indeed have reined in the commercial ambitions of some chiefs. Even if it was a 'weapon of the weak', it was not necessarily an ineffective one, as the Wilberforce case suggests.

How much have attitudes changed? As reported above, young people in the 1990s still feared chimpanzees and entertained doubts about the public-spiritedness of their elders.[25] From 1991, the forests of the eastern border of Sierra Leone with Liberia became engulfed in a rebel war promoted to control the region's diamond resources. Many of the insurgent movement's hardcore followers are deracinated youth irked by an overseas-oriented political elite making money from the diamond pits in which some of the movement's members earlier sweated (Richards 1998). The rebel aim was to overthrow a corrupt patrimonial 'old guard' and bring in a more youth-oriented regime. But venting their anger on the rural 'big men', young rebels murdered chiefs and 'Mandingo' traders without discrimination.

This was a blind violence. The rebels of the Revolutionary United Front had no better an attitude to the youth they claimed to be releasing from their bondage than the rulers who might a couple of generations earlier have sold them into slavery. Indeed recruits were as good as slaves. Teenagers and children were forcibly implicated in the murder of local authority figures to ensure they had no homes to which to return; then they were carted off into the rebel army by force. Some who could not keep up with the arduous training and forced marches died of exhaustion. Others who tried to escape were mutilated or killed. A few who succeeded in deserting fell into the hands of vengeful villagers, or were summarily executed by government soldiers.

It is as if youth in this war was simply a resource to be pushed or pulled about at will according to the needs and desires of rebel commanders or government puppet-masters alike. Even where young people rallied to the government side, often fighting loyally and bravely, their contribution was quickly forgotten in the so-called peace process. Lumped together with the rebels (Peters and Richards 1998) without any acknowledgement of their patriotic role, many of these disillusioned young volunteers, sidelined in favour of a more recently recruited 'ethnic' militia, rallied to disgruntled army commanders who mutinied against the democratically-elected government of Ahmad Tejan-Kabbah in May 1997. Although the democratic president has now been restored with the help of the Nigerian army, the rebels are not yet a spent force, and the chaos in the country continues. Young people remain putty in the hands of militia leaders.

One young man, with experience of the fighting, summed up the relationship between the political classes and youth in time of war in the following blunt terms:

> The future of Sierra Leone? I don't really know where the future is going, because it is just somehow bad, now. I have not seen any improvement. Because one thing [is for] sure, we don't respect kids, we don't respect children. In other countries, the top will know that after them the children will be next. But here they don't really know that. They just work in their own interest, and not in the interest of the children, you know. They don't listen to children in Sierra Leone . . . if you want to say something to your father or your mother, they can say 'no, don't say anything to me. I was born before you were, so I know everything.' But that is not really correct. You might be born before me, but I can see something you cannot. They don't realise that in this country . . . They don't even count children, to know what children are really about, you know. So I don't really know how the future can be good. Because if they are working in the interest of the children and try to make the children good, I think the future will be good. But if they don't care about the children, it means the future is just dropping. So I think Sierra Leone is indigent. Everybody just has to fight for themselves.
>
> (Peters and Richards 1998)

Conclusion

What, then, is the relevance of the analysis attempted above? How, in particular, does it affect chimpanzee conservation? A first obvious point is that conservationists need to know that they are dealing with a stigmatized animal, and how historically deep-rooted that stigmatization is in events associated with the slave trade, and more generally with the struggles of forest people to stay alive.

A second and less obvious point is that the politics of that struggle has tended from time to time to up-date itself. Fear of chiefs entangled by the slave trade against the interests of their farming subjects translates itself in the modern world into a general fear on the part of impoverished youth that 'big-men' will stop at nothing to make money. While these fears remain unabated, 'cannibalism' is liable to migrate across several potential 'model' species – so that when leopards become extinct it transfers to chimpanzees, and where there are no chimpanzees, such as in a modern urban context, escapes its animal avatars altogether. As the above analysis attempts to show, this is not a crisis of conservation but a crisis of leadership.

This means that conservationists must act with due caution and great political sensitivity. Some conservation projects attempt to create material incentives to good behaviour among local populations. Economists advise that everything has its price, and that the right kind of property regime, or attention to linking conservation with material development, will result in rational local action to preserve resources. But this is unlikely in the present case, since the issue is not one of incentives but of the lack of political confidence. Who would handle the economic incentives? Undoubtedly it would be the chiefs – the very persons most likely in egalitarian communities to be suspected of anti-social behaviour for personal economic gain.

Economic incentives to chimpanzee conservation might very easily have perverse results. Angry young people might well be provoked into killing off the animals as a kind of political protest. Any proposal to empower chiefs (and their local supporters) at the expense of youthful in-migrants to forest reserves should therefore be treated with extreme caution. 'Rootless' youth in the civil war in Sierra Leone have not hesitated to wreak their vengeance on the local chiefs for the injustice of social exclusion. Chimpanzees are hardly likely to escape such outbursts of anger. The basic task is to deal with the problem of 'rootlessness'.

But this is an agenda for large-scale political reform. No conservation agency could possibly contemplate becoming involved in such reform on its own initiative. To do so would be neo-colonialism, since most such agencies represent external organizations. Even so, conservationists may have to think again about the way they align themselves with social forces, within civil society and internationally, when working for governance reform. In particular, they may have to be more vigorous in lending their voice to calls for a better deal for neglected youth. This may be more important than devising 'economic' incentives.

It will not prove an easy switch to make. Much conservation starts from a Malthusian perspective on population. The implication is that there would be no problem if these young people had not been born to begin with. But on the current interpretation, local hostility to chimpanzees will prove hard to eradicate so long as the political process in Sierra Leone fails to secure the social inclusion of young people. It is ingrained in the history of the Upper Guinean forests that, when local social contracts are torn up in favour of international commerce, it is the young who bear the brunt.

One of the ways to remind local power elites of this fact is through *ngolo hinda*. For the reproach of 'chimpanzee business' to disappear, a new deal may have to be struck between the generations to end the 'commodification' of children begun by the slave trade. How well the chimpanzees in Sierra Leone have survived years of war is unclear. Longer-term survival plans may have to start from the premise of a new political deal for youth. If indeed the chimpanzee is a political animal in Sierra Leone then a simple conclusion is that good governance will contribute more to the animal's protection than the economic incentive schemes currently favoured in conservation thinking.

Notes

1 Since primatologists have used the word 'politics' to refer to chimpanzee social strategizing (de Waal 1982) I should emphasize that my concern in this chapter lies solely with human politics.
2 The most dangerous or sacred animals are those that cross boundaries in such schemes. To the Lele of Kasai the Pangolin – a scaly mammal, neither fish nor fowl – is an object of cult veneration (Douglas 1966). But it is anomalous not because, objectively, it is a mammal with some reptilian or fish-like features, but because it is linked, via cult activity, with struggles to control sexual access and fertility. It is as if Lele men orient themselves to social problems via the pangolin much as an ancient master mariner might position his ship by orienting his body and the night sky through manipulation of an astrolabe. Where, in other parts of Africa, moral dilemmas are differently configured, the pangolin is hunted and eaten without further ado.

3 A forest tree-spotter once gave me a 'new' leaf to treat a bad attack of scabies. He had arrived at the treatment by observing a chimpanzee rubbing the leaf in question on infected skin. Mills (1926: 140–141) describes a case of an old woman arriving at a skin treatment by watching a chimpanzee rub a leaf on its offspring. On chimpanzee medication, see Huffman and Seifu (1989).

4 Informants readily list the trees supplying the nuts in question, for example, *ndokei, Coula edulis*.

5 Informants dispute whether the animal beats its chest, hits tree buttresses with sticks, or bangs an instrument equivalent to the Mende *kelei* (slit drum).

6 Here is one of the clearest resonances with village ideas about 'chimpanzee business'. Informants agree that such 'cannibalism' serves no nutritional purpose, but involves mutilation of the victim to supply body parts – genitalia, fat from around the heart, skin from palms and soles of the feet, etc. – to manufacture the 'bad medicine' facilitating economic or political advancement.

7 Migeod records the villagers cared for the 'orphan' chimpanzee for a fortnight before 'it died of a cold' (1926: 167). This is odd behaviour for people with an unremitting hostility to the animal (as is sometimes alleged). Perhaps the plan was to sell the infant as a pet. But I think a better explanation is that there is a genuine local fascination with an animal that stands on the threshold of humanity. My suggestion would be that Gola Forest populations are aware of the complexity of cross-species moral obligation arising from the fact that humans and chimpanzees live in intimate proximity (this is, as it were, the opposite side of the coin of the moral discourse of human 'chimpanzees' focused upon in the rest of this chapter). Lestel (1998) has made a related point about research settings. Researchers teach language to chimpanzees while chimpanzees 'domesticate' researchers as tools for their feeding, protection etc., thus constituting a complex inter-specific cognitive nexus potentially offering insights into cognition as a socially-distributed phenomenon.

8 If we follow Mithen (1996), then this informant is making the same mistake as some scientists, of assuming the mind of the chimpanzee to be a precursor of our own, when in fact the cognitive architecture is completely different. The chimpanzee has specialized social intelligence, but not the other specialized intelligences of humans, and the evolved capacity of the human mind to cross-reference domains. According to Mithen, social intelligence has a different, and wider significance, when it can be linked (as in humans) to technical, ethnoscientific and linguistic domains.

9 Clear evidence that rice farming was based on variety management and spreading labour up and down slopes on this section of the West African coast is provided for Cape Mount in the mid-seventeenth century in Dapper (Jones 1983) and for Sherbro in the late eighteenth century in information supplied to Thomas Jefferson by Capt. Nathaniel Cutting, commissioned by Jefferson to import dry-land rice varieties to the United States (Richards 1996).

10 A number of chiefly houses in (Mende, Gola and Kissi-speaking) forest communities trace 'Mandingo' origins.

11 Fairhead and Leach (1998) suggest the need to revise commonly held beliefs about deforestation in West Africa. Their conclusions, however, are less dramatic than at first sight. They dispute only the rate and recency of forest conversion.

12 John Locke, one of the philosophical architects of seventeenth-century notions of democratic rights in a property-owning democracy, was himself invested in slave-based plantations in South Carolina. His argument was that political rights came only through the work that added value to nature. Slavery was a means to introduce indolent Africans to the meaning of work, and thus eventually to their human rights.

13 In a short but combative introduction Kalous criticizes the distinguished historian of Sierra Leone, Christopher Fyfe, for downplaying a barbarity only relieved (in Kalous' eyes) by colonial rule. For his defence of colonialism the compiler was roundly taken to task by Sierra Leonean historian Arthur Abraham (1975), but we should be grateful, nevertheless, for Dr Kalous' labours in preserving evidence that may well have been vulnerable to the confusion that has prevailed in Sierra Leone in recent years.

14 The medicine is contained in a blue baft bag known as *bôfima* (defined in Innes' *Mende–English Dictionary* (1969) as 'medicine' in the form of 'a bag containing human organs'). According to Migeod (1926), *bôfima* (or *borofima*) is a loan word from Maninka meaning 'black bag'.

15 *Babu* is Krio for chimpanzee, and is sometimes confusingly translated back into English as 'baboon'.

16 Some of the region's ruling families (e.g. the Tuckers and Caulkers) trace ancestry to English patriarchs. The Margais, providers of Sierra Leone's first two Prime Ministers, trace origins to Kono. Kono is a Northern Mande language related to Koranko, Maninka and Bambara, and in the locally loose sense of the term the Margai dynasty might count as 'Mandingo' were it not for the fact the family converted to Christianity rather than Islam.

17 From where 'leopard men' not infrequently made it into the pages of French and Belgian comic strips (Jannone 1995)!

18 Tongo divination appears to have been a speciality of the Kpa-Mende people, in the area immediately to the north of Sherbro country. Detailed material on the diviners and the Tongo 'play' is to be found in documents reproduced in Kalous (1974).

19 In the report compiled at the colonial department of agriculture headquarters at Njala in 1926, 'sasswood' was identified as *Erythophleum guineense*. A decoction is made from the bark. The 'innocent' vomit. The effect on those with a less sensitive stomach (the 'guilty') is a digitalis-like action on the circulation, with a rise in arterial pressure, numbness, stricture across the brow and severe pain in the head, leading to coma and death (Kalous 1974: 230).

20 In a perhaps excessively cynical moment Col. A. B. Ellis remarked that he suspected the murders 'were not committed by the secret society but by the Tongo people themselves, in order to create a demand for their services' (Kalous 1974: 215).

21 Due to the specialized nature of blacksmithing, originally involving iron smelting, and its spread through the forest, blacksmiths often tend to have a stranger background and a 'Mandingo' orientation. As every farming season starts, there is a long line of young farmers at the blacksmith's hut hoping to acquire tools. They often get the implements for rice farming only by agreeing to offer the blacksmith farm labour in return for tools. The blacksmith is often a 'big man' as a result of the amount of grain he commands and the number of wives he can acquire. When accusations of *bôni hinda* begin to fly,

blacksmiths are often as vulnerable as 'Mandingo' merchants and wealthy chiefs.

22 '[Some] say they are leopard men but only after being tied very tightly and a rope put around their necks which rope is tied to some part of the roof and they are allowed to hang there only the tips of their toes touching the ground' (Kalous 1974, p. 210). Acting Attorney General van der Meulen, in 1909, noted that 'No DC has ever been able to get hold of the Leopard dress, or knives, altho' models have been made from descriptions given by the accomplices' (Kalous 1974: 289).

23 The 1912 ordinance remained on the statute book, but in the later colonial period district officers generally dismissed cases, faced with evidently forced confessions. Post-colonial governments have since chosen to allow the occasional 'cannibalism' case to proceed, but perhaps only where it served political purposes to do so.

24 A Mende proverb states 'a cannibal is no relative' (*nya numu yaa kɔlɛ mɔ*).

25 The Freetown *Concord Times* (29 November 1999) reported the appearance of a human chimpanzee near Tikonko in Bo District. The creature was said to be menacing women and children searching forests for firewood, and to be wearing boots. The paper noted that human chimpanzees appear especially during or near election times.

References

Abraham, A. (1975) Cannibalism and African historiography, In A. Abraham (ed.) *Topics in Sierra Leone History: A Counter-colonial Interpretation*, Freetown: Leone Publishers.

Barrows, W. (1976) *Grassroots Politics in an African State: Integration and Development in Sierra Leone*, New York: Africana Publishing Co.

Boesch, C. and Boesch, H. (1989) Hunting behavior of wild chimpanzees in the Tai National Park, *American Journal of Physical Anthropology* 78: 547–574.

Boesch, C., Marchesi, N., Ruth, B. and Joulian, F. (1994) Is nut cracking in wild chimpanzees a cultural behaviour?, *Journal of Human Evolution* 26: 325–338.

d'Azevedo, W. (1962) Some historical problems in the delineation of a Central West Atlantic region, *Annals, New York Academy of Sciences* 96(2): 512–538.

Douglas, M. (1966) *Purity and Danger*, Harmondsworth: Penguin Books.

Douglas, M. (1999) Culture clash in American anthropology, *Nature* 400, 631–632.

Douglas, M. and Ney, S. (1998) *Missing Persons*, Berkeley: University of California Press.

Fairhead, J. and Leach, M. (1998) *Reframing Deforestation: Global Analysis and Local Realities: Studies in West Africa*, London: Routledge.

Fardon, R. (1999) *Mary Douglas: An Intellectual Biography*, London: Routledge.

Fyfe, C. (ed.) (1964) *Sierra Leone Inheritance*, Oxford: Clarendon Press.

Gittins, A. J. (1987) *Mende Religion: Aspects of Belief and Thought in Sierra Leone*, Studia Instituti Anthropos 41, Nettetal (Germany): Steyler Verlag.

Goldman, H. V. and Walsh, M. T. (1997) *A Leopard in Jeopardy: An Anthropological Survey of Practices and Beliefs which Threaten the Survival of the Zanzibar Leopard (Panthera pardus adersi)*, Marahubi: Conservation Section, Commission for Natural Resources, Revolutionary Government of Zanzibar.

Huffman, M. A. and Seifu, M. (1989) Observations on the illness of, and consumption of a possibly medicinal plant, *Vernonia amygdalina* (Del.), by a wild chimpanzee in the Mahale Mountains National Park, Tanzania, *Primates* 30: 51–63.

Hutchins, E. (1997) *Cognition in the Wild*, Cambridge, Mass.: MIT Press.

Jannone, C. (1995) Les hommes-leopards et leurs derivés dans la bande dessinée: de la secte-fantasme du colonisateur au peuple dechu (1930–1991), in *Autre et nous: scènes et types: anthropologues et historiens devant les représentations des populations colonisées, des 'ethnies', des 'tribus' et des 'races' depuis les conquêtes coloniales*, Paris: ACHAC/SYROS.

Jones, A. (1981) 'Who were the Vai?', *Journal of African History* 22(2): 159–178.

Jones, A. (1983) *From Slaves to Palm Kernels: A History of the Galinhas Country (West Africa) 1730–1890*, Wiesbaden: Steiner Verlag.

Joset, P. E. (1955) *Les sociétés secrètes des hommes-léopards en Afrique noir*, Paris: Payot.

Joulian, F. (1995) Représentations traditionelles du chimpanzé en Côte d'Ivoire: étude préliminaire de quelques critères d'humanité, in R. Corbey and B. Theunissen (eds) *Ape, Man, Apeman: Changing Views since 1600*, Leiden (Netherlands): Department of Prehistory, Leiden University.

Jusu, M. S. (1999) *Management of Genetic Variability in Rice (Oryza sativa L. and O. glaberrima Steud.) by Breeders and Farmers in Sierra Leone*, PhD thesis, Wageningen (Netherlands): Wageningen University.

Kalous, M. (1974) *Cannibals and Tongo Players of Sierra Leone*, Auckland: privately published.

Kortlandt, A. and Holzhaus, E. (1987) New data on the use of stone-tools by chimpanzees in Guinea and Liberia, *Primates* 28(4): 473–496.

Kuper, A. (1999) *Culture: The Anthropologists' Account*, Cambridge, MA: Harvard University Press.

La Fontaine, J. (1998) Ritual and satanic abuse in England, in N. Scheper-Hughes and C. Sargent (eds) *Small Wars: The Cultural Politics of Childhood*, Berkeley and London: University of California Press.

Lestel, D. (1998) How chimpanzees have domesticated humans: towards an anthropology of human–animal communication, *Anthropology Today* 14(3), 12–15.

Littlefield, D. (1979) *Rice and Slaves*, Baton Rouge: University of Louisiana Press.

MacCormack, C. P. (1983) Human leopards and crocodiles: political meanings of categorical ambiguities, in P. Brown and D. Tuzin (eds) *The Ethnography of Cannibalism*, Washington, DC: Society for Psychological Anthropology.

McDermott, W. C. (1938) *The Ape in Antiquity*, Baltimore: Johns Hopkins University Press, Studies in Archaeology No. 27.

Migeod, F. W. H. (1926) *A View of Sierra Leone*, London: Kegan Paul, Trench, Trubner.
Mills, Lady Dorothy (1926) *Through Liberia*, London: Duckworth.
Mithen, S. (1996) *The Prehistory of the Mind: A Search for the Origins of Art, Religion and Science*, London: Thames and Hudson.
Muana, P. K. (1997) The Kamajoi militia: civil war, internal displacement and the politics of counter-insurgency, *Africa Development* 22(3/4): 77–100.
Norikoshi, I. (1982) One observed case of cannibalism among wild chimpanzees of the Mahale Mountains, *Primates* 23: 66–74.
Nwaka, G. I. (1986) The 'leopard' killings of southern Annang, Nigeria, *Africa* 56, 417–455.
Opala, J. A. (1986) *The Gullah: Rice, Slavery, and the Sierra Leone–American Connection*, Freetown: United States Information Service.
Peters, K. and Richards, P. (1998) Jeunes combattants parlant de la guerre et de la paix en Sierra Leone, *Cahiers d'Études africaines*, 150–152 (XXXVIII–2–4): 581–617.
Power, M. (1991) *The Egalitarians, Human and Chimpanzee: An Anthropological View of Social Organization*, Cambridge: Cambridge University Press.
Richards, P. (1986) *Coping with Hunger: Hazard and Experiment in an African Rice-farming System*, London: Allen and Unwin.
Richards, P. (1996) Culture and community values in the selection and maintenance of African rice, in S. Brush and D. Stabinsky (eds) *Intellectual Property and Indigenous Knowledge*, Covelo, CA: Island Press.
Richards, P. (1998 [1996]). *Fighting for the Rain Forest: War, Youth and Resources in Sierra Leone*, Oxford: James Currey (reprinted with additional material 1998).
Rodney, W. (1970) *A History of the Upper Guinea Coast, 1545 to 1800*, Oxford: Oxford University Press.
Scott, J. C. (1985) *Weapons of the Weak: The Everyday Forms of Peasant Resistance*, New Haven and London: Yale University Press.
Sims, J. (1859–1860) Scenes in the interior of Liberia: being a tour through the countries of the Dey, Goulah, Pessah, Barlain, Kpellay, Sualong, and King Boatswain's Tribes in 1858, *New York Colonization Journal* 9(12) (December 1859), 10(6) (June 1860), 10(8) (August 1860).
Stanley, W. B. (1919) Carnivorous apes in Sierra Leone, *Sierra Leone Studies* (old series), March, 1919.
Suzuki, A. (1971) Carnivory and cannibalism observed among forest-living chimpanzees, *Journal of the Anthropological Society of Nippon* 79: 30–48.
Waal, F. B. M. de (1982) *Chimpanzee Politics*, London: Jonathan Cape.
Winans, E. (1992) Hyenas on the border, in C. Nordstrom and J.-A. Martin (eds) *The Paths to Domination, Resistance and Terror*, Berkeley: University of California Press.
Wrangham, R. and Peterson, D. (1997) *Demonic Males: Apes and the Origins of Human Violence*, London: Bloomsbury.

Chapter 5
Wild pigs, 'pig-men' and transmigrants in the rainforest of Sumatra

Simon Rye

Introduction

This chapter presents a case-study of environmental perception by examining a specific conflict between people and wildlife in Sumatra – that between Javanese transmigrants in Eastern Sumatra and the wild pigs which threaten their farmland. I focus on the way that these peasants from Java conceive of the wild pig or *babi hutan* (the Menes Bearded Pig or *Sus barbatus*). I shall argue that they see the wild pig as a being that enters into the construction and maintenance of distinctions between good and evil, human and non-human beings, purity and pollution and more comprehensive categories such as humanity and animality. The peasant representations of the wild pig support the view of the environment as culturally constructed. The ethnographic case-study offered here forms the basis of a critique of the theory of 'direct perception'.

The notion of 'direct perception' (Ingold 1992) represents an important new theoretical approach to the perception of the environment. I start with a discussion of the theoretical propositions behind this notion, before moving on to present the empirical data from the rainforest of Sumatra. The Sumatran example calls into question the naturalist view of environmental perception, and the notion of human interaction with nature as essentially instrumental in character, something which seems to lie at the heart of the notion of direct perception. Towards the end I shall briefly discuss possible contributions of schema theory to the study of environmental perception. I suggest that schema theory presents an alternative both to constructivist and naturalist notions of environmental perception.

A central tenet of ecological anthropology, writes Tim Ingold, is that relations between humans and their environments are mediated by culture (1992: 39). In some of his recent work he contests this proposition, and criticizes what he sees as the cognitivism of anthropological accounts of environmental perception. He rejects the idea of humans as meaning-makers who merely impose their symbolically constituted designs upon the external world, an influential view he attributes to anthropologists like Clifford Geertz (1964) and Mary Douglas (1966). Accordingly, he refutes the supposition that people know or act upon their environments primarily through the medium of cultural representations. Ingold starts from 'an ontology of dwelling' which implies a notion of mutualism of person and environment achieved through practical and perceptual engagement with the dwelt-in environment. This notion of mutual envelopment of person and the environment, which departs from the notion of minds detached from the world and the Cartesian dualisms on which constructivist anthropology is based, is inextricably tied to a continuous intercourse between people and their environments.

The substitution of the Cartesian dualisms is made possible by an alternative theory of perception that shows how it is possible to engage in *direct* perception of the environment through practical activities in it. Such a theory is, Ingold maintains, available in the ecological psychology developed by Gibson (1979). Drawing on Gibson, Ingold sees the process of perception as a process of action: we perceive the world as, and because, we act in it, and contrary to constructivist anthropology (which contends that people mentally construct their environment), the theory of direct perception asserts that people '*discover* meaningful objects in their environment by moving about in it' (Ingold 1992: 47, original emphasis). In accordance with this view, language and symbolic representation are not preconditions for people's contact with their environments in productive activities. Hence, symbolic representations may be indispensable for knowledge-sharing about the world, but not for knowing it in the first place; 'cultural construction of the environment is not so much a *prelude* to practical action as an (optional) *epilogue*' (ibid.: 52, original emphasis). Ingold argues that the meanings that people find in their environments are already there in the information that people extract in the act of perception; the source of meaning is somehow supposed to reside in the object, as an intrinsic quality. Hence, meaning is not added on to the object by the perceiver. On the contrary, knowledge about objects is gained in terms of what the objects *afford* for the consummation of certain kinds of action (see Gibson 1979; Ingold 1992). The presence of a tree that affords elevation and safety for the human escaping an attacking predator, or the cave that affords shelter from a thunderstorm, are examples of environmental affordances.

But can we also apply the notion of affordances to more elaborate, but still adaptive, behaviour? Hunting constitutes a category of action that can be interpreted as a function of human need for protein, available technology and what nature affords in the form of wild game. Yet we also know that hunting, as a category of action, encompasses a wide variety of elaborate cultural practices and beliefs; we know that hunters do not perceive animals as sources of protein only. Similarly, it can be claimed that the tree that offered safety for the escaping human is not perceived only in terms of its affordance of elevation; it may also, for example, be the abode of ancestor spirits. We know, as it were, that 'animals are good to think', as well as to eat. The anthropological literature abounds with accounts of how humans perceive of and relate to animals in terms of elaborate cultural representations; the literature on totemism and animal food taboos offer but two examples (see, for example, Douglas 1966 and Lévi-Strauss 1966; see also Feld 1990, and for recent literature on environmentalist constructions of nature, see Milton 1993 and Freeman and Kreuter 1994).

The theory of direct perception also touches on fundamental and eternal questions in the philosophy of knowledge, particularly those that grapple with what it means to know the physical world. Ingold seems to support a realist or naturalist view, not primarily by maintaining that there is a world of physical objects 'out there', but by proposing that humans apprehend it independently of the specific cultural categories that we, by imposition of a constructivist perspective, bring to bear in the act of perception. Here, it will have to suffice to point out that these realist views seem to represent a break with anthropological theories about knowledge formation and symbolic representation, which have been influenced by constructivist theory. If we apply Ingold's ideas, we cannot, as it were, any longer be 'thinking through cultures' (Shweder 1991) about the environment.

As a further consequence of this reasoning, which seems to suggest that the environment is apprehended in similar ways by any group of subjects in their active engagement with it, the established distinctions between the world as given to the detached observer, and the construction of it by 'the natives', cannot be maintained. Various terms have been used to coin this distinction; *emic* and *etic* is but one example (Geertz 1983). In the field of ecological anthropology Rappaport's terms *operational* and *cognized* models refer to the same distinction, i.e. between 'people's knowledge of their environment and their beliefs concerning it', in contrast to 'the same ecological system in accordance with the assumptions and methods of science' (Rappaport 1979: 97) – that is, scientific ecology. The reason we cannot maintain this distinction, if we apply a notion of direct perception, is that this notion rejects the idea that the perceived environment (which is equivalent to Rappaport's *cognized models*) is a separate cultural domain that is the outcome of a process of cognition, and that such cognition is a necessary guide to action. As Ingold sees it, the environment is not separately cognized; it is by their action in the world that people know it and come to perceive what it *affords* for the pursuit of action (Ingold 1992).

On the basis of Ingold's proposition, it seems possible to suggest the following more general argument: if cultural representations are not decisive for human apprehension of the environment, it follows that any group of subjects will apprehend a given environment in essentially similar ways, irrespective of their cultural differences, as long as they engage in similar behaviour and make use of or confront the same environmental affordances. Thus, different perceptions of the environment are contingent only upon the pursuit of different activities in it. Since we know that different ethnic groups (or, certainly, scientists and 'natives') may pursue different activities in the same forest, we should be able to maintain that they will apprehend the forest in different ways, according to the nature of the activities they engage in (for example, hunting and gathering versus cultivation). Although we are thus able to explain differences in people's perception of their environment in terms of behavioural variation, such an account will be far removed from the rich and culturally sensitive accounts of cultural anthropology.

Assuming that people move from one environment to another, is it not likely that they will perceive and relate to their new environment in terms of what they know, that is, in terms of cultural representations? Can we, as an alternative trajectory, expect them to 'adjust' their perceptions according to the affordances that the new environment offers? The following ethnographic account of migrants' perceptions of pigs in the rainforest of Sumatra will show that affordances have no objective existence independent of our apprehension of them *as such*. This apprehension takes place with reference to prior experience and accumulated knowledge. It can also be argued that affordances are, in fact, the result of human productive activity, and that they have to be seen in relation to their creation as affordances through human action upon nature. Hence, affordances are cultural constructs and not inherent qualities of objects to be discovered by humans. Furthermore, objects in nature must also be seen within a comprehensive context of cultural representations that lends relevance to their non-utilitarian qualities (notwithstanding the cultural meanings ascribed to the objects themselves).

In order to study human adaptation, we have to study culture and the ways cultural meaning systems inform human interaction with the environment. Hence, since I maintain that we should not dismiss the culture concept altogether, some clarification is needed as to what the term should mean.[1] At the risk of being unfashionable, I see culture as consisting of learned and to some extent shared systems of meaning having representational, affective as well as directive functions whereby people act in and upon their natural and social environments (D'Andrade 1984; Geertz 1983). However, recent developments in culture theory have brought our attention to the particulate, elusive and socially distributative character of cultural knowledge, and to the intimate relationship between cognition and bodily and social experience. These developments have paved the way for views that challenge both structuralist and interpretative notions of culture.

The defence of the culture concept in the study of human adaptation does not necessarily imply the interpretivist notion of culture as a set of 'shared meanings'. Nor does it imply that language and symbol systems *determine* what we experience, or indeed the constructivist notion of people as detached meaning-constructors who 'clothe their environment with meaning' without entering into active engagement with it. It does, however, imply that we endow people with the capability of creating cultural entities that cannot be reduced to being a reflection of the affordances of nature (in Gibson's sense). We see adaptational knowledge not merely as the outcome of subjective experience *vis-à-vis* non-human objects in nature, but as the outcome of an intersubjective process of knowledge formation and accumulation.

Having said this, I must also say that I go along with those who have pointed to the dangers of cognitivism and the linguistic bias in culture theory (see, for example, Bloch 1991). It is, however, unnecessary to revert to reductionism (which, by implication, lies at the heart of a theory of direct perception) in order to say that humans can perceive their environment without constructing it first. We need, I think, to maintain that there is a difference between seeking shelter in a cave and building a house, although both offer protective affordances, and that humans (unlike animals) are capable of doing both.

Cultural representations of nature, or indeed, of any phenomenon, are not just 'matters of meaning' devoid of functions. As Barth has put it, cultural representations have 'jobs to do' in the sense that they provide people with cognitive means that can be used in order to render the natural world intelligible; people create and apply such representations 'in a struggle to grasp the world, relate to it, and manipulate it through concepts, knowledge and acts' (Barth 1987: 87). Exploration of representations about nature can only be fruitful if it also includes an appreciation of the context of the practices from which they spring, that is, the 'real world' of nature in which people engage in adaptational practice. Accordingly, in the words of Barth, we should focus on 'this widest compass: a natural world, a human population with all its collective and statistical features, and a set of cultural ideas in terms of which these people try to understand and cope with themselves and their habitat' (ibid.: 87).

Javanese migrants in the Sumatran rainforest

As part of the Indonesian state's attempt to address the problem of overpopulation on the island of Java, a large-scale transmigration policy has been pursued in which 'surplus' Javanese are relocated to outlying islands, including Sumatra. Eastern Sumatra is one of the major sites of Javanese transmigration; in 1992 I carried out fieldwork in the Riau province of Sumatra, and studied Javanese migrants who had taken up rice cultivation on the edge of the forest.[2]

Javanese transmigrant farmers blame the wild pig for their steadily diminishing returns from agricultural labour and their consequent neglect of their fields. Originating mostly from rice-growing areas in the neighbouring island of Java, the people who moved to Sumatra in 1981 had hoped to realize their lives there as secure rice cultivators. Transmigration was presented to them as the road to a better life and relief from penury. However, for most of them that road led to a future hardly any brighter than that available to them in overpopulated Java. Some of the better-off migrants have spent their savings on the journey back to Java or to some other settlement in search of better prospects.

For the approximately 600 migrant households that remain in the resettlement village, the swamps of eastern lowland Sumatra represent the point of no return. After an initial period of two to three years, the marginal agriculture of most migrant households collapsed; the farming systems introduced by the government, and on which the economy of the migrants depended, turned out to be ill-suited for the lowland rainforest environment.[3] Each household was allocated 2 hectares of land upon arrival. Out of these 2 hectares, 1 hectare had been cleared before the migrants arrived. The remaining hectare was supposed to be cleared by the migrants (which only very few had managed to do even ten years after their arrival). The initial government plan was for the migrants to establish permanent rice cultivation, either irrigated (*sawah*) or rainfed (*ladang*), on their plots and thereby to become self-sufficient rice cultivators.

This scenario was never realized, mainly because of the lack of ecological insight among those responsible for the location of the settlement, and in the inadequate means to curb the degradation resulting from an attempt to reproduce permanent rice agriculture in a rainforest environment.[4] Today, cultivation takes place almost exclusively in the gardens that surround each house, except in the case of a few households that cultivate land along a small stream where *sawah* cultivation is possible. The lack of farming viability in the settlement, combined with the expansion of plantation enterprises in the area, has turned the majority of migrants into wage-dependent plantation workers rather than self-sufficient farmers.

The migrants themselves identify two causes of agricultural collapse. The first is the loss of soil fertility. The second is the damage by wild animals that attack and ruin virtually all types of crops, except mature stands of fruit trees. In addition to depletion of the inherently poor soils, attacks by marauding wild pigs have increased dramatically since 1984. At the time of fieldwork in 1991–1992 wild pigs were said to far outnumber people and to pose the most serious threat to cultivation.

The migrants have tried to counteract the impact of the wild pigs in several, not very successful, ways. One of their measures is poisoning; the seeds of the poisonous *tuba* plant are prescribed for killing pigs in Java.[5] The intractable pigs in Sumatra, however, are known to avoid the poisonous seeds when, according to informants, they 'see what happens to other pigs'. Hunting is another strategy. But hunting is considered dangerous, and, again, the hunters are said to fall short of the ability of the pigs to outwit them. Although hunting is known to have produced some results in other settlements in the area, hunting expeditions are seldom organized, the main constraint being the absence of men due to continuous labour migration. Another reason for the absence of hunting may be that the returns to labour spent on hunting are small as long as crop cultivation is in any case almost non-existent and Muslim food-taboos prohibit consumption of pig meat. The migrants' fear of the many spirits in the forest and their lack of hunting skills also contribute to the low returns from labour spent on hunting.

Cultural representations of the 'pig-man'

The majority of the migrants are Muslims, and dislike of the wild pig is common among adherents to Islam. But cosmological dimensions of the pig relate to more than its condemnation in the Qur'an. As mentioned above, the mystical capacities of the pig are often referred to in order to explain the pigs' resilience and cleverness or, in a similar vein, to account for the inability of the migrants to fight them. Not only is the pig regarded as a polluting creature imbued with taboos. It is also considered as a competitor to human beings, and as an evil creature hiding in the surrounding forest, which is experienced as a continuous threat to cultivated land.

For people from Java, the contrast between forest and cleared land is not merely one of vegetation cover. The forest is non-human space, uncultivated and potentially threatening, and the abode of malevolent beings and spirits. The forest spirits commonly referred to by the migrants as *hantu hutan* (literally 'spirits of the forest') are one example. In contrast, the village and the cleared land, including the fields located between the village and the forest, are regarded as space controlled by humans, even though it is under threat from forest-dwelling beings. Coming from intensively cultivated Java, the migrants have no particular experience of the forest, nor are they comfortable with the creatures and spirits that inhabit it. Clifford Geertz writes in a passage about the history of spirits in Java: 'As Javanese culture advances and the heavy tropical forest turns into rice fields and house lands, the spirits retreat to the remaining woods, the volcano cones, and the Indian Ocean' (Geertz 1960: 28). The island of Sumatra contains a large share of these spirit-infested woods, and it is exactly these woods next to which the Javanese migrants have been placed.

Pak Wirio is a Sundanese *dukun*. (The Sundanese are one of the two main ethnic groups on the island of Java.)[6] He introduced me to his representations of wild pigs and to the wider field of cultural representations of which pigs are a part. The term *dukun* refers to several functions that a man or a woman may have in ritual and ceremonial life, but the term is often used among people from Java in relation to curing. Pak Wirio can best be conceived of as a curer and as a particularly knowledgeable person on issues related to the workings of the spiritual world in human life. His small house and his abandoned plot of land are located on the fringe of the dense forest where he has often encountered the wild pigs, especially in the evening or early in the morning.

One evening Pak Wirio asked me to accompany him on a walk to *tanah babi* – the land of the pigs on the edge of the forest. He wanted me to see it with my own eyes – he wanted me to see *orang babi*, the 'pig-man'. Once we were out there, after having forced our way through almost impenetrable *alang-alang* thickets,[7] we waited, listened and stared into the green chaos that surrounded us. But we could neither hear nor see anything that indicated the presence of the pig-man, or other mystical creatures. As we sat there, the contours of the tree canopy became almost invisible against the black sky, and the silence of the day gave way to the cacophony of the nocturnal forest. Pak Wirio commented that the pig-man was probably watching us from its hiding place, or it had returned to the pig people and would come back later during the night. On our way back to Pak Wirio's house, he pointed to the place where he had last seen a herd of wild pigs accompanied by the pig-man.

It was later, when we were sitting on the little patio outside his house, that Pak Wirio introduced me to the world of the pigs:

> Here we are in the land of the pigs, we can do nothing to harm the pigs or protect our land from them, they are superior here because they have the *ilmu babi* [the secret and powerful knowledge of pigs, or the pig spirit], which we do not have. There are two kinds of pigs; *babi tunggal* or *orang babi* [the solitary male pig known as the pig-man, or one of the pig people] and the *babi biasa* [the ordinary wild pig].[8] It would not be so difficult to handle the ordinary pigs if it was not for *babi tunggal*. *Babi tunggal* is the head of the pigs, he leads the other pigs and teaches them how to trick us, and it is *babi tunggal* who commands the ordinary pigs into our gardens. *Babi tunggal* is clever. Whenever I heard or saw a pig near my garden back in Java I could say a spell and then something like 'your food is served in the garden of Pak Dirjo', and point in the direction of Pak Dirjo's garden. Then the pig would make its way into Pak Dirjo's garden instead of my garden. But here [in Sumatra] you never see the pig until it has entered your garden, and the spells I used to say in Java have no effect here ... *Babi tunggal* is clever, very clever, he hides in the forest and waits for the right moment because he knows our thoughts, he knows our next move.

Babi tunggal is half-man half-pig, and it is believed to have the mental capacity of humans. In some cases it may also have the bodily features of a man with the head of a pig. This pig, with human features, is believed by the migrants to be one of the *orang babi* – the pig people – whom they believe live in the forest further up in the Cinaku river valley. There, in the riverine forests where the migrants seldom or never set foot, live the *orang suku* – the tribal peoples who are believed by the migrants to possess the magic power to turn themselves into pigs. The *orang suku* seldom come close to the resettlement, and the migrants have only vague knowledge about them. When the term *orang suku* is used by the migrants in Titian Resak, it usually refers to the indigenous Talang Mamak people.[9] It may also refer to the Malays, although they are most often referred to as *orang Melayu*, meaning Malay people. In the question of pig magic the distinction between Talang Mamak and Malays is of some significance since only Talang Mamak are believed to have the capacity to turn themselves into pigs.[10] The fact that the Malays are Muslims prohibits them, in the view of the migrants, from possessing and using pig magic. Hence, although different, the Malays are included by the migrants in a Muslim moral community which excludes the non-Muslim Talang Mamak.

The Talang Mamak, who number about one thousand people, are a forest-dwelling group who used to subsist on swidden cultivation supplemented by hunting and gathering of forest products, and who have recently become sedentarized in permanent villages. Both the Talang Mamak and the Malays are considered to be *keras* by the migrants: coarse, rude and spiritually unrefined. But only the Talang Mamak reveal 'pigness'. In accordance with this characterization, the migrants believe that the Talang Mamak possess pig magic and have the power to turn themselves into pigs and thereby to become pig-men. The control of pig magic is believed to be confined to certain Talang Mamak families or kin groups among which the *ilmu babi* (the secret pig knowledge or power) is passed on from one generation to the next, following the male line.

Explaining 'pig-man' beliefs

To return to the introductory discussion about direct perception versus cultural representations of the environment, it seems pertinent to ask how we are to explain migrants' ideas without recourse to a concept of cultural representations. How interesting or useful would such an account be? It is obvious that migrants' representations say something about pigs as objects in nature, and that they somehow refer to experiences from practical, perceptual interaction with the rainforest environment, notably those that relate to their unsuccessful attempts to engage in rice cultivation. But they also say a lot more. They disclose the symbolic properties of knowledge that is brought to bear in the very act of perception. For the migrants there is no way that pigs can be perceived as affordances independent of a cultural context. Pigs enact an array of cultural meanings that span from Muslim food taboos rooted in ideas about purity and pollution to distinctions between dangerous wilderness and human space. Pak Wirio's discursive representations of the malevolent nature of pigs can hardly be seen as in any way discontinuous with his perception of pigs in his garden or in the forest.

Steven Feld's rich account of the relationship between bird sounds and human sentiments among the Kaluli of New Guinea points to a similar connection. Among the Kaluli, bird sounds are simultaneously heard as the 'talk' of the dead, and it appears in Feld's account that the representations evoked by bird sounds are not epiphenomenal to the hearing of the sound (Feld 1990). Hence, perception is not a prelude to a representational epilogue; both are simultaneous (and possibly interdependent) processes. Pigs and birds thus take on the character of symbols that enact a broad 'fan of cultural meaning' which cannot be encompassed by a notion of affordances.

One of the problems with the notion of affordances is its link to utilitarian thinking and to studies of animal behaviour. This link is obvious in Gibson's definition of affordances (which Ingold builds upon): 'the affordances of an environment are what it offers the animal, what it provides or furnishes, either for good or for bad' (1979: 127, cited from Ingold 1992). It is clear that transmigrant or Kaluli cultural representations about the environment encompass a lot more than the use-value of a given object or organism in nature for their life-sustaining activities, or constraints in relation to the consummation of life-sustaining behaviour. How, then, are we to explain this 'excessive knowledge', and how are we to distinguish it from knowledge about affordances in Gibson's sense? In other words, what are we to make of knowledge about the environment that cannot plausibly be explained in terms of affordances? How can we, for example, account for the fact that migrants seldom engage in logging of valuable timber in the rainforest even though nobody would stop them if they did? The reason mature *kulim* hardwood trees, that timber purchasers would pay high prices for, are not 'affordances' for the migrants is that the latter fear the spirits which reside in these trees.

What, then, can the theory of direct perception contribute to ecological anthropology, or more specifically to a culturally sensitive ecological anthropology? And how useful can it be if it has little to tell us about the role of culture in people's interaction with their environment? Let us return to the pigs. As we have seen, the antagonistic relationship which pertains between humans and wild pigs in Sumatra offers no resolution and clearly favours metaphorical elaboration. The migrants' notions may be seen as cultural representations put to work in order to handle the discontinuities associated with a new and inhospitable environment. Although these representations of wild pigs are fascinating in themselves, as fragments of what Croll and Parkin (1992) have aptly termed *eco-cosmologies* in the making, their social and moral relevance surfaces only when they are placed within the social context of their formation. We have to explore the connection, which the migrants conceive of, between the *orang suku* and the wild pigs as harmful, polluted and taboo creatures. This leads to an enquiry into how wild pigs become metaphors for migrants' thinking about their neighbours who live in the rainforest. It leads into themes of general and long-standing anthropological interest: the ascription of inferior cultural traits to other social groups, the symbolic construction of otherness in terms of civilization and savagery, and the way in which derogatory cultural constructions may enter into relations of power and dominance.[11]

The migrants conceive of the *orang suku* of Seberida in derogatory terms, and they do this by imposing on them interpretative schemes that encompass notions of morality as well as causal relationships. The plausibility of the link between hostility, vandalism and wild pigs is rooted in representations which the migrants have brought with them from Java to Sumatra. These representations are put to work as schemes for interpreting the hostile behaviour of the wild pigs as behaviour wrought by *orang suku* possessed by animal spirits. The way the migrants put their intact representations to use in the Sumatran context provides a telling example of how a set of ideas can be successfully adapted to a new situation. One of these representations, which clearly brings out the link between moral breaches and 'pigness', was conveyed to me by Sundanese migrants.

Sundanese migrants told me that in the remaining forest patches of a place in West Java lives a *guru babi* (a pig guru or teacher) who has the power to pass the *ilmu babi* on to other people. Interestingly, the migrants apply this notion in the Sumatran context. In expanded form, they bring it to bear on their perception of the social environment so that it also encompasses moral evaluation of neighbouring ethnic groups. In Seberida, the *guru babi* is believed to be one of the Talang Mamak people, and to be responsible for the recruitment of novices among those who later become *babi tunggal* and leaders of *babi biasa* – the ordinary wild pigs. Any person with evil intentions may seek out this *guru* to be endowed with the body and powers of a wild pig in order to undertake actions that are socially prohibited. One instance of such actions that was often referred to by informants was theft of land: people were known to have transformed themselves into pigs, and to have ruined people's land in order to force the owner to abandon it and then take it over for their own use. After having accomplished his murky business and consulted the *guru babi* again, the pig-man is believed to regain his human features.

In the forest further up along the Cinaku river, there is, according to Pak Wirio, a big rock in the shape of a pig with water running from its mouth. This rock is the source of the *ilmu babi*:

> The *guru babi* will take the pig novice to the rock a number of times and teach him the ways and language of the pigs. The novice has to learn a secret mantra by heart, which is revealed to him by the *guru*. Then, after some time, the novice is told to return to the stone alone. This time he will have to take off his clothes, kneel down in front of the rock and drink of the water that runs from its mouth. After this, the novice will whisper his wishes to the pig spirit which resides in the stone and say the mantra before and after. Upon doing this the novice will turn into a pig-man. After the transformation, his clothes will be taken away and kept with the *guru*. The first thing a man will do when he has become a pig, and rid himself of his human nature and his knowledge of human conduct, is to make his way to somebody's garden, dig up the roots, destroy the banana-plants and gorge himself on edible crops. The man will remain a pig as long as he needs to in order to accomplish his tasks, and he will live in the forest as a pig. When he wants to regain his human nature, he will seek the *guru* who will then hold his clothes up in front of him. Upon the sight of his clothes, the pig-man will try to put them on, and then slowly regain his human features.

Although they are broadly similar, there is one feature that distinguishes the pig-man believed to live in the rainforest of Sumatra from that of Java – his alleged immortality. The pig-man in Java can be injured and even killed, whereas the pig-man in Sumatra is regarded as immortal, something which makes him even worse than his counterpart in Java. This immortality supports the idea held by the migrants that the pig-man is a manifestation of evil forces that cannot be conquered by humans.

But for what reason do the migrants believe that the Talang Mamak turn themselves into wild pigs and ruin their gardens? What lends relevance to the myth about the pig-man in the Sumatran context? It is interesting to find that the idea about the close linkage between wild pigs and the *orang suku* goes together with the transmigrants' notion they are not welcome in Sumatra, that the *orang suku* are jealous of them and that the plague of the wild pigs is conceived of as an attempt by the indigenous people to make life so unbearable to the migrants that they will give up and leave. It is this belief that so clearly establishes the parallel between the *orang suku* and the imposter-thief who forces peasants off their land in Java in the story told by Pak Wirio.

The large influx of migrants to the area, in combination with extensive logging and mining projects, has increased the pressure on land and turned even the Malays into a minority. This development is not celebrated by the people who had lived there before the migrants arrived, and their hostility is not, therefore, implausible. To the migrants, however, the *orang suku*, in the form of hostile pig-men, are responsible for much of the misery that they experience in Sumatra. The perception of the latter group as scapegoats and scoundrels may be seen as the consequence of explanatory as well as legitimating schemes put to work. I shall return to this below.

Transmigrants' representations as forest schemas

Ingold contests the role of culture in the human perception of the environment. The answer that he offers implies, as I have tried to show, that we embark on a route that may eventually lead us to discharge the concept of culture in human adaptation altogether. But are there no other ways out of the overly constructivist models of culture and the linguistic biases which have shaped so much of modern anthropology? Schema theory is a field within cognitive science which has caught the attention of anthropologists (see Bloch 1991; Strauss 1992; D'Andrade 1995). In this section I suggest that schema theory can contribute to an understanding of migrants' experiences with the rainforest, and of environmental perception more generally.[12]

Schema theory suggests that most cultural knowledge, unlike language, is not organized in linked linear propositions and categories (Bloch 1991: 184). According to schema theory, we comprehend events, tasks and objects in the world through the activation of internalized schemas; we comprehend situations and objects by instantanously comparing them to more or less established configurations of features that have been created through earlier experience, not by checking off a list of features of the object or situation at hand (Bloch 1991). Bloch's example of the Malagasy cultivator who makes an assessment of the suitability of a forest plot as a swidden by a short glance at it, provides an apt illustration (ibid.).

Another useful contribution to schema theory has been made by Mandler, who offers the following useful description of schemas:

> Schemas are built up in the course of interaction with the environment... The schema that is developed as a result of *prior experiences* with a particular kind of event is not a carbon copy of that event; *schemas are abstract representations of environmental regularities. We comprehend events in terms of the schemas they activate*... Schemas are also processing mechanisms; they are active in selecting evidence, in parsing the data provided by our environment, and in providing appropriate general or specific hypotheses.
> (Mandler 1984: 55–6, in D'Andrade 1995: 122, emphasis added)

From the perspective of schema theory, the investigation of cultural understandings involves more than the features of particular categories. It involves the investigation of how constituent parts may activate entire schemas that are brought to bear in perception and interpretation. It is interesting that Mandler does not distinguish between the perceiver and the comprehender, and this touches upon an important feature of schema theory: the schema instantanously creates complex interpretations from minimal perceptual inputs. Hence, as appears from the Kaluli case, humans are perceivers and interpreters in the same instance.

If we apply the notion of schemas in the case of migrants' perception of their environment, I believe it is possible to delineate a Javanese or Sundanese cultural schema for the *forest* (*hutan*). It seems clear to me that what was actually being conveyed through informants' discursive representations about their environment in Sumatra was an abstract account which relates or connects certain features that together make up the migrants' cultural schema for the *forest*. These features include *trees, spirits, malevolence* and various kinds of birds and animals among which *pigs* stand out as the most symbolically potent. Because it is the most potent in terms of social meaning, the wild pig has come to 'stand for' the forest in a way that makes it like a 'key symbol' in Ortner's terms (Ortner 1973). In other words, wild pigs can be seen to activate the forest schema as symbolic instantiations of it.

The schema for the forest is not, however, a rigid structure. As the case of the migrants so well illustrates, schemas are flexible configurations that can incorporate new inputs. The way the migrants incorporate the *orang suku* in their schemas, or the way the pig-man in Sumatra is conceived of as immortal, clearly demonstrate that there is room for *bricolage*. However, as noted by D'Andrade, in order for schemas to have interpretative and representational functions, they must to some extent be resistant to change; if the schemas we employ in interpretation are themselves continuously changing, we would not be able to interpret changes in our environment as we would lack a reference frame for comparison. Hence, we may distinguish between weak and strong, well-formed schemas, the difference being not absolute but one of degree. Unlike weak schemas, strong schemas have the power to create illusory correlations and organize knowledge in the form of memory (D'Andrade 1995: 142).

I suggest that the migrants' cultural schema for the *forest* is a strong schema, not only because it has the power to create illusory correlations and hence has a considerable explanatory potential, but because it also encompasses normative and moral evaluations of human action associated with the forest, and thus to more comprehensive schemas, particularly Islam and contingent notions about civilization and savagery, purity and pollution and taboo. On this basis, we can argue that the migrants' schema for the forest makes possible explanation as well as legitimation. This understanding brings us close to Berger and Luckman's concept about the process of justification whereby the world is not only rendered plausible, but whereby its 'inevitable imperatives are also infused with "moral dignity"' (Berger and Luckman 1967). This example clearly brings out the normative and moral aspects of schemas, which may seem to be missing in cognitive schema theory.

In this chapter I am mostly concerned with interpretative and representational schemas. However, as noted by D'Andrade (1995) there are as many schemas as there are kinds of things; there are orientational schemas, propositional schemas, image schemas and so on. Schemas can also be action-oriented, and this points to an important aspect of the migrants' schema for forest. As a result of their background in Java, where they have seldom or never engaged in interaction with forest environments, their cultural schemas for the forest remain largely representational; they draw most of their interpretations from shared mythical representations. Furthermore, it can be assumed that their lack of practical expertise for handling the forest environment in Sumatra favours a representation of the forest and its malevolent inhabitants as invincible. The pig-man conceived of as immortal stands out as a strong manifestation of such beliefs. Contrary to the migrants, the indigenous Talang Mamak make active use of the forest through hunting and gathering, as well as swidden cultivation. Both forest schemas are representational, but only the Talang Mamak schema incorporates the forest and the animals in it as objects for human action; hence, we may argue, the Talang Mamak schema *also* represents the forest as affordances. This clearly demonstrates the necessary link between the concept of affordances and human action upon nature.

Conclusion

Let us return to environmental perception, which I think provides a good example of the usefulness of schema theory. If we take a look at certain well-established ideas in anthropology about how humans experience the world, Ingold's argument may in fact be well taken. One convincing example can be found in Marshall Sahlins' quotation of Leslie White's formulation: 'Between man and nature hung the veil of culture, and he could see nothing save through this medium . . . permeating everything was the essence of words' (Sahlins 1978: 105, from D'Andrade 1995). Similar general assertions about the role of language and culture in how we experience the environment are common in anthropology (Douglas 1966; Leach 1976; Sahlins 1978). This anthropological 'metaphor of cultural symbols as a veil' between humans and their environment stems from the idea that 'language and other symbol systems *determine* what we experience' (D'Andrade 1995:148–149, original emphasis). The veil metaphor implies, if we paraphrase Ingold, that humans, as meaning-makers, 'dissolve the reality of the environment' (see Ingold 1992: 46).

According to schema theory, the veil metaphor is misleading because it makes invisible the correspondence between cultural representations and the external environment. Schemas are open and flexible configurations that have a great capacity for receiving and adjusting to new information, and their correspondence to the external environment occurs through a continuous interaction with it. Such correspondence applies both to physical objects that are part of the natural world, like trees and animals, and to the behavioural regularities that are part of social life (D'Andrade 1995). From this follows that migrants' representations of wild pigs are not wholly constructions of their imagination; they bear resemblance to wild pigs as organisms in nature that in fact damage crops. This correspondence or isomorphism, does not, however, imply a simple naturalism in which individual and cultural representations merely mirror our perception of the world.

Schema theory thus presents an alternative both to the 'metaphor of culture as a veil' employed by constructivist anthropology, and to the naturalism implied by an idea of direct perception. As I see it, schema theory supports the idea that the environment is perceived in terms of cultural knowledge. It, does, however, offer a more nuanced account of the complex processes by which knowledge is formed, stored and brought to bear in human experience than does constructivist theory. In his argument, Ingold takes up the question posed by Steward more than forty years ago about the 'cultural factor' in ecological anthropology. Steward noted that what 'to do about this cultural factor in ecological studies has raised many methodological difficulties' (1955: 31). Steward himself did not come anywhere near to clarifying the cultural factor, and Ingold suggests rhetorically that perhaps the answer may be to leave it out of the ecological equation (1992: 53), opting instead for a theory of direct perception based on a concept of environmental affordances. As I have tried to show, that is not the only option. Schema theory may provide a possible way out of the impasse between constructivist and naturalist approaches to human perception of the environment.

Notes

1 Although he does not join the camp of post-modern critics, Ingold's argument may be seen as (a naturalist's) contribution to the attack on the culture concept, and to the 'existential doubt' experienced by most anthropologists over what we are to mean by the discipline's core concept. He does not seem, however, to present us with an alternative except to discharge the culture concept in the study of human adaptation.
2 This fieldwork was carried out as part of the inter-disciplinary NORINDRA research project.
3 See Holden and Simanjuntak (1994) and Hvoslef (1992) for analyses of farming systems among migrants in the Seberida district.
4 See Geertz (1963) for a description of the agro-ecological differences between the so-called 'inner' and 'outer' islands of the Indonesian archipelago. The 'inner' islands comprise Java, Bali and Madura whereas the 'outer' islands comprise Sumatra, Kalimantan, Sulawesi, Nusa Tenggara, Maluku (the Moluccas) and Irian Jaya (Western New Guinea).
5 *Tuba* is a bush belonging to the *Euphorbiaceae* family (Hvoslef 1992).
6 The population of Java comprises two main ethnic and linguistic groups: the Javanese and the Sundanese in addition to the smaller groups of Tenggerese and Badui peoples living in the highlands of eastern and western Java. The ethnic Javanese occupy the eastern and central parts of Java, whereas the western part is inhabited by Sundanese. Ethnicity was of little importance to the migrants, and although my main informant on the issues that I discuss here was Sundanese, it would be quite mistaken to view his representations about the pig-man as exclusive to the Sundanese.
7 *Alang-alang*, or elephant grass, is known to invade abandoned fields in much of Southeast Asia, and to transform them into what Geertz (1963) called 'green deserts'. Its scientific name is *Imperata cylindrica*.
8 There are two categories of wild pigs: the solitary boar and the sows with their piglets. The boars and the sows live separate lives. *Babi tunggal* refers to the former category whereas the term *babi biasa* refers to the latter. Hence, only the boars are believed to be pig men whereas the sows are devoid of mystical powers.

9 The term *orang suku* also encompasses the indigenous Kubu people. However, most of the Kubu live across the border in the neighbouring Jambi province (Øyvind Sandbukt and Lene Østergaard, pers. comm.).
10 Although there are some diverging views on this issue, most migrants agree that the capacity to use pig-magic is restricted to the Talang Mamak people.
11 This is an interesting and comprehensive theme that merits detailed investigation, particularly with regard to the possible political implications that the derogatory construction of the indigenous population might come to have in a near future characterized by increasing inter-ethnic conflicts over resource use.
12 This presentation must be short and superficial, and it will have to suffice to point out some of the possibilities that seem to open up by the application of schema theory. For a review of the schema concept, see e.g. Holland and Quinn (1987), D'Andrade (1995), and also Shore (1996) for a recent contribution to a discussion of schemas and cultural models.

References

Barth, F. (1987) *Cosmologies in the Making: A Generative Approach to Cultural Variation in Inner New Guinea*, Cambridge: Cambridge University Press.
Berger, P. and Luckman, T. (1967) *The Social Construction of Reality: A Treatise in the Sociology of Knowledge*, London: Allen Lane.
Bloch, M. (1991) Language, anthropology and cognitive science, *Man* 26: 183–198.
Croll, E. and Parkin, D. (1992) Cultural understandings of the environment, in E. Croll and D. Parkin (eds) *Bush Base: Forest Farm. Culture, Environment and Development*, London: Routledge.
D'Andrade, R. (1984) Cultural meaning systems, in R. A. Shweder and R. A. LeVine (eds) *Culture Theory: Essays on Mind, Self, and Emotion*, Cambridge: Cambridge University Press.
D'Andrade, R. (1995) *The Development of Cognitive Anthropology*, Cambridge: Cambridge University Press.
Douglas, M. (1966) *Purity and Danger*, London: Routledge and Kegan Paul.
Feld, S. (1990) *Sound and Sentiment: Birds, Weeping, Poetics, and Song in Kaluli Expression*, Philadelphia: University of Pennsylvania Press.
Freeman, M. M. R. and Kreuter, U. (eds) (1994) *Elephants and Whales: Resources for Whom?* Amsterdam: Gordon and Breach Publishers.
Geertz, C. (1960) *The Religion of Java*, New York: The Free Press.
Geertz, C. (1963) *Agricultural Involution: The Processes of Ecological Change in Indonesia*, Berkeley: University of California Press.
Geertz, C. (1964) The transition to humanity, in S. Tax (ed.) *Horizons of Anthropology*, Chicago: Aldine.
Geertz, C. (1983) *Local Knowledge*, New York: Basic Books.
Gibson, J. J. (1979) *The Ecological Approach to Visual Perception*, Boston: Houghton Mifflin.

Holden, S. and Simanjuntak, R. (1994) An agroeconomic analysis of transmigration settlements in Seberida, Riau Province, Sumatra, in Ø. Sandbukt and H. Wiriadinata (eds) *Rain Forest and Resource Management: Proceedings of the NORINDRA Seminar, Jakarta 1993*, Jakarta: Indonesian Institute of Sciences (LIPI).

Holland, D. and Quinn, N. (eds) (1987) *Cultural Models in Language and Thought*, Cambridge: Cambridge University Press.

Hvoslef, H. (1992) *From Volcanoes and Sawah to Pigs and Cassava: Homegardens of Javanese Transmigrants in Sumatra, Agroecological Constraints and Evaluation of Potential Solutions and Declining Productivity*, Master degree thesis, Noragric, Agricultural University of Norway.

Ingold, T. (1992) Culture and the perception of the environment, in E. Croll and D. Parkin (eds) *Bush Base, Forest Farm: Culture, Environment and Development*, London: Routledge.

Leach, E. R. (1976) *Culture and Communication*, Cambridge: Cambridge University Press.

Lévi-Strauss, C. (1966) *The Savage Mind*, Chicago: University of Chicago Press.

Mandler, J. M. (1984) *Stories, Scripts, and Scenes: Aspects of Schema Theory*, Hillsdale, NJ: Erlbaum.

Milton, K. (1993) Introduction: environmentalism and anthropology, in K. Milton (ed.) *Environmentalism: The View From Anthropology*, London: Routledge.

Ortner, S. (1973) On key symbols, *American Anthropologist* 75(5): 1338–1346.

Rappaport, R. (1979) *Ecology, Meaning and Religion*, Berkeley: North Atlantic Books.

Sahlins, M. (1978) *Culture and Practical Reason*, Chicago: University of Chicago Press.

Shore, B. (1996) *Culture in Mind: Cognition, Culture, and the Problem of Meaning*, Oxford: Oxford University Press.

Shweder, R. A. (1991) *Thinking Through Cultures: Expeditions in Cultural Psychology*, Cambridge, MA: Harvard University Press.

Steward, J.H. (1955) *Theory of Culture Change*, Urbana: University of Illinois Press.

Strauss, C. (1992) Models and motives, in R. D'Andrade and C. Strauss (eds) *Human Motives and Cultural Models*, Cambridge: Cambridge University Press.

Chapter 6

Animals behaving badly

Indigenous perceptions of wildlife protection in Nepal

Ben Campbell

> The landscaping of Disneyland is rarely less than brilliant, with each different habitat and playground screened from its neighbours with carefully controlled sight lines, plantings and sound baffles. The animals in these landscapes always perform perfectly on cue as the tourists pass by, because most are machines that reproduce the appearances of nature without its bothersome misbehaviours.
>
> (Cronon 1995: 40)

Introduction

Unlike the conditions pertaining in a theme park, the spectacle of wildlife for tourists in protected areas such as national parks is often only visible on the constrained sufferance of local human communities. For forest-dwelling subsistence producers, the loss of food crops to wildlife can make all the difference between livelihood sufficiency and deficit. This chapter attempts to relate the politics of wildlife within a protected area to local cultural understandings of animals and their 'bothersome misbehaviours'. It raises some tricky questions for those who advocate incorporating indigenous knowledge into conservation projects, both in terms of the local perception of wildlife as pests and in terms of the sorts of indigenous knowledge to which conservation agencies pay attention.

Subsistence production is particularly vulnerable to wildlife in the Langtang National Park of central Nepal. Villagers depend on a highly vertical distribution of ecological niches where terraced fields may be cultivated and livestock pastured. The transhumant agro-pastoral range in the area is generally between 1,000 and 4,500 m in altitude. The extensive dispersal of landholdings presents severe problems for crop protection.

In November 1997 I revisited some of the families who had been the focus of previous research in the Tamang-speaking village of Tengu.[1] This time I was specifically asking about crop damage by wild animals. I traced the movements of families the previous year in the shifting locations of their livestock and field cultivation and asked about the crops in each place. One family had impressed me before in having a relatively low-lying, well-consolidated area of terraced fields, where they spent much of the year and produced a variety and abundance of crops. Speaking about the harvest from this location they said, 'There's been nothing left by the wild animals. Langur monkeys, macaques, bears, pigs, porcupines, they've eaten the lot.' They added that this year the father of the family had been ill and unable to guard against damage. The previous year they had harvested twenty baskets of maize; this year hardly four.

The day before I left Kathmandu one of the English language newspapers even carried a front page article about the misery caused by wild animals in the Langtang National Park. Something is obviously stirring. The current relationship between the park and the people is unsustainable and has been recognized as such in certain quarters. Hence, as with other parks, there is now a policy to introduce 'buffer zones' to recognize that some area of explicit exchange needs to mediate between nature and society. I shall return to this later.

Most of the other families I revisited told of similar stories of damage. One of them has terraces about a hundred metres above those of the first family.

> We stayed in Kolmajet for June–July to protect the maize. Porcupines, langurs, macaques, bears, they ate it till it was finished. We sowed seven tin measures of maize seed [that's a whole *pathi* – approx. 3.5 litres (1 gallon) – and one tin], and got back not one kernel. It's ruined in Kolmajet, we had no other fields of maize.

The animal attacks are not spatially random. Those located at the forest margin are most at risk. This family's other fields at a higher location are situated in the middle of a densely cultivated slope. The previous year's wheat crop there was excellent, amounting to thirteen baskets of unthreshed ears, or enough to grind into flour to feed their small family of three for about six months.

A third family had persisted in the attempt, abandoned by most other villagers, to grow a high-altitude rice variety first introduced in 1990. The woman of the house had spent most of September and October with her ten-year-old daughter guarding the ripening crop on an isolated slope of terraces. She told me she was afraid of the bears who come to eat the rice.

> You have to throw stones and shout. They ate the paddy on three nights. They ate the finger-millet below [the paddy] one night. They ate nine or ten gallon [34–38 litres] measures of paddy. They probably ate one basket of finger-millet, that's four gallons [15 litres] of grain.

The previous year this family hadn't been able to harvest any rice either. Then it had been wild pigs that were responsible.

On another set of terraces at the very edge of the village territory by a stream, the same family lost its maize crop. They had spent most of March manuring, ploughing and sowing maize on the fields that take two whole days for one man to plough.

> The wild pigs ate it. We didn't get one kernel[2] of maize . . . This year we have no maize seed at all. We had sowed one gallon of maize seed. It wasn't porcupines. It wasn't monkeys. The wild pigs ate it.

Because of the present and future uncertainties of agricultural production, this family has tried its best to find employment for the oldest son, who is about twenty, as a jeep or truck driver. They had sold five goats for a total of five thousand rupees (approx. £50) to pay for the costs of procuring a driving licence. Goats and sheep are often sold to meet such cash requirements. They would have had more to sell that year but for the leopards which carried off two goats, one of them pregnant. This does not exhaust the accounting of annual animal damage for this family. Wild pigs and birds ate another gallon of wheat, and wild pigs and porcupines ate 25 gallons [95 litres] of potatoes.[3]

The lists of damages continue, for which there has been no financial compensation from the national parks. The park these days charges 1,000 rupees to each trekker passing through (roughly £10 in 1998). Ten thousand trekkers now come through Langtang National Park annually. The deal under discussion regarding the introduction of buffer zones is that if village committees prepare a management plan agreed with the park for a specified area to be demarcated as under their control, then between 30 and 50 per cent of park income will be made over to the committees as compensation for crop damage, on condition that areas outside buffer zones are left untouched.

From my case study survey, it appears that crop damage is not evenly distributed across socio-economic categories in the same village. Out of the nine households which I most closely looked at, the two which reported least damage were the wealthiest. One of these households happens to be that of the only village man who is employed by the National Park, as a game scout. According to his daughter-in-law, three terraces of potatoes were damaged, but their main fields of wheat were untouched, and their maize had not been damaged at all, despite being located in the same grouping of fields as the earlier man whose crop was completely devastated. The son of the rich, leading village politician also reported to me that, 'this year wild animals did not come in big numbers, neither the potatoes, nor finger millet, maize, nor wheat were eaten'.

The poorest of all the interviewees also has a few terraces in the same area. He said that at this place 'There are so many wild animals. You have to chase them off as much as you can manage. All day, all night you have to be on guard.' His widowed mother added that they had tried to get the title to some land which had belonged to her younger brother, now deceased. She has to pay back a bank loan for the land of 5,000 rupees, and selling the potato crop from that land seemed like the best way of repaying the loan. They had planted 40 gallons [150 litres] of potato seed, but the wild pigs ate the lot. The reason for the contrast in damage with the wealthiest households is that the rich have acquired prime agricultural locations, have the resources to erect walls and fences, and have the person-power to devote to nocturnal guarding of crop-maturing sites situated far from where the herd and living shelter might be.

The administration of nature

In 1974 the ideal conditions for setting up the Langtang National Park were given in the Government's 'LNP Preliminary Development Plan' as to be 'as free as possible of human interference, and [in] particular of agricultural settlement and domestic livestock' (SAGUN 1995: 5). This unfortunately misanthropic initial position, based on the Yellowstone model of nature protection (Stevens 1997), invites conflict over unfeasible and contradictory objectives. The reality is that human 'interference' is encouraged by other state agencies. Apart from the conflict over crop damage, the siting of two cheese factories (set up by Swiss development initiatives) within the area that became the park, has created an inevitable tension between seeing the forest as providing fodder and fuel for small-scale commercial dairying on one hand, and as a wildlife sanctuary on the other.

The *Kathmandu Post*'s front-page article of 20 December 1997 reported that when the King visited the LNP area twenty years ago he was asked by a local man, 'on behalf of his entire tribe, "your majesty which is superior – an animal or a human?"'¹ The article says that at the time the King only smiled, but the question remains unanswered to date. It reports from villages further up the valley tales of nocturnal wild pig damage similar to those recounted above. The journalist interviewed the Park Warden who mentioned, in support of the park's position, that hunters were brought in from the royal palace to kill wild pigs. But it then quotes the dismissive comments of a local politician: 'It's useless bringing hunters from outside . . . they would shoot only if the villagers cornered the wild pigs to a shade. If the villagers were given rifles they wouldn't miss a single pig even at crags and steep slopes.' The piece ends with the demand for action or compensation.

LNP contains about 1,250 households within its boundaries. From the outset it was hardly a policy option to exclude entirely the local population, as was done in only a minority of the national parks in Nepal (for example, Chitwan, see Müller-Böker 1995). Rather, certain human activities such as hunting, swidden agriculture, pasture burning, and trade in forest products were banned, and the military presence of several hundred men enforces the bans. Agriculture on registered fields is permitted, but the usage of forest products for domestic purposes such as timber and bamboo officially requires licences to be purchased from the park authority. Building timber has become especially expensive and new houses are often targeted for checks on proper documentation. Tin roofs have now almost completely replaced the traditional fir-tree shingles.

Villagers do not always observe these official restrictions on park access and exploitation. Bamboo is taken regularly from stands that are reportedly never patrolled, though twice a year villagers march off to pay a nominal fixed sum and carry home their official quota. Hunting within the park also occurs. I have eaten wild pig, barking deer, and porcupine (even though I am usually a vegetarian) from the park. I have also been asked by local people for poison to be used against bears and leopards of the park. The punishment for such activities is quite severe, usually involving a period of incarceration followed by negotiations over the fine.

A report on the relationship between the LNP and the local people written by an NGO, which initiated demonstration plot trials for the introduction of the 'buffer zone' concept, mentions the intention of undertaking a study on Indigenous Knowledge of Biodiversity in the area. This well-intentioned NGO argues against a very reluctant constituency within the park bureaucracy and the military who tend to see the local people as straightforward criminals and the local women as prostitutes. Some members of the NGO are well attuned to critical perspectives on the relationship between development and indigenous knowledge.[4] But what concerns me is that the idea of 'Indigenous Knowledge of Biodiversity' is likely to be handled in a very limited way, focusing on 'ethnobiology' in terms of lists of plants for economic use, and other formulations of local knowledge deemed worthy of codification for the strict purposes of policy argument over conservation.

Pragmatically viewed, such limited steps are necessary to support the view that local knowledge deserves any attention at all. But this argument needs to be made carefully and in measured doses. In the rest of this chapter, I explore what certain forms of local knowledge can tell us about the thieving miscreants of the forest. Moving from the older generations' memory of hunting, and even the domestic rearing of wild pigs, I turn to cultural narratives about animals collected from the Tamang-speaking population of the LNP. How does animal misbehaviour feature in their oral tradition? In pursuing this track I am attempting to counter the arguments put forward by certain cognitivists such as Atran (1990), who claim to be able to isolate 'commonsensical', empirically founded indigenous understandings of the environment from the mythical imagination. At the same time, it has to be recognized that a non-bowdlerized indigenous environmental knowledge presents clear problems for advocacy in the *realpolitik* of nature protection. There are certain kinds of knowledge which are unlikely to promote the indigenous cause in the eyes of conservationists.

Recalling the time before the park

Villagers' memories of how they used to interact with animals and how the state participated in production from the forest and the hunting of animals, can provide an insight into current attitudes and practices regarding wildlife. To show this, I present below an account of how things were before the Park, from a seventy-three-year-old villager with a sharp memory.

> In the old days before this park came into being, it took a whole day to follow the trail of the wild pig and chase it. Then inside the nest the mother would say 'o'o'r', the piglets would say 'che'e'. [They make] their nest dug into the ground with a bedding of leaves. They were bought by people from Timling [outside the present limits of the park]. They gave 3–400 rupees each. They took the

piglets to the west, and made enclosures to put them in. When they grew big they went to sell them in Kathmandu, and were given 10 to 20 thousand rupees. [You had to say] 'Bu'ui na na na' to call them. Some used to bite, and those ones had to have their snouts tied up. To raise the piglets you must feed them buffalo milk, and as much grain as they could eat three or four times a day. You need to put some flour in the milk. When they get big they can eat brewing mash. The wild pigs give birth in April–May. You have to catch them in June. [I] went ten times to catch them. Many people went. If there were not many people, the male pig could kill you. [The wild pig] is not even afraid of leopards. The tusks are long.

After they have been up high, they make a nest down below the field of Kolmajet. A few give birth high up, most give birth lower down, like around the cliff of the cemetery ridge. You need to strike them with a sharpened spear. Now no-one brings out a spear, not openly. There used to be one gun [a musket] in the headman's house. In this village only one [gun]. The year before last the government sent hunters from Kathmandu to kill wild pigs. They killed one pig. In Bharku village [14 km to the north] they killed eight. [The wild pigs] eat finger-millet, wheat, maize, potatoes, barley and paddy . . . Langur monkeys eat finger-millet, soybeans, germinated wheat seedlings. Their meat smells [i.e. the idea of eating it is repugnant].

I asked him about a great fire which burned its way up the valley in 1995.

For five months the forest was on fire. The fir trees died. The people from Brabal [LNP headquarters] couldn't put it out. In the old days there was never such a fire. In those days bush-burning did not set the forest on fire too much.[5] This was Royal forest. The government cattle herds came to pasture in these high meadows. People from Dhunche, Boldung, Grang [and Tengu] had to carry storage baskets, and wooden milk pots. They had to cut up and supply wooden boards. Collect and supply building stones. We the poor had to pay tax [in this way]. In the old days, another government herd stayed in the western side of the valley, up the Mailung side river at Phedor, the place they call 'Alder Bottom'. The government herd kept buffaloes, cattle, goats and sheep. It was looked after by government herders . . .

Before the park, the goral [in Tamang *tangsar*; nemorhaedus goral or Himalayan chamois], barking deer, and porcupine [were often caught]. For trapping the goral you set a rope net, weaving it from ropes, and setting sticks in it. The goral got caught in the rope trap and tumbled over. You needed many people, thirty or so, and about one kilometre of rope . . . Fifteen or so goral were caught at a time. Thighs [of meat] were given to the government. Some were killed in the rope trap. The government wanted three or so live ones, mothers and young ones, to breed down in Kathmandu . . . Barking deer were caught in rope traps. If caught alive, they were taken to Gorkha or Kathmandu . . . For porcupines, where they eat maize, you kill them with a snare of bamboo-strip cord. Some say the people of the west valley eat leopard meat, and that the liver is tasty.

Even in old times the bear's gall bladder, the porcupine's *podet* [an innard of some kind], and the foetus of barking deer, were used to cure respiratory illness. These days we are not allowed to kill them.[6]

This old man is a shaman. He finished the conversation by talking about his specialist knowledge of the sacred landscape, in particular the sites of Shyibda, the territorial guardian deity and Lord of the animals, usually associated with commanding ridge points. He mentioned about eight such places in the entire village territory. At these sites milk should be offered at full moon. He said if you don't offer milk, leopards will come, you'll fall off cliffs, slip over when crossing streams, and Shyibda will generally get angry. On other occasions I have heard of landslides, hailstorms and lightning bolts being attributed to Shyibda. Hunters will not have success without honouring Shyibda.

A conversation with another old man led on to further hunting subjects. Musk deer is one of the endangered species supposed to be protected by the park. He told me it was specialist hunters, Tamangs from the west, outside the park, who came to hunt them, 'it wasn't us'.

Our grandfathers killed leopards, tigers, deer and wild pigs. A man-eating tiger was killed with a gun. A man-eating tiger came along Prayer-wall Ridge and swallowed a man's arm and his knife. It was killed with a gun. I don't remember it [i.e. he was told about it]. A tiger ate a postman. Only one thigh was left, all the rest was eaten by the tiger.

The next village to the north from Tengu is known in Nepali as Bokhajhunda, meaning 'The Hanging Goat'. I was told this is a corruption of the original 'Baghjhunda' ('the Hanging Tiger'), a reference to a tiger that was shot and hung from a tree by the nineteenth-century ruler of Nepal Jang Bahadur Rana on a military expedition to Tibet.

The former plenty of game was frequently suggested to me by people recounting how headmen, who had guns, used to order a pot of water to be put on the fire, and before it had boiled, returned with a pheasant to plunge into the water. Overall, the ban on hunting is seen as unwarranted given the actual numbers of animals. In the past, state officials had participated in both hunting and livestock-dairying in the area, as well as commercial timber-felling. Thus for the state to ban hunting is seen as running counter to its historical relationship to the forest and the people who live there, and as running counter to the known personal proclivities for game meat among state officials.

Tales of animal misbehaviour

Beyond the accounts of crop damage and memories of hunting, is it possible to postulate a more deeply rooted zoophobia in Tamang cultural representations? I was treated to a number of stories which played on narratives of animal mischief. These stories are known typically in Tamang as *arta* or *ugen*. They are clearly meant for amusement, and elicit hilarity, even when I read them from my notebook. The comedy they contain is, I shall argue, a valuable window on to the Tamangs' sense of natural affinity. In the myths animal species are credited with a relational intentionality common to sentient beings. There is a kinship of species, but, as between the species-like clans of humans, cross-species relations are particularly fraught with danger and suspicion.[7] Of all animals it seems to be the jackal who has the worst reputation.

The pheasants and the jackal

There was once a family of eight pheasants inside their house. Then a jackal came and sat up on the handle of the flour-mill. [He asked one of the little ones] 'Little girl,[8] where have your mother and father gone?' 'They have gone to look for food, uncle,'[9] she said. He came again the next day, 'Where have your father and mother gone?' he asked. 'Gone to find food.' The jackal had come to eat the pheasant family. The father and mother said, 'He has come to eat us all, stay quiet!' Saying that the jackal might hear them, they got inside an earthenware pot. 'He'll eat all our family now.' Then the pheasant farted and the pot burst open. The jackal slipped off with surprise, got his bum stuck on the handle of the flour-mill, and then ran off. The pheasants clapped in delight till their eyes were red.

The predator adopting kinship terms with the intended prey repeatedly invades domestic space. Terror is transformed into delight through an involuntary flatulent outburst, booming out of a pot used typically for fermenting grain into alcohol. The jackal had perched menacingly on the symbol of household culinary provision. That he injures himself on this handle of sustenance satisfies a hunger for comic defiance of predatory relations.

As I collected more and more of these stories it became clear that it is the very possibility of a relationship between animals, and the conceptual entertainment of reflection on what we might want to distinguish as the sociality of nature, and the nature of sociality, that makes these stories pertinent. I argue elsewhere (Campbell forthcoming) that, fundamentally, the distinction between nature and culture in terms of sociality is inappropriate for the Tamang framing of relationship because marriage itself is seen as a coming together of species-like difference. Humans, like animals, seek relationships with other kinds that are fraught with tension and the possibility of deceit. In the corpus of narratives it is the jackal who figures as a consummate trickster.

The bear, the leopard and the jackal

Back in the beginning of time, before there was soil, before there was stone, before people had originated from Ganeyül. Then people began to speak. And then it is said a leopard, a bear and a jackal became all three ritual friends.[10] Then one of the friends [was told] 'Go find some sauce for us to eat food.' A sheep was stolen and brought back. 'You two friends eat. As for me [said the leopard], I should not eat cooked [food]. I will eat raw [food].'

Then traders came up walking quickly from downhill carrying loads of rice. The jackal barked on the path, and [the people saying] 'Look, a jackal has come' and began to chase it away. The bear in turn carried off the rice. The leopard then went off, leaving two friends behind. 'How much food will you eat?' asked [the jackal]. 'I will eat five pint measures,' said the bear. Then they cooked five pints of food. When it was cooked the jackal said, 'Let's sew up your anus.' The jackal sewed it up. Then he asked the bear, 'Friend, how much will you eat?' The jackal repeated respectfully 'Friend how much will you eat?' 'I will eat three pints of food,' said the bear, 'I haven't had enough yet.' 'It's going "potok potok",' [said the bear] for he couldn't shit. The jackal said, 'Ok, I'll look for an omen.' He took one pint and looked for an omen. 'Friend, you have to eat one pint of food and you'll get better,' said the jackal. With this [the bear] was close to death. 'Ah friend, we need to go and look for an omen. We need to take a pint of rice and see a priest.' 'Friend after eating two pints more I'm dying.' The jackal was sat below the bear's anus. He touched the thread [he had sewn], and it split apart, covering him with shit. The jackal went off to clean himself in the Tsangku river.

He returned and wandered off. Later the two friends met up again. They went off to buy thread in a shop. They brought back the thread and made a swing to play with. 'I can almost see my mother and father,' [the bear] said. 'Push me in the swing,' said the bear. 'Gosh! Now, friend, can you swing up so you can see your mother and father?' said the jackal. 'Let's see mother and father,' said the bear. Then as the swing dropped low down the cliff, the bear fell off and died.

So one friend went off, one friend was left fallen down the cliff. 'Now I'm going to get inside a chicken hutch,' thought the jackal. He carried off a chicken. [The people] said, 'The chicken's gone, what took it?' In the path where the jackal came they made an image of a person. 'Who is this? Who is this person sitting in the path? Who is it in the path where the king of quarrels walks, I will hit you with a stone.' The image caught the stone. 'Who is the person who caught this stone? I shall kick you with my foot. Who has caught my foot? I'll kick you with my right foot.' His two feet were caught. 'I have my right fist.' As the image saw the fist coming it caught the jackal's hand. It caught the jackal's left hand. Now both feet and hands were caught. 'I will bite you with my mouth.' The mouth was caught. The chicken thief was now caught. The jackal's head shook. 'Don't kill me, let go of my mouth.' The villagers meanwhile were in dispute. 'Hey friends, they say an ox gave birth to a calf' was what they were saying. 'Let me go,' [said the jackal]. 'As you are arguing, I'll go to the river to wash, and coming back will give judgement on this.' 'Will he come now, will he come now?' the villagers watched out. 'Where have you been all this time?' [they asked] the jackal. He said, 'The Tsangku river caught fire, it's easy to catch fish there.' What did the village chiefs say? 'Has the river caught fire?' 'And you say an ox has given birth?!' said the jackal to the chiefs. The jackal was victorious.

Later, the jackal remembered his friend the leopard. He had killed many goats and sheep. Then [people] had made a pound to [trap and] kill the leopard. In half of it they put goats, thinking to trap the leopard. The jackal saw how to get inside as he was small. 'It's easy to get in,' he said to the leopard. He pushed the leopard into the pound. Once inside the villagers killed the leopard. 'Now I am the king of all quarrels,' said the jackal, and left.

In a remote past the three animals were sworn to friendship. They connive to steal a sheep, and then grain, but the narrative then charts the perfidious moral descent of the relationships. The king of quarrels tricks human porters into leaving their loads for his friend the bear to make off with and gorge himself to super-satiation. Eventually disposing of the bear at the downturn of his foolish attempt to catch sight of his parents, the jackal is then trapped by the mysterious human technology which defies every effort of the jackal to gain the upper hand. Once imprisoned by humans, however, he plays on their disputatious wrangling and gullibility to outwit them by logically exposing the natural impossibility of their belief that the river could catch fire or an ox give birth. The jackal completes his treachery by sending his last friend, the leopard, into certain entrapment, lured by a goat-pen.

Several years before recording this account I had heard a conversation which the jackal's story brought back to mind. At a big social gathering, a mourning feast of one man's ritual friend's mother, the visitor had expressed disquiet at the manner in which he had been received as a guest. He said words to the effect of, 'I might as well have been a jackal as a ritual friend'. The jackal embodies distrustful nature. He is the king of misbehaviour, the 'baddest' of them all. He epitomizes suspicion in relations between species.[11]

The message of this tale seems to be that in spite of their similar instincts to avail themselves of human affordances, the three animals cannot cooperate even in common predation directed at human production. We have the leopard as pure hunter, the jackal as deceitful opportunist, and the bear as infantile glutton. The ritual kinship of the three species fails to overcome the mutual incompatibilities of animal desire, and to sustain the social bonds necessary for collective predatory enterprise, in spite of their common intent to conspire in stealing human food.

The toad and the monkey

Here is another comedy of ill-fated animal friendship.

A long time ago, in primordial ages, it is said that a monkey [langur] and a toad became ritual friends. They walked and walked and came across an orange tree. The monkey was able to climb up the tree. The toad stayed below, and said, 'Friend, throw me one down.' The monkey said, 'Just wait.' At last he chucked one orange down. It rolled off downhill, and an old woman who was fetching water gobbled it up. 'My friend threw that down grandma, I'm hungry.'

'If you're hungry let's go to my house,' said the old woman. They went off and the monkey followed later. [The woman] asked about food, 'Will you eat cooked flour or rice, what do you want to eat?' The toad replied, 'I'm just an ugly toad, I'll eat flour.' The old gran then asked the monkey respectfully, 'Would you like to eat rice for your meal or flour?' 'I am a chief. I'll eat rice' (wearing a white turban he made himself out as important). To the toad who said he would eat flour the old woman gave rice, and to the monkey who said he would eat rice she gave flour.

They stayed at the old woman's house. Then she asked the toad, 'Would you like to have a milking cow, or would you like to have a ploughing ox?' The toad replied, 'Give me an ox as I am a toad who sits beneath the ox.' Again the old woman asked the monkey, 'Will you take a milker or a plougher?' 'Gran, I'm a chief, I'll take the milker,' said the monkey. The toad was given the milker, the monkey was given the ox. The monkey led away the ox, the toad took the pregnant cow. The two friends went off together and reached home: the monkey in his house, the toad in his house. Eventually the cow gave birth to a calf. At night the monkey stole the calf.

The toad then searched the whole area. He couldn't find [the calf] anywhere. Thinking maybe it had gone to his friend's, he went to have a look. And indeed it was at his friend's house. Then he said, 'My friend has taken my calf.' 'Gosh!' said the monkey, 'My ox has born a calf. The ox has given birth!' The toad went off downhill to make a report at the law court. 'Look, my calf has been stolen by my friend. He said his ox gave birth, and won't give it back,' he told the judge in his report.

'When will you come?' he asked the judge. 'I won't be coming today, I won't be coming tomorrow.' Eventually he came. 'What took you so long?' asked the toad. The judge arrived with a fish stuck behind his ear, and what did he say? 'I have been going around from place to place, the river caught fire, and I've eaten lots of fish,' he said. The monkey had joined them. 'You have been all around and the river caught fire? Where have you seen this?,' asked the monkey. What did the judge say? 'An ox has given birth indeed, in what place have you seen this?' He gave the calf to the toad and the toad took it away.

Again the theme is that of betrayed ritual friendship between different species. Is there anything here of relevance to actual animal behaviour? Isn't this story simply an allegory about dominance and hierarchy in human society? Ritual friendship makes social bridges across species-like differences of caste among people, but the motives for entering ritual friendship are highly variable and it must be doubted whether ritual friendship can ever transcend basic hierarchical identities. The animal world provides characters for comic play on chiefly delusions of grandeur. The langur has white trimmings linking him to human emblems of chiefly authority. In Tamang society this chiefly position was historically much abused, but the chiefly lineages never managed to elevate themselves completely above their origins in a society which demands that even chiefs should defer on occasion to reversible hierarchies. The state-patronized Tamang elite indeed preferred rice and did accumulate others' milking cattle (and labour) for their personal enrichment, but their authority was seen as deriving from external political realities, and only secondarily through internal processes of legitimation.[12]

With the narrative inversion of nature's shadows of social relations, the lowly humble creature is given the more valuable opposite of his request, while the arrogant one is given less. The opposition of flour and rice meals is one of the clearest indicators of lifestyle status in Nepali rural society: 'you are what you eat' sets apart the rich and poor. The milking cow is valued over the ox, and the toad locates his due position as beneath the ox, suggesting a simple symbolic salience of 'beneath' (*tirang*). Here the notion of just natural hierarchy itself is the butt of the joke – both in terms of the absurdity of the lesser animal owning the greater, and then in terms of the monkey's pretensions in claiming to deserve the more valuable gift options, which are foiled by the humans (the old woman and the judge) who decide on the just deserts. Entering the human domain by first chasing the orange, the toad and monkey fall out over the distinctions of abundance that the human-controlled world affords them. As for the stumbling block of the monkey's trickery, we are treated to a surprising, sudden intervention of rational scepticism in the narrative, as limits of credulity come to apply even in fairy tales when it comes to bovine male pregnancy.

The animal stories I have told are from a numerous oral corpus among the Tamang, and if they cannot be taken and simply transformed into ethno-ethological understandings for biodiversity programmes, it is because they speak rather to a different level of generality.[13] They too readily invite commentaries of an interpretative and politically symbolic nature.

Animal kingdoms

To discuss the politics of wildlife, a deeper stratum of the archaeology of the nature/society dichotomy needs to be revealed than the standard underpinnings of Cartesian dualism, the Enlightenment's discovery of universal humanity, and the separation of human populations from natural environments produced by urban industrialism. The dichotomy certainly receives a particular, sacralized cultural formulation with North American notions of de-humanized Wilderness, and the creation of national parks (Olwig 1993), but there are significant medieval roots to these notions that current biodiversity programmes might do well to remember. It might be recalled that the New Forest in England was created by the forced evacuation of Saxon farmers by William the Conquerer. He was written about as loving his stags as a father and by implication not loving his human subjects. The medieval definition of forest is governed by the idea of royal privilege, granted by the King to his wildlife (Harrison 1992: 72). The royal hunt is at the core of European, and probably Asian, notions of wildlife sanctuary (Gold and Gujar 1997). The category of forest is at base a political one.

Robert Harrison's (1992) work on a cultural history of forests quotes some discussion of *The Treatise of the Laws of the Forest* written by John Manwood, a gamekeeper of Waltham forest in the time of Elizabeth the First.

> In the Middle Ages the struggle of the barons against the king had as its goal to restrain royal privileges, deemed exorbitant. One had to protect men against the royal forest . . . [In Manwood] the proposition is the opposite: one must protect the forest against men, so that it might endure and continue to serve as a refuge for animals.
>
> (ibid.: 256)

There is also, in Harrison's book, a discussion of historical shifts between comedy and tragedy in narrative genres set in forests. I find his association of tragic forests with polytheistic antiquity, and comic forests with monotheistic Christianity somewhat inappropriate to the discussion here, but his remarks on forests as themselves sites of comedy are of interest. The logic of comedy is of the absurd. Absurdity becomes comedy 'when there is an unmasking of deceptive appearance' (ibid.: 79). The medieval forest outlaws, in particular, unmask 'the institutions that conceal behind the cloak of legitimacy their perversion of the law' (ibid.: 79).

> [F]orests also provide the scene for disguise, tricks, gender reversals, confusion of identity, and so forth, becoming the site where conventional reality loses its persuasion and gets masked or unmasked in a drama of errors and confusion. If one of the main functions of comedy is to dramatise the instability or absurdity of the world as human beings define it, forests represent a natural scene for the enactment of its ironic logic, thanks to their shadows of exteriority with regard to society.
>
> (Harrison 1992: 80)

Do the tales recounted above further our understanding of Indigenous Knowledge of Biodiversity? Hard-nosed environmental agenda-setters would presumably be dismissive, and say that what is needed is forms of knowledge that can advance the comparison of quantitative scientific indicators of changing biodiversity. But that would be to relinquish the setting of the agenda to 'eco-crats' (Sachs 1993). Jane Guyer and Paul Richards in 'The invention of biodiversity' (1996) have written about this problem in Africa, and asked how the concept of biodiversity can be domesticated to African needs and perspectives. They mention that it is rural communities who are often the direct custodians of biodiversity, despite what states and international agencies may think.

I would see a genuine Indigenous Knowledge of Biodiversity as one that understands the range of ways in which natural species figure as both useful and meaningful to people in this position of de facto custodianship. That knowledge should include the possibilities natural species afford for ridiculing human pretension and the absurdities of human attempts to control nature. Tamang representations of animal misdemeanours invoke a common field of struggle between wilful agents that spills over into human relations. There is a 'phenomenological unity' (Viveiros de Castro 1998) across the animal–human divide, and the stories of animal exploits play with interpretative reversals between animal and human worlds. The intervention of legalistic judgements into the narratives has salience with regard to the Tamangs' tradition of occasional brigandage: the animals' thieving of grain and livestock is not unlike the Tamangs' historical predation on passing traders.

This chapter is entitled 'Animals behaving badly' in order to highlight the harm that protected wildlife cause to village agriculture, but also because in Tamang cultural representations such harm appears to be all they can do. I do have one story in which a son-in-law is set a number of Herculean tasks by his royal father-in-law, and it is with the assistance of animals that he accomplishes these, but it is through normally unwelcome animal activities (for example, wild pigs ploughing up a huge area of soil with their snouts, and pigeons devouring enormous quantities of grain) that the tasks are achieved. Animals lack the distinctly human property of *sem* or moral conscience, which, interestingly, is deemed to take effect in humans at twelve years old, after completing the first cycle of the twelve animal years. There are indeed stories in the Buddhist canon about the compassionate turtle and so on, but I think they are unknown to the Tamang who are conversant with a more oral, shamanic tradition.

In 1997 I recorded a chanting of the origin of society in nature, in which warm-blooded animals are noticeable by only the briefest of appearances in participating in the foundation of domestic ecology. From mineral origins and life forms in watery domains, original trees eventually emerge occupying the distinctive altitudinal points of Himalayan ecology. From the buds on their branches flowers blossom and are inhabited by gods and spirits. Humans are born from divine parents, and with the arrival of blacksmiths construct the original house of wood. In this divine evolutionary ecology of domestic life, the first four of the twelve animal years are sited in the corners of the house: rat, bull, tiger and cat.[14] Unfortunately, the pig and the monkey are not featured, being numbers eleven and twelve of the cycle of years. This chant (The Song of Primordial Eternity) clearly gives priority to factors of geological verticality and vegetation in setting the eco-cosmological foundations for humans' social reproduction, to the virtual exclusion of zootic referents. It does, however, finish with a blessing for long life and prosperity, bountiful crops and productive herds of livestock.

Conclusion

I began this chapter with the details of one man's crop damage by a host of wild animals. That was hard fact. During the interview some indigenous knowledge of biodiversity was being put to use to try to rescue the calamitous situation of their newly bought and very pregnant buffalo having fallen and broken a leg. The man's initial idea was to kill it, but he was told it is illegal to kill a pregnant buffalo in Nepal. I described the scene in my diary that day.

> I went down to Buduru's just below the old path in Godam. He had a big saucepan on the fire and I asked him what the leaves and bits of wood in it were for. It was medicine for the sick buffalo. [Asked about the contents of the saucepan] he mentioned a story that once a man and his *mha* [sister's husband] went hunting but quarrelled after they had got their prey and forgot about the meat which had been all cut up. The next day they found the meat had joined up together again and realized the plants they had wrapped it up in must be medicine [the plants boiling away in the pot]. [Another friend] commented on this when I mentioned it last night 'Is it nonsense or true?'

Is it as fanciful as the river catching fire, or should these stories be listened to? Whether such stories or even the knowers of them are listened to depends on the politics of environmental knowledge. The storyline of nature as threatened by local people has powerful listening constituencies, especially in the alliance between international environmentalists and national park authorities in Third World states, not generally noted for their indulgence of fanciful ideas or for their sense of humour. William Cronon writes in 'The trouble with wilderness' that:

> The dream of an unworked natural landscape is very much the fantasy of people who have never themselves had to work the land to make a living . . . The romantic ideology of wilderness leaves precisely nowhere for human beings actually to make their living from the land.
> (Cronon 1995: 80)

Indigenous Knowledge of Biodiversity is claimed to be an avenue for hearing the voice of local people who have interests in protected areas. If IKB is to reflect a genuinely holistic cultural perception, then unfortunately for the Tamang their apparent quasi-zoophobia is unlikely to meet sympathetic ears. Of course 'zoophobia' is suggested here with playful intent. It is not a general antipathy to wildlife. Porcupine quills and Tibetan antelope horn are essential items of shamanic technology, for example. The point of all this is rather that relations between species (as between clans, and castes) are characterized by dispute and difficulty over their difference. The Tamang make this explicit, in contrast to the disengaged, de-socialized vision of nature held by conservationists.

In recent ecological anthropology we have been offered ideas of the forest as metaphorical parent-like unconditional giver (Bird-David 1993), and, against this view, of nature offering unmetaphorized affordances to humans (Ingold 1996). I am suggesting the material discussed in this chapter requires both these ideas to be inverted. Society affords directly perceivable plenty to nature, and misbehaving nature takes it without asking. Animals have little time for the false dichotomy of nature and society and the villagers speak sardonically of their crops as 'food for the wild pigs'.

Will the animals' predation on human production be addressed in the creation of buffer zones? For the villagers a buffer zone would mean an acceptance that they should have the right to protect their crops from damage by controlled culling of the animals, or at least some meaningful compensation from the coffers of the Department of National Parks. My impression is that, for the park authorities, the buffer zone will only be acceded to if villagers' activities are then limited exclusively to the buffer zones, leaving the parks with people-free zones for which tourists would pay special rates for access: in other words, the zones would enable the re-assertion of a nature off-limits to society, except for paying visitors. I have no doubt that villagers would never agree to these restrictions, but then their agreement was not part of the original imposition of a state of bewilderment. They will more than likely continue their own bothersome misbehaviours in the face of attempts to regulate the social–natural interface, so long as these attempts do not address the problematic mutuality of humans' and animals' engagement with each other.

Notes

1 The research for this chapter was funded by the Economic and Social Research Council (award R000237061, *Himalayan Biodiversity and Human Interests*).
2 The Tamang word used is *phum*, meaning a generic round-shaped grain-fruit-produce.
3 In all these estimations of quantities, I hold a high level of confidence as to their broad accuracy.
4 Mukta Singh Tamang in his MA dissertation states that 'Although the present perspective has acknowledged the importance of the knowledge held by indigenous communities in sustainable resource management, modernist

assumptions have continued to dominate the development discourses. Indigenous knowledge is viewed as a "body" or "stock" which can be extracted for incorporation in the development process.' (1996: 86).
5 Talking with other environmental researchers I seem to have frequently heard of damaging fires increasing in occurrence when human activity is strictly controlled or prohibited.
6 One of the threats to wildlife is said to be the trade in animal parts for Chinese medicine. Indeed, I have seen dried, shrivelled up gall-bladders produced from secreted hiding places. Leopard bones are also supposed to command a price.
7 For more on the species nature of human clans, see Campbell (1998).
8 *konme* – Sister's daughter, or wife's brother's daughter (man speaking).
9 *ashyang* – MB or FZH.
10 *leng* – 'male ritual friend'. Ritual kinship in human society establishes a special morality across the relational gulfs of species-like castes.
11 It could be possible to read some allegorical political commentary into narratives of treacherous ritual friends. It is a widely held belief that the small Tamang kingdoms which encircled Kathmandu till the eighteenth century were betrayed by the encroaching Gorkha powers. The Tamang kings were reportedly invited to meet with Prithvi Narayan Shah beside rivers for ritual friendship ceremonies. As the Tamang parties arrived, the Gorkha soldiers produced swords hidden in the sand and killed them (personal communication Mukta Singh Tamang).
12 See my 'Dismembering the body politic . . .' Campbell (1995).
13 Current research in animal behaviour would, however, suggest that the Tamangs' attribution of intentionality to animals is far from fanciful. Manning's review of Whiten and Byrne's *Machiavellian Intelligence* states the following: 'If true deception occurs, it must imply some knowledge of the result of one's actions. A deceiving false alarm call cannot as ethologists originally conceived, be simply driven out of an animal by the perception of danger. This capacity must surely be an important step towards the recognition of self and of consciousness. Must it also imply a recognition of others, distinct from oneself, to whom one attributes a nature and thus a responsiveness the same as one's own? It certainly does in ourselves, and there is plenty of evidence for apes as well. It is particularly important that some observations in monkeys suggest stage one but not stage two.' *TLS* 28 August 1998 p.5.
14 I understand these associations are significant astrological co-ordinates in Tibetan architecture (Personal communication Maria Phylactou).

References

Atran, S. (1990) *Cognitive Foundations of Natural History: Towards an Anthropology of Science*, Cambridge: Cambridge University Press.
Bird-David, N. (1993) Tribal metaphorisation of human-nature relatedness: a comparative analysis, in K. Milton (ed.) *Environmentalism*, London: Routledge.
Campbell, B. (1995) Dismembering the body politic: contestations of legitimacy in Tamang celebrations of dasai, *Kailash* 17 (3–4): 133–146.

—— (1998) Conversing with nature: ecological symbolism in central Nepal, *Worldviews: Environment, Culture, Religion* 2: 123–137.

—— (forthcoming) Identity and power in a conflictual environment, in *Proceedings of the First Conference of the European Bulletin of Himalayan Research, September 1998*, Paris.

Cronon, W. (ed.) (1995) *Uncommon Ground: Rethinking the Human Place in Nature*, New York: Norton.

Gold, A. G. and Gujar, B. R. (1997) Wild pigs and kings: remembered landscapes in Rajasthan, *American Anthropologist* 99(1): 70–84.

Guyer, J. and Richards, P. (1996) The invention of biodiversity, *Africa* 66(1): 1–13.

Harrison, R. P. (1992) *Forests: The Shadow of Civilization*, Chicago: University of Chicago Press.

Ingold, T. (1996) Hunting and gathering as ways of perceiving the environment, in R. Ellen and K. Fukui (eds) *Redefining Nature*, Oxford: Berg.

Manning, A. (1998) The potential of parrots: do animals try to deceive each other? *Times Literary Supplement* 28 August, 4–5.

Müller-Böker, U. (1995) *Die Tharu in Chitawan: Kenntnis, Bewertung und Nutzung der natürlichen Umwelt im südlichen Nepal*, Stuttgart: Franz Steiner Verlag.

Olwig, K. (1993) Sexual cosmology: nation and landscape at the conceptual interstices of nature and culture; or, what does landscape really mean?, in B. Bender (ed.) *Landscape Politics and Perspectives*, Oxford: Berg.

Sachs, W. (ed.) (1993) *Global Ecology: A New Arena of Political Conflict*, London: Zed Books.

SAGUN (1995) *Participatory Biodiversity Management: Langtang National Park*, report submitted to Department of National Parks and Wildlife Conservation, Kathmandu.

Stevens, S. (ed.) (1997) *Conservation through Cultural Survival*, Washington: Island Press.

Tamang, M. S. (1996) *Indigenous Knowledge Systems and Development: An Ethnoecological Case Study of Mewahang Rai from Arun Valley in Eastern Nepal*, MA dissertation, Tribhuvan University, Kathmandu.

Viveiros de Castro, E. (1998) Cosmological deixis and Amerindian perspectivism, *JRAI* 4: 469–488.

Chapter 7
Culling demons
The problem of bears in Japan
John Knight

Introduction

One of the major problems faced in the field of wildlife management is divided public opinion. Certain wild animals are pests which arouse antagonism among rural publics and generate demands for pest control. But these same animals may also be culturally valued or the object of conservationist concern. This problem is especially serious in the case of large wild predators such as bears, wolves or tigers that inspire both fear and reverence, hatred and respect, and antipathy and sympathy. The issue of wild predators can pit the city against the country, the conservationist against the livestock farmer or the rural dweller more generally. In North America, grizzly bear conservation has been criticized as 'a burden placed on the rural minority . . . by the government to satisfy the aesthetic preferences of the urban majority' (in Primm 1996: 1032), and grizzly bear re-introduction programmes have encountered local opposition (Merrill *et al.* 1999).

Yet, on closer inspection, attitudes towards wild predators may prove more complicated than the depiction of a simple urban–rural divide suggests. Within rural areas wild predators may be appreciated as pest-killers (i.e. of crop-raiders) and not just feared as pests; they may inspire reverence as well as excite fear; and they may even become the object of human identifications. Despite the anxiety they can undoubtedly arouse, wild predators are often multi-faceted in the significations attached to them by local human populations.

Bears in Japan trigger contrasting emotions. The bear is an object of fear and hatred. Notorious bear attacks in the past have fixed a popular image of the bear as an aggressor, a mankiller, and even a maneater. The bear has been characterized as a 'fearful demon' (*kyôfu no oni*) (Azumane 1997: 33), a 'black devil' (*kuroi mashin*) (Maita 1998: 60), and a synonym for fear itself (Katô *et al.* 1986: 2). An illustration of the bear's power to frighten was when the image of a bear on a roadside billboard (warning of wild animals crossing the road) had to be replaced (by the image of a raccoon-dog) because it was too shocking to passing drivers and a cause of road accidents (Azumane 1997: 32). Real bears encountered on roads are even more shocking, and can elicit extreme human reactions. When (in Hokkaido) a bear appeared before a bus, the driver – encouraged by passengers who demanded that he 'hit it!' – put his foot on the accelerator and drove the bus flat out into the bear, knocking the animal off the mountain cliff to its death (Honda 1998: 20–21).

But bears also elicit affection, sympathy, admiration, and reverence. As an animal which 'stands up' on two feet, has tracks that resemble human tracks, has an omnivorous diet, and carries out prolonged nurturance of its young, bears readily invite anthropomorphic representations. In Japan the bear is characterized variously as a 'mountain man' (*yamaotoko*), a 'mountain uncle' (*yama no ossan*), a 'mountain father' (*yama no oyaji*), a loving mother, and a child.[1] As a solitary animal in the forest (in contrast to gregarious monkeys and deer), the bear is represented as a sad, lonesome figure and referred to as a 'lonely person' (*sabishigariya*). For some observers, the bear is the very embodiment of virtue.

> Have you ever seen the eyes of a bear that lives in the mountains? They are soft, gentle eyes, eyes that are innocent and without malice. Sometimes they have a golden shine. Those are, of course, the eyes of a bodhisattva.
>
> (in Yamazaki 1996: 15)

The bear's link with religion extends to an association with the mountain spirit (*yama no kami*) (Ogura 1993: 99–100).

Both negative and positive evaluations of the bear are evident among the mountain villagers of the Kii Peninsula (in western Japan), where I have carried out fieldwork, in a number of different spells, in the late 1980s and in the 1990s. The old name for this region, Kumano, literally means 'Bear Plain' (despite its mountainous character), and first appears in the eighth-century *Kojiki* in a passage which describes the founding ancestor of the Japanese imperial line slaying a bear.[2] In the years I have spent in the Kumano area, much of it in and around the forest, I have never seen a bear, nor have most local people. Yet bears are much talked about. Everyone knows that there are bears in the mountains and there is considerable fear of encountering them. Posted signs along forest roads warn about the presence of bears. When people talk about the dangers of the night-time mountains – for example, when a herb-picker fails to return to the village by sunset – bears immediately come to mind. When in 1988 the partially eaten corpse of an old man was found in the mountains near Hongû, there was instant speculation that a bear had attacked him (the attack was eventually attributed to feral dogs). Tales also circulate about the terrible injuries and mutilations that bears can cause.

However, the bears of the peninsula also elicit concern of another kind. In the Kumano regionalist movement, calls are sometimes made for the region to make a special effort to conserve the eponymous bear at a time when bear numbers are dwindling. Among young people, the perception of the bear is infused by the cuddly, cute bear imagery that nationally circulates in the media and the world of commerce. Peninsular children (following national trends) have T-shirts, bags and stationery imprinted with images of childlike bears, play with soft, furry teddybears and other bear toys, and watch television cartoons featuring rotund, friendly bear figures. Among the local souvenirs that tourists in the peninsular spa resorts can buy is an assortment of items carrying bear logos (the latest of which, in January 1999, was the teddy bear of Mr Bean).

In this chapter these two sets of representations of bears in Japan are examined. The first part of the chapter describes upland Japan's 'bear problem' (*kuma no mondai*), both the damage done by bears and the human culling of bears in response. The second part focuses on the criticism that has been levelled at bear-culling. To a large extent, this criticism emanates from outside conservationists, but concern over the plight of bears also exists within mountain villages themselves. In Japan, the bear is not just a nationally divisive animal, but – in upland areas – a locally divisive one as well.

Japanese bears

There are two species of bear on the Japanese archipelago: the black bear (*Selenarctos thibetanus japonicus*), known in Japanese as *tsukinowaguma*, found in Kyushu, Shikoku and Honshu; and the larger brown bear (*Ursus arctos yezoensis*), known in Japanese as *higuma*, found in Hokkaido. The Japanese black bear, a subspecies of the Asiatic black bear, has a distinctive (V-shaped) white crescent on its upper chest, and its Japanese name *tsukinowaguma* literally means 'crescent bear'. The adult black bear averages 1.4 m in body length and 80 kg in weight, the brown bear 1.8 m in body length and 200 kg in weight (Maita 1996a: 2–3). The population of wild bears in Japan is estimated to be around 16,000 animals – 13,000 black bears and 3,000 brown bears (Maita 1998: 29).

The original habitat of the Japanese black bear spanned high sub-alpine conifer forests (1,500–2,300 m), cool-temperate forests (500–1,500 m), and low warm temperate forests (below 500 m), but this range has narrowed and bears are now restricted to elevated forests of 500 m and above (Azuma and Torii 1980: 71). The modern Japanese forestry industry has transformed Japan's forests, and in the process displaced bears from much of their former territory. In the postwar period a large area of the primary and secondary forest has been replaced with monocultural timber plantations which, along with the extensive network of forest roads built to service them, have destroyed bear habitat and isolated bear sub-populations.

This large-scale habitat loss is the background to conservationist fears of bear extinction.[3] The situation is particularly serious in the western half of the Japanese archipelago, where the bear has disappeared from the islands of Kyushu and Shikoku. One of the few remaining regions of bear habitat in western Japan is the Kii Peninsula, but even here there are estimated to be only around 150 bears left. The 1991 *Red Data Book*, published by the Environment Agency, warned that there was 'a high danger of extinction' on the part of the peninsula's bear population (in Hazumi 1992: 297–298), while other scholars predict that 'the disappearance of bear groups [on the peninsula] is just a question of time' (Hazumi and Kitahara 1994: 15).

In upland Japan bears have long been hunted for their hides, meat, organs (especially the gall bladder) and other body parts and substances. These bear products were both put to local use and traded for money. This tradition of bear-hunting is largely associated with the east (especially northeast) of the main island of Honshu, but is also found in the west. On the Kii Peninsula bear parts were valuable commodities traded by local hunters, and bear gall is still used for its medicinal value (it is viewed as a general panacea and as a tonic for the weak and the elderly). But, in general, the bear has become an animal which threatens rather than supports upland livelihoods.

People–bear conflict

Bear predations on livestock are reported in the French Pyrenees (Camarra 1987), the Cantabrian Mountains in Spain (Clevenger and Campos 1994), and central Italy (Cozza *et al.* 1996). In the Andes spectacled bears are a threat to cattle (as well as to corn and squash) (Urton

1985: 271; Goldstein 1991). Bear attacks on people are reported in western Canada where grizzly bears are responsible for 'mugging hikers' (Marty 1997: 30) and where black bears attack foresters, hunters and hikers (Shelton 1998). In northern Canada polar bears drawn to populated areas by the prospect of food have mauled and killed people (Comeau 1997: 58). Bear attacks on people have also been reported in Asia, for example, attacks by sloth bears in Nepal (see Nepal and Weber 1995). When bear attacks occur they tend to attract considerable media attention, but it should be emphasized that, in fact, human injury or death due to bears is rare (see Floyd 1999).

People–bear conflict has long existed in Japan. In remoter areas of Japan the bear is a farm pest which damages fruit, vegetables and honey. Bears feed on cultivated bamboo shoots in the spring, on plums, watermelons and corn in the summer, and on persimmons, sweet potatoes and rice in the autumn (Maita 1998: 167). Throughout the summer, bears feed on cultivated honey; every year in Japan around 3,000 bee-hives are damaged by black bears (Maita 1998: 21). Bear damage to farms often seems wasteful and wanton to the farmer. When a bear feeds on a water melon or pumpkin crop, it goes only for the seeds in the middle, and ignores the fleshy part of the fruit (Watanabe 1984: 185). Bears do not just feed on the crop but seem to vandalize the plant as such. They snap orchard tree branches in the process of feeding, disfigure the tree and adversely affect future harvests. Villagers complain that their chestnut and persimmon trees are eventually turned into 'bonsai trees' by the attentions of bears. Livestock (fish [on fish farms], chickens and even cows) is another (albeit less frequent) target of bears (Watanabe 1984: 186).

Second, the bear, along with the deer and the serow, is a major forestry pest in Japan. Bear bark-stripping greatly damages timber plantations, leading to defoliation and even the death of the tree. In the late 1970s the annual area of bear damage to conifers in Japan ranged between 400 and 1,200 ha, affecting trees aged between 15 and 30 years (Watanabe 1980: 67–68). A majority of the trees in a plantation may be affected, leading to great economic loss on the part of the forest landowner. Moreover, there are signs that bear bark-stripping may be becoming more serious still; according to a recent report, fully mature plantation conifers of up to 70 years old (commanding the highest of market values) have been bark-stripped by bears (*Nihon Keizai Shinbun* 19/1/1997). The bear seems to feed on the trees, gnawing and eating the exposed sapwood; as one observer put it, 'when the bear has its afternoon snack, it costs money' (Hida 1967: 61–62).

Bear damage to farms and plantations has to do not just with economic loss, but also with the symbolism of these crops. Bear damage to farms affects produce earmarked for other family members as much as market crops. The exchange of cultivated food between elderly villagers and their migrant relatives in the cities has an important role in maintaining family ties that have become stretched in the course of outmigration to the city, and it is in this connection that bear damage has its full impact. The following plea for help from one rural grandmother makes the point. 'Please help me, the bear has ruined the peaches, and I don't know what to do. The peaches I was going to send to my grandchildren in Hiroshima [City] have now all been eaten up!' (in Maita 1998: 9). Timber trees, grown over decades by two or more family generations, are an even stronger symbol of family unity in upland Japan; the maintenance of trees planted by a grandfather or a father is an important family duty. The damage done to such trees by bears threatens to negate the ancestral labours of the past.

Outbreaks of bear crop damage lead to a general sense of vulnerability among mountain villagers, and heighten local fears of bear attacks. In addition to encounters between farmers and crop-raiding bears, every year there are bear incidents involving foresters, hunters, herb-gatherers, mushroom-pickers, nut-collectors, hikers, anglers and other forest recreationists. Forest workers can inadvertently disturb denning bears – for example, by stepping on or falling into a den at the base of a plantation tree (an increasingly common site for denning), or by waking them up with the loud noise of their chainsaws (Ōta 1997: 126). Forest workers are also vulnerable to encounters with roaming bears at other times of the year. Many attacks occur through sudden encounters on the bends of winding mountain paths when neither bear nor human can take evasive action. Bears seize the rucksacks of hikers, knowing that they are likely to contain riceballs or other foodstuffs. Attacks also occur when bears forage for human foods in and around forestry stations, tourist camping sites or garbage dumps.

Although most bear attacks are not fatal, there are occasional deaths. In the period 1979–1989, nine people were killed by black bears and 182 people were injured in Japan (Yoneda 1991: 149). In Akita Prefecture ninety-six people suffered bear attacks in a nineteen-year period from the mid-1970s to the mid-1990s; these figures include fifty-nine serious injuries and six deaths (Torii 1996: 4). In Hokkaido, '[d]uring the first 57 years of this century, when accurate records began to be kept, 141 people died in bear attacks and another 300 were injured' (Fujiwara 1988: 28).

Even where no attacks take place, bear encounters (or just sightings) generate considerable disquiet among local people. One bear conservationist who has visited villages affected by roaming bears characterizes this phenomenon as 'spiritual damage' (*seishinteki higai*) to the villagers (Maita 1998: 27). Bear-sightings render familiar spaces dangerous and frightening. A bear-sighting in a field or a timber plantation can deter villagers from working in those areas (in some cases ruining a crop – for example, melons – by the delay in harvesting). Bears also visit village graveyards, where they feed on the edible offerings made to the dead, and again can make these places off-limits. Bear incursions are even more threatening still where they involve the domestic spaces of the village. Bears climb on to roofs, break windows, invade houses and enter kitchens; there are even reports of startled housewives finding bears sitting in front of the television (Maita 1998: 27)! Bears can induce a general air of anxiety and insecurity in remote areas, to the point where villagers observe a de facto night-time curfew.[4]

Culling

Upland areas respond to the bear threat in a variety of ways, including fencing, olfactory repellents (such as bear fat), scarecrows (mannequin dolls) and guard-dogs. Bear sightings occasion a state of emergency during which access to the forest is restricted, billboard warning notices put up, small bells distributed to the local population, schoolchildren escorted to and from school, armed patrols mounted around the village and police reinforcements called in.[5] Large-scale military-style operations, involving Japanese troops, have even been mounted against bears. In Hokkaido in 1966, in response to a bear alert, 'a literal army of 148 hunters with the support of 260 self-defence force members, 50 regular vehicles, 5 snow vehicles and 4 helicopters, killed 39 bears' (Moll 1994: 34).[6]

The main response to problem bears is culling. According to official figures, 77,564 black bears were killed in Japan between 1946 and 1994 (Maita 1998: 49). In this post-war period, bears have been increasingly killed as pests rather than as game animals. Of the 1,695 bears (black and brown) killed in 1994, over half were killed as pests, but in some prefectures the figure for pest-kills reaches 80 per cent (Maita 1998: 50). Bounties are offered for bears by local municipalities, and bear culling squads (known as 'bear extermination groups' or *kuma bokumetsukai*) have been established in many regions (Torii 1989: 196–197). Bear-culling generally takes place outside the winter hunting season (during which bears are in their dens), usually in the autumn before denning and in the spring after denning. Summer and autumn culling takes the form of a pursuit of particular 'problem bears' (*mondaikuma*) by a party of armed hunters with dogs (while springtime culling represents the precautionary elimination of bears). Bears are also caught using honey-baited cage-traps (and sometimes wire traps).

Bear-culling has become the target for criticism in recent times. Conservationists condemn the high level of bear-culling as a threat to the integrity of regional bear populations. It is claimed that much bear-culling is unjustified and that the danger posed by bears is greatly exaggerated. For example, it has been pointed out (for Hokkaido) that for every bear attack that takes place, there are one thousand bear encounters or sightings which pass off peacefully, and that the number of bear-caused human deaths pales into insignificance when compared with the number of deaths caused by road accidents (Abe *et al.* 1986: 106–108). Some critics charge that the scale of bear-culling in Japan is due to the commercial value of bear body parts (especially the gall bladder) as much as to the economic loss due to bear damage (Mizoguchi 1992: 33; Hazumi 1994: 147).

Despite these outside criticisms of bear-culling, bear-cullers or bearhunters (generally, the same people) locally appear as the protectors of upland society from a serious threat to it. A common idiom applied to problem bears is that of crime. Farmers denounce the bear as a 'criminal' (*hanzaisha*) and a 'thief' (*dorobô*) (Wada 1995: 35). The bear's farm raiding often resembles human theft: bears are said to break off the branches of fruit trees and take them back to their forest hideaway to eat the fruit, or to lift up bee-hives with their arms and walk away with them (Ue 1983: 324–325; Matsuyama 1994: 75, 86–87). Bear incidents provoke newspaper headlines featuring references to 'Violent Bears' (*bôryoku kuma*), 'Heinous Crimes' (*kyôakuhan*), 'Death Penalty for Mr Bear' (*kumakô shikei*), 'Habitual Offender' (*jôshûhan*), and 'Shooting the Criminal' (*hannin o itomeru*), along with photographs of hunters in shooting poses next to bear carcasses (Maita 1996a: 152–153). While such media accounts do sensationalize the conflict, they also strike a chord among local people. As the people responsible for apprehending these ursine 'criminals', hunters become, in effect, the village's policemen in the mountains.

However, because of its power and ferocity, the bear is no simple criminal. In this connection, one particularly notorious bear attack should be mentioned. In Hokkaido in 1915 there took place what has come to be known as the Tomamae Incident (*Tomamae jiken*), a bear attack in which seven people died and three people were seriously injured. Accounts of the attack portray scenes of horrific carnage in which women and children are devoured by a frenzied giant beast (the bear was weighed at 340 kg) which directs its murderous impulses against a whole village (see Maita 1996b: 16–17; Honda 1998: 11–16). The Tomamae bear attacked this village not once but twice – returning the following night, during the pre-funeral vigil for the earlier victims, to resume its killing.

The village responded by mobilizing large numbers of armed men to go after the killer bear. When the animal was itself finally killed, the avengers reacted with spontaneous shouts of 'banzai' ('Long Live the Emperor', literally 'ten thousand years'), as though celebrating a great military victory. Afterwards, a monument and a museum were established in Tomamae to commemorate the terrible attack. But arguably the true legacy left by the Tomamae bear lies less in these material forms than in the popular consciousness of the bear it has helped to generate. The Tomamae bear attack is often explicitly referred to in present-day media reports of bear incidents (for example, *Asahi Shinbun* [hereafter AS] 2/6/1990) and is believed to be largely responsible for the widespread Japanese perception of bears as bloodthirsty maneaters (Maita 1996b: 15–17).

It is this elemental fear aroused by the bear that makes bear-culling a special kind of village protection. One phrase that regularly appears in newspaper headlines and other publications in connection with bear-culling is 'Bear Conquest' or *kuma taiji*.[7] The term *taiji* occurs widely in Japanese folklore in connection with an assortment of malevolent monsters and other creatures and spirits (witches, ghosts, serpents etc.) which must be vanquished. One of the classic objects of *taiji* is the demon (as in *oni taiji* or 'demon conquest') (Maruyama 1994), and it is perhaps on account of its image as a 'demon' (*oni*) that the bear readily attracts the term *taiji*. But it is not only the bear that resonates with mythological imagery in media accounts of the bear problem. In his analysis of mass media coverage of bear damage, Maita Kazuhiko identifies the recurrence of a particular kind of narrative, the *buyûden* or 'martial tale', in which the bear appears as an evil figure vanquished by the hunter/culler who is cast as the brave 'hero' (*eiyû*) of the tale (Maita 1998: 45). The demonic status of the bear establishes the heroic status of the bear-culler.

This public image of bear-culling as selfless heroism is supported by the self-image held (and projected) by bearhunters. Bearhunters maintain that the ability to confront a bear face-to-face without losing one's nerve is the test of whether or not a man is truly 'a man of courage' (*dokyô no ii hito*) (Taguchi 1994: 93) and whether he possesses the bearhunter's 'spirit' (*konjô* or *matagidamashii*) (Hida 1972: 71–79). 'The encounter with the bear is always a matter of life and death', where the bearhunter says to himself, 'if I don't kill this rascal, I'll be killed myself' (Fujiwara 1979: 36). This extraordinary spirit is sometimes expressed in the nicknames given to successful bearhunters – for example, 'Kiyoshi the Lion' (Taguchi 1994: 294–295), as though it takes a lion to catch a bear.

Bearhunters tend to admire the qualities of strength and power associated with the bear. In Japanese, the term *yuhi no shi* or 'bear man' is applied to 'men who are intrepid like the black bear or the brown bear' (Takahashi 1997: 104), and the term *tetsuguma* or 'iron bear' is applied to hardy men able to withstand the cold (Ōnishi 1998: 122). Male children are named after the bear; there are a variety of personal names containing the Chinese character for bear, *kuma* 熊, including Kumaichi, Kumaji, Kumao etc. ('Kuma' is also a popular name for boarhounds among hunters.) In upland areas of Tôhoku there is a custom known as 'bear-riding' (*kumanori*), according to which male children are placed on the back of the hide of a recently killed bear, all the while being offered words of encouragement such as 'go on mount [it], you'll become strong' (Amano 1999: 162–163). Men, especially those destined to hunt bears, should show the spirit of the bear. In upland Japan it takes a bear to catch a bear.

It is because of this emphasis on spirit that some bearhunters object to winter den hunting (Satô 1979: 111). The true bearhunter is one who faces the bear out in the open, risking his life in a straight confrontation, rather than killing the bear through the 'guerrilla tactics' (*gerira senpô*) of den-stalking (ibid.). A similar objection arises among hunters to the shooting of trapped bears (Maita 1998: 13). The hunter risks his life in neither case. There is also a belief that the bear problem in part arises from human cowardice. This is because cullers who opt to shoot at a safe distance rather than go in close frequently fail to kill the bear outright and instead create a wounded, angry animal all the more disposed to attack people (ibid.: 57). Weak men are often the cause of dangerous bears.

The life-risking dimension of the bear-hunt can induce an almost religious sensibility in the bearhunter. For example, the famous bearhunter Fujiwara Chôtarô (who claims to have killed 200 bears) refers to bearhunting as 'ascetic training for the heart' and as 'the only path to enlightenment' (Fujiwara 1979: 36). Implicitly, Fujiwara, like other writers on hunting, invokes the ideals of *bushidô*, the 'Way of the Warrior'. Like the medieval samurai warrior, the bearhunter lives his life in the face of imminent death. It is as though the existence of true men is inextricably bound up with the existence of wild bears.

This heroic status of the bearhunter as the defender of the village depends on the frightening image of the bear. It is the perception of fearsome bears, as epitomized by the Tomamae bear, that allows the bearhunter to appear as the champion of upland society. But, despite the emergence of the 'bear problem', this image of the bear as a rampaging demon no longer seems so credible in the upland Japan of the 2000s.

Local-national divisions

The bear is the object of growing conservationist concern in Japan. There is a widely expressed sentiment that the bear should not be allowed to become extinct as the wolf did one hundred years earlier. In the 1990s there emerged a movement for the reintroduction of the wolf into the Japanese mountains, as a means of restoring the natural environment, widely seen to have been destroyed by industrial modernization (see Knight 1998). This same sentiment, of protecting 'nature' threatened by the forces of modernity, finds expression in bear conservationism in Japan. Conservationists argue that the bear is the representative large mammal of the Japanese forest (Kawasaki 1993: 151); that there can be no real Japanese forest (*mori*) without the bear because 'if the bear disappears the forest becomes empty' (in AS 10/12/1994); and that 'to protect the bear is to protect the forest' (in AS 25/11/1995; see also Watanabe 1984: 220). The state of bear habitat is sometimes seen as a barometer of forest ecology (Takahashi 1995: 117; see also Noss *et al.* 1996). One bear conservationist makes this point by quoting an elderly Ainu hunter: 'it is thanks to the bear that nature in Hokkaido has been preserved and passed down' (Odajima 1993: 28). One of the keywords that appeared in media reports on the bear in the 1990s was 'coexistence' (*kyôzon*), along with the message that the Japanese people must learn to 'coexist' with the bear.

These calls for people–bear 'coexistence' can elicit negative responses among the people who actually live in bear country. One Hokkaido conservationist recalls how, whenever he mentioned the issue of bear conservation in rural areas, people would react with disbelief and ask him if he were 'a fool or a madman' (*baka ka kyôjin ka*) (Odajima 1993: 26). Bear conservationists find themselves challenged along the lines of, 'Which is important, human life or the bear?' (Watanabe 1984: 215; see also Maita 1998: 13). Local hostility to bear conservationists can take the form of attacks on property and other threatening behaviour: the smashing of windows, nuisance telephone calls late at night and even physical threats. The bear conservationist Maita Kazuhiko found scratchmarks on his car and a note left on the car windscreen stating that there was 'no need for bear research' (Maita 1996a: 179). It is as though some villagers decided to teach the bear conservationist what it is like to suffer damage to property, as they regularly do because of the bears he protects.

Implicit in the conservationist argument for people–bear 'coexistence' is the idea that the survival of the bear is important to humanity. But some remote rural dwellers dispute that the continued existence of the bear is of any local benefit; indeed, given the damage caused to farms and forests, the bear's existence appears to lead to considerable local costs. Some remote villagers in Hokkaido, where the notorious 1915 Tomamae bear attack is still remembered, explicitly wish that there were no bears left. 'When you see [bear] tracks near the field, you are startled. It doesn't matter [to us] if the brown bear becomes extinct' (AS 2/6/1990). Similarly, Maita Kazuhiko recalls that during his fieldwork in upland areas he has often been challenged in the following way: 'In Kyushu [one of the main Japanese islands to the southwest], since the bear became extinct, not one person has suffered as a result. What is the reason that bears should exist?' (Maita 1996a: 190).[8] At least some mountain villagers believe that they would be better off without bears.

This strength of reaction can, to a large extent, be attributed to a deep-seated fear of the bear. Harato Shôjirô recorded the following comments in rural Hiroshima.

> When [outside] people talk about 'co-existence, co-existence', it is not a joke. It is crazy to talk about co-existence with bears. You are talking about a savage animal, while we are human beings – mostly old people. This is not the bear's land, this is a place where we have lived since long, long ago. Please give a thought to us!
> (Harato 1994: 109)

This sense of grievance is only heightened when rural dwellers, in whose own area a moratorium on bear culling is in place, see that whenever a bear emerges in a nearby city it is immediately shot dead (AS 25/11/1995). Even though the likelihood of a bear encounter is far greater in upland areas than in the city, mountain villagers believe that they receive less protection from bears, and that, in government circles, public safety in remote rural areas counts for less than in the city.

Such hostility to conservationists suggests a deep-seated rural antipathy to the existence of bears. Yet the bear conservationist Maita Kazuhiko, himself a victim of rural anger over bears, offers a somewhat different interpretation: mountain villagers have become hostile to bear conservation not so much because of the damage they have incurred, but because of the indifference of the wider society to this damage (Maita 1996a: 151–152). National concern for the bear expressed in the calls for conservation contrasts all too starkly with national neglect of upland society. Moreover, local people see themselves as inordinately incurring the burden of the national policy objective of bear conservation.

There is a further dimension to the fear of bears in upland Japan. In addition to the physical damage they cause, bears can inflict a kind of symbolic damage on the villages they visit. In Japan bears have long been a symbol of rural backwardness and even primitiveness. Upstream villagers have even been stigmatized as being 'hairy like bears' by their downstream neighbours (Sakurai 1990: 599). (This sentiment is perhaps most pronounced in Hokkaido where the Ainu have long been the object of a stigmatizing association with bears by majority Japanese.) 'Until the 1960s, the very existence of the brown bear symbolized undevelopment, [and the bear] was viewed as an enemy of civilization' (Mano 1991: 158–159). From this perspective, eradication of the bear was part of the process of modernization and the extension of civilized standards to the Japanese mountains.

This sensibility persists, to some extent, in the 1990s. In recent decades local governments in upland areas have reacted to postwar decline with an aggressive modernization drive in which they attempt to project their municipalities as places of 'culture' and 'civilization'. To this end, the resettlement of the inhabitants of scattered upstream villages to concentrated downstream residential areas has taken place, modern factories, shops and other workplaces have opened, and impressive new public buildings (town halls, post offices, schools, gymnasia etc.) have been erected. Great effort is expended by remote localities (through their municipal governments) to appeal to outsiders – to come and invest in the locality, to consider settling locally, and to visit as tourists. But these efforts at projecting an attractive modern image are believed to be undermined by bear sightings and (even more so) bear attacks because of the great publicity such incidents attract.[9]

Bears not only discourage outsiders from coming in, but also encourage local people to leave. One category of refugees are farmers who, after repeated bear damage to their fields, decide to abandon the land altogether (Palmer 1983: 332). But bears are also said to deter other villagers from committing themselves to the locality. In a newspaper report on fatal bear attacks in remote villages in Yamagata Prefecture in 1988, the fear was expressed that, at a time when there is already a local shortage of brides, the incident might make getting married even more difficult for local men (AS 29/10/1988). This same fear is expressed by the bear conservationist Hazumi Toshihiro in a passing reference he makes to the rural prejudice 'that brides are not attracted to the kind of place where bears are found' (Hazumi 1992: 308). The background to this remark is that upland areas of Japan tend to be afflicted by high rates of bachelorhood. The fear is that the furore over bears will make such places even less appealing to would-be brides and therefore accelerate their depopulation and abandonment. Proximity to bears is a source of stigma for remote villages and an extra reason for leaving them. Bears adversely affect villagers not just through damage to person and property, but also *by association*.

Local divisions

Antipathy to bears in upland Japan is based on the threat posed both to human livelihoods and to human life. Yet antipathy to bears is far from universal in upland Japan. Indeed, bears elicit sympathy from hunters, foresters and other mountain villagers.

Hunters are on the front line in the upland struggle against bears. They are the ones who actually seek out and confront the animal in the course of the hunt (or cull). As we have seen, the killing of bears is, as a measure of manly status, of considerable symbolic significance among bearhunters, but it can also generate mixed feelings among them. In a famous story by the writer Miyazawa Kenji, a bearhunter explains to a dead bear why he had to shoot it.

> Don't think I killed you, Bear, because I hated you. I have to make a living, just as you have to be shot. I'd like to do different work, work with no sin attached, but I've got no fields, and they say my trees belong to the authorities, and when I go to the village nobody will have anything to do with me. I'm a hunter because I can't help it. It's fate that made you a bear, and it's fate that made me do this work. Make sure you're not re-born as a bear next time.
> (Miyazawa 1993: 61)

The hunter is forced to kill bears because of his lowly social position. He takes no pleasure in his job, and indeed regrets what he has to do.

Even among present-day bearhunters, who otherwise celebrate their struggle with the bear, mixed feelings are sometimes apparent. Fujiwara Chôtarô tells of how, when on a culling mission to dispatch problem bears, through his binoculars he caught sight of a family of bears on a facing mountainside.

> When I saw this innocent scene of the parents and cubs together, even I, who has made a living by killing bears, lost my hunting desire. My heart was attacked by this all too wonderful scene, which I just stood watching, forgetting myself.
>
> (Fujiwara 1979: 36–37)

The literally disarming sight of bear family life has been reported more widely. Tabuchi Jitsuo recounts a hunter's observation of a mother bear in deepest winter: too dehydrated to continue suckling her cub, the bear uses her last reserves of energy to leave the den to drink mountain water in order to resume her maternal duties back in the den (Tabuchi 1992). Tabuchi states that no self-respecting hunter would shoot such a bear.

Rural sympathy for the bear extends to other mountain villagers who (reportedly) accept occasional bear crop-raiding with equanimity. According to Watanabe (1989: 8), the visit of a bear might set villagers talking for a short while, but nothing more would happen. Hida (1971: 196–197) mentions a village where there is a matter-of-fact recognition that there will be some years when, because of a shortage of forest nuts and berries, bears must descend to the village to feed. The villagers simply state that 'if the bear does not feed, it cannot hibernate in the winter', and so when every few years a bear does appear they allow it to eat what it likes and return to the mountains to begin its winter sleep.

Maita describes a scene in which a family of bears (a mother and two cubs) comes to a village to feed on a persimmon tree. As the village dogs bark wildly, three old women watch the bears feeding, absorbed by the spectacle; one woman says to another, 'they are hungry', and then, to the bears, she mutters the words 'go ahead and eat' (*taben'sai*) (Maita 1998: 42). At a time when bears had become a serious problem in such remote areas, Maita was impressed at the lack of fear or hatred of the bears shown by the women.

> Perhaps in this lonely hamlet, the bear is [seen as] just a neighbour in the forest. For the grandmothers, even if their persimmons are being eaten up, the feeling is, 'oh, you're back', like they are waiting for the bears to appear each year.
>
> (Maita 1996a: 52)

Among Japanese urban dwellers, the bear appears a vulnerable, pitiable figure, and bear-culling therefore cruel and unnecessary: 'To kill the bear is not fair. We should protect the bear' (in Maita 1996a: 175). But this perception of the bear as a 'cute' (*kawaii*) figure in need of protection is also present in upland areas. A not uncommon response in the Kumano area to the culling of a bear is *kawaiisô* or 'poor thing' (literally, '[how] pitiable'), an expression suggesting that the bear is more a helpless victim than a dangerous demon. I recall one peninsular housewife (admittedly an urban-born woman) who condemned the tendency among hunters to kill 'cute' animals like the monkey, the deer and the bear. Bear-cullers find themselves criticized for killing 'Mr Bear' ('Kuma-chan' – the suffix *chan* expresses intimacy or familiarity, and is often used for children).

If bears have always been anthropomorphized in upland areas, their more recent, unnatural behaviour can elicit a special pity and concern. Bears are said to be smaller than before; as a result of the shortage of nuts, hunters no longer catch large fat bears. Bears are not seen in their traditional areas, but are instead encountered in new places such as near roads and even in town centres (AS 12/7/1994; Azumane 1997: 111–112). Bears are increasingly unable to find suitable trees for winter denning, and are forced to den in the most inappropriate of places, such as near noisy roads, in timber plantations, in old charcoal kilns, or in abandoned mines. The bear population also appears to have atomized. As a result of displacement and falling numbers, individual bears have become isolated and have difficulty finding mates.

Foresters recognize that bears are victims of the human transformation of the mountains. One forest-worker on the Kii Peninsula draws a parallel with the situation of the young men of the villages.

> For bears and people alike, their home has been ruined. Just as the bear must come down from the now bald mountain peak to the plantations, so people must leave the village to work outside. Also, as their numbers have decreased, bears have great difficulty meeting a spouse. For example, in the southern mountains of the peninsula, there are isolated bears who will probably end up as lifelong bachelors. Is this not a rather similar situation to that of those mountain village youth who cannot find brides?
>
> (Ue 1983: 366–367)

The plight of roaming bears is likened to that of upland dwellers driven to leave their villages for the cities. As animal migrants, driven out of their forest home by the forces of modern development, bears readily elicit sympathy among villagers whose sons have likewise been driven to out-migration. Bears viewed in relation to the forest recall people in relation to the village.

We saw above how the bear is characterized as a criminal. But the bear may also be seen as a victim of crime. 'The situation today is that, because of the damage to the forest, bears and people have together received a great blow. They are both victims [*higaisha*] who have been robbed [*shudatsu sareta*] by the high-growth economy' (Ue 1983: 367). This 'robbing' of the bears by modern Japanese society is a largely invisible crime, for which there is neither a police investigation nor any redress. But modern human society does not completely get away with its theft from the bear. As though seeking redress, the bear descends to feed in human space – to eat the food of those who robbed it. From this perspective, the 'crimes' that bears commit against people and property are to a considerable extent a consequence of this larger crime committed against them. There is awareness of the larger context of bear pestilence, and therefore recognition of the human dimension of the bear problem, a counter-perspective which the anthropomorphic character of the bear tends to promote.

In upland areas, there is a belief that the remote mountains are the bear's 'country' (*kuni*). As we have seen one costly expression of the bear's claim to the mountain forest is the animal's bark-stripping of trees, including the conifers of the timber plantations. A common interpretation of this behaviour is that, through its marking of trees, the bear asserts its 'right of occupancy' over the area to other bears (Hida 1971: 200), but the effect of freshly bark-stripped conifers is to frighten away foresters from the area too. Watanabe Hiroyuki makes a similar point when he recounts how, in Kyoto, bears chew the painted red posts placed in the forest by surveyors, knocking them over in the process. While Watanabe himself attributes such incidents to the bears' partiality to the taste of paint, nearby villagers interpret the bears' behaviour as active defiance of human attempts to survey the mountains. 'For the mountain people, it showed that the bears were angry at this brazen attempt, without permission, to place landmarks in the natural forest which they [the bears] think of as their own country' (Watanabe 1984: 203).

There has been a large-scale loss of bear habitat. Planted conifer forest has replaced much of the fruit-bearing forest vegetation on which bears depend. Golf-courses and ski-slopes are also responsible for deforestation and habitat loss. A hunter in Iwate Prefecture characterizes the bear's plight in the following terms.

Whether you look to the right or look to the left, where there used to be chestnut and acorn forest there is [now] nothing but ski-slopes. It's like a ski-slope has been built right through the middle of the bear's fields [*kuma no hatake*]. If you are a bear [in this situation], you start to want to descend to the [village] fields, don't you?

(in Azumane 1997: 109)

In these remarks it is the bear's 'fields' which are being invaded and the bear which is the victim of (human) pestilence. On the Kii Peninsula the conservationist Higashiyama Shôzô makes a similar point when he depicts the bear as the victim of human 'pests' (*gaijû*) (see Takahashi 1984: 92; Maita 1998: 80). Bear farm damage is a consequence of human society denying the bear its means to livelihood. It is because the bear has lost its forest 'fields' that it decides to come and feed in village fields.[10]

Conclusion

In parts of upland Japan bears are a threat to farms, to timber plantations, and to people. In addition to this physical threat, bears represent a symbolic threat. The presence of bears in an area is a testament to its backwardness and even calls into question whether it is a fit place for people to live in. The presence of a bear in and around human settlements generates a panic both among local residents about their safety and in local government circles about its effect on wider public perceptions of the locality. In this chapter, I have shown that calls for people–bear 'coexistence' collide with these negative associations of the animal among Japanese mountain villagers.

Yet there is another side to bear imagery in Japan. In recent years there has taken place a shift in the image of the bear in Japan. The animal no longer seems so powerful. One reason for this lies in the much-publicized physical displacement of the bear in upland areas; the bear increasingly appears a vulnerable animal, and even a pathetic migrant forced to roam the mountains to survive. In place of the bloodthirsty victimizer of the Tomamae Incident, the bear becomes a wretched victim of the larger forces of modern human society which have displaced it from its mountain home. A second reason for the bear's diminished status as threat is that, in addition to its *physical* displacement, it has undergone an *imaginative* redefinition. Reflecting national and international trends, the wild bear has become associated with the cute, childlike and helpless bears that appear in the spheres of media, entertainment and commerce. Bear stories in the Japanese media are now more likely to be about *saving bears from people* than *saving people from bears*.

Just as the bear's association with power has waned, so too has its association with backwardness. Indeed, backwardness would seem to be something that is increasingly associated with *human violence against the bear*, rather than with the bear as such. Japan has attracted international criticism both for its high annual rate of bear mortality and for endangering overseas bear populations through the trade in wildlife parts (Hazumi 1992: 297). Japanese conservationists point out that, despite its status as an economic superpower, Japan has acquired an international image as 'uncivilized' (*yaban*) when it comes to wildlife management, especially in relation to bears (ibid.). At the national and international levels, bear conservation thus comes to be redefined as 'civilized' and modern conduct.

Finally, this changing image of the bear has implications for the position of the hunter. The ursine invasion of human space in recent decades legitimated the hunter as the defender of the village from the 'fearful demon' from the forest. But hunters are themselves becoming victims of the very sensibility that underlies bear panics. Japan's preoccupation with public safety is directed not only at bears and other wild animals, but also at the hunters who pursue them. In the 1980s and 1990s, hunters have come to be viewed as a threat to public safety – through their strayfire, their out-of-control hounds, and the dangerous wounded animals they create (especially bears and wild boars). Hunters are responsible for more human injuries and fatalities than bears are. Moreover, when the Japanese mass media reports that hunting weapons find their way into the underworld, where they are used in bank robberies and other violent crimes, hunting comes to be directly associated with crime. The hunter, for long the village's 'policeman' in the mountains who kept in check 'criminal' bears, is crossing the line to appear a kind of criminal himself.

The future of wild bears in Japan is in serious doubt. The Japanese bear exists in a country where there is no longer a true wilderness for it to inhabit and where it cannot but wander in and around human territory. Given this environmental context, the 'bear problem' is set to continue, even as bear numbers diminish further and the demonic bear imagery of the past softens. But if Japan's endangered bears remain dangerous, they increasingly share the status of public enemy with the hunters who pursue them.

Acknowledgements

Field research on the bear problem in Wakayama in the winters of 1996–1997 and 1998–1999 was supported by the International Institute for Asian Studies in Leiden. I would like to thank Higashiyama Shôzô for giving up his time to explain to me his work on bear conservation in Wakayama Prefecture. I would also like to express my gratitude to Watanabe Hiroyuki of Kyoto University, Watanabe Osamu of the Sapporo Nature Research and Interpretation Office, and Torii Harumi of the Nara University of Education for sharing with me their expertise on the issues of bear pestilence and bear conservation in Japan. I owe a special debt of gratitude to Tanagami Kazusada for his assistance in field research and for the many stimulating conversations about wildlife issues we have had.

Notes

1 On bear as 'mountain uncle', see Hida (1971: 203); on bear as 'mountain father', see Kaneko (1993); on bear as loving mother, see Tabuchi (1992).
2 See *The Kojiki*, Volume II, Section 45. This passage seems to describe a bear fight. As Kamu-yamato-ihare-biko – i.e. Jimmu Tennô – reached the village of Kumanu, 'a large bear came out of the mountain, and forthwith disappeared into it. Then His Augustness . . . suddenly fainted away, and his August army likewise all fainted and fell prostrate' (Chamberlain 1981: 164). A 'Kumanu' villager then arrived bearing a sword which was accepted by Jimmu Tennô at which point the 'savage deities of the mountains of Kumanu all spontaneously fell cut down' (ibid.). The bear slain, Jimmu Tennô proceeded on his journey to establish the Japanese nation.
3 See, for example, Watanabe (1981: 583), Miyao (1989: 207), Yamazaki (1996: 38) and Azumane (1997: 143).
4 Detailed accounts of such local reactions to bear sightings are given by Miyao (1989: 199), Watanabe (1984: 185), *Asahi Shinbun* (16/10/1992), *Asahi Shinbun* (12/7/1994), *Asahi Shinbun* (25/11/1995), and Takahashi (1995: 103).
5 See Torii (1996: 6), *Asahi Shinbun* (11/8/1995), *Asahi Shinbun* (29/4/1996) and *Asahi Shinbun* (12/7/1994).
6 The war idiom often occurs in connection with the bear, especially in Hokkaido. The post-Meiji colonization of the bear is often characterized as a 'war' (*tatakai*) between bear and settler. See Mano (1991: 158), Odajima (1993: 27), Chiba (1995: 93), and Honda (1998: 300).
7 See *Asahi Shinbun* (17/10/1993), Kudô (1996: 166), and Watanabe (1984: 211).
8 For reports of similar local sentiments, see Watanabe (1989: 8) Yamazaki (1996: 38), and Azumane (1997: 34, 86).
9 For example, bear attacks have been cited as the cause of a decline in forest tourism in the late 1990s in Gunma Prefecture (see *Mainichi Shinbun* 10/9/1999).

10 One response to the bear problem has been to try and supplement the bear's feeding opportunities in the mountains. Emergency food supplies (such as potatoes) are scattered in bear territory and fruit-bearing trees are planted to help restore bear habitat (AS 16/5/1996; Harato 1994: 108–110). Under the catchphrase, 'fruit for the bear, wood for the town', one rural town planted 15,000 chestnut trees on 6 ha of municipal land (Maita 1996a: 188). The same trees would benefit both bears and villagers in a practical example of potential people–bear coexistence. Human attempts to enhance the bear's food supply in the mountains even extend to the establishment of cornfields in forest clearings – 'bear fields' (*kuma no hatake*) which, unlike the human fields in the village, wild bears are at liberty to harvest (Maita 1998: 164).

References

Abe, H., Tawara, K., Hattori, K. and Saitô, S. (1986) Higuma no hogo (Conservation of the brown bear), in S. Saitô (ed.) *Higuma – sono, ningen to no kakawari (Brown Bears: Their Relations with People)*, Tokyo: Shisakusha.

Amano, T. (1999) *Kari no minzoku (The Folklore of Hunting)*, Tokyo: Iwata Shoin.

Asahi Shinbun 29/10/1988 Mori ni owareta tsukinowaguma (Bear chased through the forest).

Asahi Shinbun 2/6/1990 Higuma hogo e ippô (One step towards brown bear conservation).

Asahi Shinbun 16/10/1992 Kuma shutsubotsu aitsugu Tajima chihô (Successive bear encounters in the Tajima Region), Hyôgo.

Asahi Shinbun 17/10/1993 Dôbutsutachi no himojii aki (The hungry autumn of the animals).

Asahi Shinbun 12/7/1994 Ie ni kuma, hitori kega (A bear in a house, one injured), Osaka.

Asahi Shinbun 10/12/1994 Kuma o sukue, hito to no kyôzon hôhô saguru (Saving the bear, finding a way of co-existence with people).

Asahi Shinbun 11/8/1995 Kyanpujô chikaku ni kuma shutsubotsu' (Bear encounter near camp-site), Yamaguchi.

Asahi Shinbun 25/11/1995 Kyôzon no michi motome hogo mosaku (Groping for conservation and the path to co-existence), Osaka.

Asahi Shinbun 29/4/1996 Kuma ni gochûi (Beware of bears), Tochigi.

Asahi Shinbun 16/5/1996 Kuma to no kyôzon, jissen o isoge (Coexistence with bears, hurry up with realizing it!), Maeda Naoko.

Azuma, S. and Torii, H. (1980) Impact of human activities on survival of the Japanese black bear, in *Bears: Their Biology and Management, International Conference of Bear Research and Management*, Vol. 4, Bear Biology Association Conference Series, Morges, Switzerland: IUCN.

Azumane, C. (1997 [1993]) *SOS tsukinowaguma (Bear SOS)*, Morioka: Iwate Nippôsha.

Camarra, J. J. (1987) Changes in brown bear predation on livestock in the

western French Pyrenees from 1968 to 1979, *International Conference of Bear Research and Management* 6: 183–186.
Chamberlain, B. H. (1981) *The Kojiki: Records of Ancient Matters*, Tokyo: Charles E. Tuttle.
Chiba, T. (1995) *Ôkami wa naze kieta ka (Why Did the Wolf Disappear?)*, Tokyo: Shinjinbutsu Ôraisha.
Clevenger, A. and Campos, M. (1994) Brown bear *Ursus-Arctos* predation on livestock in the Cantabrian Mountains, Spain, *Acta Theriologica* 39(3): 267–278.
Comeau, P. (1997) Dangerous liaisons, *Canadian Geographic* 117(5): 56–60.
Cozza, K., Fico, R., Battistini, M. L. and Rogers, E. (1996) The damage–conservation interface illustrated by predation on domestic livestock in central Italy, *Biological Conservation* 78(3): 329–336.
Floyd, T. (1999) Bear-inflicted human injury and fatality, *Wilderness and Environmental Medicine* 10(2): 75–87.
Fujiwara, C. (1979) Kuma nihyakutô shakaku no waga satori (My enlightenment after shooting two hundred bears), *Shuryôkai* 23(3): 33–37.
Fujiwara, E. (1988) Wildlife in Japan: crisis and recovery, *Japan Quarterly* 35(1): 26–31.
Funato, S. (1993) Shizen kyôiku no kyôzai ni – 'kowai' imeji (Materials for nature education: the frightening image), in Gifuken Honyûrui Dôbutsu Chôsa Kenkyûkai (ed.) *Horobiyuku mori no ôja: tsukinowaguma (The Imminent Extinction of the King of the Forest: The Black Bear)*, Gifu: Gifu Shinbunsha.
Goldstein, I. (1991) Spectacled bear predation and feeding behavior on livestock in Venezuela, *Studies on Neotropical Fauna and Environment* 26(4): 231–235.
Harato, S. (1994) Kôyôju fubatsu no mori koso (The idea of a forest of unfellable broadleafed trees), in Yamada Kunihiro (ed.) *Satoyama torasuto (The Satoyama Trust)*, Tokyo: Hokuto Shuppan.
Hazumi, T. (1992) Kikiteki jôkyô ni aru tsukinowaguma – chiiki kotaigun no hogo kanri keikaku no teian (Current status and management of the Asian black bear in Japan), *WWFJ Science Report* 1(2): 293–333.
Hazumi, T. (1994) Status of the black bear, *International Conference of Bear Research and Management* 9(1): 145–148.
Hazumi, T. and Kitahara, M. (1994) Tsukinowaguma no bunpu (The distribution of the black bear), in Toyama-ken (ed.) *Kuma to ningen – tsukinowaguma, mukashi to ima, soshite (Bears and Humans: The Black Bear in Early Times, the Present-day, and Hereafter)*, Tateyama: Toyama-ken Tateyama Hakubutsukan.
Hazumi, T. and Yoshii, R. (1994) Tsukinowaguma no genzai soshite mirai (The present-day situation of the black bear and its future), in Toyama-ken (ed.) *Kuma to ningen – tsukinowaguma, mukaishi to ima, soshite (Bears and Humans: The Black Bear in Early Times, the Present-day, and Hereafter)*, Tateyama: Toyama-ken Tateyama Hakubutsukan.
Hida, I. (1967) *Yamagatari nazo no dôbutsutachi (The Animals in Mountain Tales)*, Tokyo: Bungei Shunjû.

Hida, I. (1971) *Yamagatari – nihon no yasei dôbutsutachi (Mountain Tales: The Wild Animals of Japan)*, Tokyo: Bungei Shunjû.

Hida, I. (1972) *Yamagatari – daishizen no dôbutsutachi (Mountain Tales: Nature's Animals)*, Tokyo: Bungei Shunjû.

Hirata, T. (1995) *Hokkaidô wairudoraifu ripôto (Hokkaido Wildlife Report)*, Tokyo: Heibonsha.

Honda, K. (1998) *Kitaguni no dôbutsutachi (Animals of the North)*, Tokyo: Asahi Shinbunsha.

Ishida, K. (1993) Kegawa no riyô (The use of the hide), in Gifuken Honyûrui Dôbutsu Chôsa Kenkyûkai (ed.) *Horobiyuku mori no ôja: tsukinowaguma (The Imminent Extinction of the King of the Forest: The Black Bear)*, Gifu: Gifu Shinbunsha.

Kaneko, H. (1993) Nushi, oyaji (Owner, father), in Gifuken Honyûrui Dôbutsu Chôsa Kenkyûkai (ed.) *Horobiyuku mori no ôja: tsukinowaguma (The Imminent Extinction of the King of the Forest: The Black Bear)*, Gifu: Gifu Shinbunsha.

Katô, T., Tsujii, M., Yoshizaki, M. and Saitô, S. (1986) Imêji no sekai no higuma (The world of imagery with regard to the brown bear), in S. Saitô (ed.) *Higuma – sono, ningen to no kakawari (Brown Bears: Their Relations with People)*, Tokyo: Shisakusha.

Kawasaki, T. (1993) Kokusaitekina hogo dôbutsu (An internationally protected animal), in Gifuken Honyûrui Dôbutsu Chôsa Kenkyûkai (ed.) *Horobiyuku mori no ôja: tsukinowaguma (The Imminent Extinction of the King of the Forest: The Black Bear)*, Gifu: Gifu Shinbunsha.

Knight, J. (1998) Wolves in Japan? An examination of the reintroduction proposal, *Japan Forum* 10(1): 47–65.

Kudô, J. (1996) *Kamoshika no mori kara (From the Serow's Forest)*, Tokyo: NTT Shuppan.

Mainichi Shinbun 10/9/1999 Ken, shika kujo ni hongoshi (Prefecture serious about deer culling), Gunma.

Maita, K. (1996a) *Yama de kuma ni au hôhô (Ways to Encounter Bears in the Mountains)*, Tokyo: Yama to Keikokusha.

Maita, K. (1996b) *Kuma o ou (Pursuing Bears)*, Tokyo: Dôbutsusha.

Maita, K. (1998) *Ikashite fusegu kuma no higai (Preventing Bear Damage)*, Tokyo: Nôbunkyô.

Mano, T. (1991) Ezohiguma hogo kanri no mondaiten to kadai (Problems and tasks in the conservation management of the Hokkaido brown bear), in NACS-J (ed.) *Yasei dôbutsu hogo – 21 seiki e no teigen (Wild Animal Protection: A Proposal for the 21st Century)*, Tokyo: Nihon Shizen Hogo Kyôkai.

Marty, S. (1997) Homeless on the range: grizzlies struggle for elbow room and survival in Banff National Park, *Canadian Geographic* 117(1): 28–39.

Maruyama, H. (1994) Onitaiji (Demon conquest), in K. Inada *et al.* (eds) *Nihon mukashibanashi jiten (Dictionary of Japanese Old Tales)*, Tokyo: Kôbundô.

Matsuyama, Y. (1994) *Inadani no dôbutsutachi (The Animals of Inadani)*, Tokyo: Dôjidaisha.

Merrill, T., Mattson, D. J., Wright, R. G. and Quigley, H. B. (1999) Defining landscapes suitable for restoration of grizzly bears *Ursus arctos* in Idaho, *Biological Conservation* 87(2): 231–248.

Miyao, T. (1989) *Tsukinowaguma: owareru mori no sumibito jûnin (The Black Bear: A Fugitive Forest Dweller)*, Nagano: Shinano Mainichi Shinbunsha.

Miyazawa, K. (1993) The bears of Nametoko, in *Once and Forever: The Tales of Kenji Miyazawa*, translated by John Bester, Tokyo: Kodansha International.

Mizoguchi, M. (1992) *Mori no dôbutsu to ikiru gojû no hôhô (Fifty Ways of Co-existing with Forest Animals)*, Tokyo: Buronzu Shinsha.

Moll, J. P. (1994) Western influences on the management of brown bears in Hokkaido, Japan, unpublished Master of Science dissertation, University of Montana.

Nepal, S. K. and Weber, K. E. (1995) The quandary of local people-park relations in Nepal's Royal Chitwan National Park, *Environmental Management* 19(6): 853–866.

Nihon Keizai Shinbun. 19/1/1997. 'Yasei dôbutsu to do kyôzon?' (How to co-exist with wild animals?).

Noss, R. F., Quigley, H. B., Hornocker, M. G., Merrill, T. and Paquet, P. C. (1996) Conservation biology and carnivore conservation in the Rocky Mountains, *Conservation Biology* 10(4): 949–963.

Odajima, M. (1993) Idainaru yamanokami 'kimun kamui' ('Kimun kamui', the grand mountain spirit), in Rizôto Gorufujô Mondai Zenkoku Renrakkai (eds) *Yasei seibutsu kara no kokuhatsu (Wildlife Indicts Us)*, Tokyo: Recycle Bunkasha.

Ogura, I. (1993) Kuma to yama no kami (The bear and the mountain spirit), in Gifuken Honyûrui Dôbutsu Chôsa Kenkyûkai (ed.) *Horobiyuku mori no ôja: tsukinowaguma (The Imminent Extinction of the King of the Forest: The Black Bear)*, Gifu: Gifu Shinbunsha.

Ônishi, N. (1998) *Boku no mura no takaramono (The Treasures of My Village)*, Tokyo: Jôhô Sentô Shuppankyoku.

Ôta, Y. (1997) *Matagi – kieyuku yamabito no kiroku (Matagi: A Record of a Disappearing Mountain People)*, Tokyo: Keiyûsha.

Palmer, E. (1983) Rural depopulation in post-war Japan, with reference to remote rural settlements of the Tajima region, unpublished PhD thesis, School of Oriental and African Studies, University of London.

Primm, S. A. (1996) A pragmatic approach to grizzly bear conservation, *Conservation Biology* 10(4): 1026–1035.

Sakurai, T. (1990) *Minkan shinkô no kenkyú: Sakurai Tokutarô chosakushû 4 (Research on Folk Religion: The Collected Works of Sakurai Tokutarô Volume 4)*, Tokyo: Yoshikawa Kôbunkan.

Satô, Y. (1979) Fuyugomori chokuzen no kuma o karu gokai na ôgata haundo no ryômi (The hunting style of exciting large hounds used in bearhunting prior to winter denning), *Shuryôkai* 23(3): 109–111.

Shelton, J. G. (1998) *Bear Attacks: The Deadly Truth*, Hagensborg, Canada: Pogany Productions.

Tabuchi, J. (1992) Chichishiro mizu, in K. Tanigawa (ed.) *Dôshokubutsu no fôkuroa 1 (Animal and Plant Folklore Volume 1)*, Tokyo: Sanjûichi Shobô.
Taguchi, H. (1994) *Matagi – mori to kariudo no kiroku (Matagi: A Record of the Forest and its Hunters)*, Tokyo: Keiyûsha.
Takahashi, S. (1995) *Yasei dôbutsu to yaseika kachiku (Wild Animals and Feral Livestock)*, Tokyo: Daimeidô Hakkô.
Takahashi, S. (1997) *Dôshokubutsu kotowaza jiten (Dictionary of Animal and Plant Proverbs and Sayings)*, Tokyo: Tôkyôdô Shuppan.
Takahashi, Y. (1984) *Inakagurashi no tankyû (Investigating Country Life)*, Tokyo: Sôshisha.
Torii, H. (1989) Shizuoka-ken ni okeru tsukinowagumaryô to sono rinboku higai (Bear-hunting in Shizuoka Prefecture and bear damage to forest trees), *Shinrin Bôeki (Forest Pests)* 38(11): 195–202.
Torii, H. (1996) Tsukinowaguma no higai to higai bôji (Bear damage and damage prevention), *Ringyô to Yakuzai (Forestry and Drugs)* 135: 1–8.
Ue, T. (1983) *Yamabito no dôbutsushi (A Mountain Villager's Record of Animals)*, Tokyo: Fukuinkan Shoten.
Urton, G. (1985) Animal metaphors and the life cycle in an Andean community, in G. Urton (ed.) *Animal Myths and Metaphors in South America*, Salt Lake City: University of Utah Press.
Wada, K. (1995) Shizen to yasei chôjû no hogo ni mo (The conservation of nature and wild beasts), *Shuryôkai* 39(4): 33–35.
Watanabe, H. (1980) Damage to conifers by the black bear, in C. J. Martinka and K. L. McArthur (eds) *Bears – Their Biology and Management (International Conference of Bear Research and Management 4)*, Bear Biology Association Conference Series, Morges, Switzerland: IUCN.
Watanabe, H. (1981) Black bear damage to artificial regeneration in Japan: conflict between control and preservation, in IUFRO (ed.) *XVII IUFRO World Congress Proceedings*.
Watanabe, H. (1984 [1974]) Tsukinowaguma no hanashi (Tales of the black bear), in Mizuhara, Y. *et al.* (eds) *Zenshû nihon dôbutsushi 26 (Collected Works on Japanese Animals Volume 26)*, Tokyo: Kôdansha.
Watanabe, H. (1989) Tsukinowaguma – sono hogo o megutte (The black bear: towards its conservation), *Dôbutsu to dôbutsuen (Animals and Zoos)* 41(470): 8–11.
Yamazaki, T. (1996) *Fukui no tsukinowaguma to genpatsu (The Fukui Bear and Nuclear Power Stations)*, Tokyo: Hachigatsu Shokan.
Yoneda, M. (1991) The status of the Asian black bear in the western part of Japan, in N. Maruyama, B. Bobek, Y. Ono, W. Regelin, L. Bartos and P. R. Ratcliffe (eds) *Wildlife Conservation: Present Trends and Perspectives for the 21st Century*, Tsukuba: Japan Wildlife Research Center.

Chapter 8

The wolf, the Saami and the urban shaman

Predator symbolism in Sweden

Galina Lindquist

Introduction

In the pre-Christmas days of 1995 Stockholmers witnessed an unusual incident. It took place on a small elegant square, Stora Torget, a historic place in the middle of the Old City which, weeks before Christmas, was full of street vendors from different corners of Sweden selling popular arts and crafts as Christmas presents. A group of Saami reindeer herders pulled their trucks into the square and filled it with dishevelled corpses of reindeer, covered with frozen blood. This was a Saami protest connected to the government ban on the hunting of wild predators.

This incident, and media representations of the conflicts behind it, dramatize the tension between two different views of wild predators in contemporary Sweden. Among Saami reindeer herders of the north, wild predators, especially wolves, are seen as a threat to livelihood, and even to the Saami way of life. In some parts of the wider national society, the wolf is held up as a symbol of the nation's wilderness and a symbol of authenticity. This pro-wolf sentiment, shared by a range of environmental groups, forms the background to the wolf conservation measures passed by the Swedish polity in recent times. In the 1960s wolves and other wild predators (such as wolverines and lynxes) were put under legal protection in Sweden. Despite the low numbers of predators overall, in some areas of Saami territory their concentration is quite high and the source of some disquiet among local people. In Sweden, as elsewhere, the wolf occasions a conflict between a rural population of livestock-herders and a national-level conservationism intent on maintaining predators in the wild.

This chapter examines this divergence in perspective by contrasting the Saami view of the wolf with that of a particular group of Swedish urbanites. Neo-shamanism is an urban subculture of spiritual seekers within the New Age movement. One of my main research interests has been shamanic techniques, and in the course of fieldwork on this theme I discovered that wild animals in general, and wild predators in particular, occupy a prominent place in the world-view of these new-agers as a positive symbol of authenticity. It was in the course of my research in the 1990s that the Saami controversy blew up, and I found myself struck by the stark contrast between these two views of the wolf – as bloodthirsty threat to Man and as spiritual guide of Man. This chapter is an attempt to explore this contrast in views of the wolf, and its larger significance in terms of attitudes to nature in Western societies.

I begin by describing the Swedish neo-shamans I studied, and the importance of wild predators to them. The second half of the chapter focuses on the Saami struggle with the wolf. This chapter is based on fieldwork carried out among neo-shamans in Sweden (but also in Denmark, England and France) in the period 1993–1996 (see Lindquist 1997). I have not conducted fieldwork among the Saami; the following description and discussion of the Saami draw on the ethnographic literature on the Saami, and especially on the work of the anthropologist Hugh Beach.

Neo-shamans

Neo-shamanism can be seen as a form of animism, reflexively constructed by practitioners, which is based on a knowledge of traditional religions and is informed by a broad environmental awareness. The neo-shamanic world-view can be seen as a kind of 'sacralized environmentalism' in which the Divine is seen to dwell in nature-at-large, in the woods, the rivers, the seas and the forests, and in the wild animals which inhabit these spaces. It is premised on the conscious rejection of the Christian view of Man as the crown of creation and master of nature. Instead, in neo-shamanic theology human beings occupy a humble position, on a par with all other living creatures.

Many Scandinavian neo-shamans come from the environmental movement. Some of them perceive this movement, as well as other mainstream forms of political activity, as bureaucratic and as lacking a spiritual dimension. Other practising neo-shamans, who have chosen 'to work on different planes of reality', participate in mainstream environmental groups (where they tend to be reticent about their spiritual persuasions). Many neo-shamanic rituals in Sweden seek to achieve the same goals as those of regular environmental groups, like saving green areas from residential construction or protecting endangered animal species. During my fieldwork a number of rituals were performed to save the population of wolves in Sweden. Thus, in contrast to many conservationist groups, the neo-shamans try to achieve conservation goals not (or not only) by accepted means of public protests and gathering signatures for petitions, but also by performing ecstatic ceremonies with drumming, dancing and chanting in which they journey to different 'non-ordinary' realities and recruit the help of spiritual beings to secure environmental and other social ends.

Shamanism is also seen as the spirituality of traditional peoples. Shamanic practices are considered to be basic to the cultural and spiritual survival of traditional peoples, whom neo-shamans revere as a source of wisdom and a model of an ecologically benign lifestyle. It is often said that the West should learn from the traditional people to live in harmony with nature, and it is understood that their wisdom will lead the Western world out of its present-day blind alley. Thus, neo-shamanism is constructed on the image of the exotic Other, and this Other has a dual character. First, it is an abstract 'natural' Other, conceived as nature-at-large with wild animals as its specific manifestation. Second, it is an abstract 'cultural' Other, traditional peoples, seen as an icon of social good.

In terms of its cultural forms, neo-shamanism can be defined as a set of practices for altering one's state of consciousness that uses the instruments and techniques derived from various tribal peoples. Among these are drumming, rattling, chanting, dancing, and ceremonies modelled on Native American heritage, including ritual baths (modelled on sweat lodges), vision quests (when people sit out in the woods without food or water for days) and day-long dances around the Tree of Life (based on the Native American sun dance).

The main technique of core shamanism is the shamanic journey. Under monotonous drumming, the practitioner comes to an altered state of consciousness and perceives herself as journeying to another realm of reality, the Alternative or Non-Ordinary Reality, which unfolds in the consciousness of the journeyer as sequences of mental imagery. A shamanic drum journey is based on the technique of visualization and the work with imagery that is an integral part of many modern alternative therapies. The beings one meets there, the spirits, are expected to become the source of advice, healing and practical help. Beginners receive instruction and are expected to meet their Spirit Helpers who take the form of wild animals.

Swedish neo-shamans are a loosely defined group that is difficult to quantify. The technique of shamanic journeying has been taught on courses and introduced at numerous New Age fairs and festivals in Sweden since the 1970s. There are thousands of what I elsewhere call 'neo-shamans of low engagement' (Lindquist 1998). These are people who have gone through these courses and who have some kind of experience of the images of alternative realities and of Power Animals as Spirit Helpers (see below). There are considerably fewer *actively* engaged individuals in neo-shamanism – people who live their lives within the Swedish neo-shamanic community and who take part in its rituals and annual celebrations. There are probably around fifty core people in Sweden responsible for generating new cultural forms and maintaining existing ones. There may be about two hundred people participating in the festivities and attending advanced courses on a more or less regular basis, although people can disappear from the shamanic scene for several years to try something new.

The neo-shamans of both low and high engagement come from the ranks of the New Age movement. While the New Age scene in the USA and Western Europe is a predominantly middle-class movement, in Sweden the picture is somewhat different. During my fieldwork I came across a number of industrial workers and service sector employees, as well as people living on the social margins – on unemployment benefits, disability pensions, and the like. Academics are prominent (the natural sciences are only sparsely represented, while social sciences are over-represented). One also meets many social workers and artists of all kinds. Since the ideological premises of neo-shamanism in Sweden have strong roots on the political left and in environmentalism, people from the upper class, banking and industrial management are not represented in this movement.

Power Animals

The spirits that the beginners meet on their drum journeys manifest themselves in the form of wild animals. These cultural expectations start to be built up even before the seekers enrol in courses in shamanism where socialization into the new cultural system usually takes place. Before ending up at these courses, many of the aspiring students of shamanism will have read the now classic manual of the founder of neo-shamanism, the American anthropologist Michael Harner (1982). This text states explicitly that only wild animals can be Power Animals. Cows, pigs and hens are not eligible. Nor are dogs unless they are rather wild and look wolfish. If the journeyer meets certain kinds of domesticated animals and interacts with them on the journey, they may well become the main source of supernatural help. For example, cats turn up in people's narratives of their journeys quite often, probably because the cat is seen as never wholly domesticated but always somewhat wild and mysterious (witness the role the cat plays in popular culture, for example, in Steven King's horror stories [popular in Sweden, as elsewhere] as the bearer of dark supernatural forces). Otherwise, domesticated animals are of marginal importance.

Generally, there is a good deal of uniformity in the kinds of animals people meet on their journeys. The majority of Power Animals are wild predators. There are lots of lions, tigers, panthers, leopards, pumas and other exotic felines. For Swedes and Danes there are often wolves, white and brown bears, lynxes and foxes. There are also whales, and there are always dolphins, the favourites of the New Agers (the dolphin is considered to have an especially high intellect, to be capable of emotions, and, generally, to be closest to man).[1] There are many birds of prey: eagles, condors and kites. I have never heard of people bringing back hyenas or skunks as Power Animals, and no wonder – these representatives of the animal kingdom are in Western culture the bearers of obviously negative qualities. Wild predators dominate the fauna of the Non-Ordinary Reality of Scandinavian neo-shamans.[2]

When people meet animals on their journeys and communicate with them, finding answers to the burning questions of their lives or receiving useful advice, these animal figures may thereafter become key figures for them – 'significant others' in G. H. Mead's sense (1972). The interaction with, and the feedback that people get from, their Power Animals may have little or nothing to do with these animals' real-life characteristics. A twenty-year-old student of humanities that I met in the field had a polar bear as one of his spirit helpers. The bear helped him in healing the different physical ailments he suffered from. When the young man first met the bear (on a drum journey on the beginners course), he was plagued by a bad cough that did not respond to conventional medicines. On the journey the boy asked the bear how to cope with the cough and received concrete advice, which he subsequently applied and succeeded in curing his cough. Thereafter the bear helped him to give up smoking and, on the journeys, gave him special treatment that, according to that young man, alleviated his headaches and bouts of influenza.

Another neo-shaman I knew, a female academic in her mid-thirties, had a wolf as a special helper. The wolf first came to her on a journey at a time when she was trying to work out an abusive relationship with her partner and to cope with her timidity and fear of open conflicts and direct confrontations. The wolf on that journey was fierce and bared its teeth at the overbearing partner from behind the woman's shoulder. This non-ordinary wolf was helping her to overcome what she perceived as her weakness in ordinary reality. When I talked to her again a couple of years later she reported that the wolf remained with her as one of her Power Animals. It kept turning up in her imagination in real life on similar occasions when she was confronted with pressure and hostility and overcome by fear. In one case, in her mind's eye, she saw the wolf baring its teeth at her enemy. She said that this confrontational person, as a result, behaved differently towards her in real life. It was as if something had changed in her own demeanour, as if she was now giving out the message that she was not to be trampled on.

According to this woman, the fierce wolf, even though it did not turn up so often, was of great help in her everyday life. The imaginary wolf rectified her behaviour in real life and helped her change some of her behaviour patterns that she perceived as debilitating and destructive. In this example, the wolf is used by an urbanite as a representation of an abstract quality of 'fierceness', which in the context of her life translated into the ability to stand up for herself, to resist the pressure others put on her, and to overcome her timidity and proneness to give in to force. The ability to 'show teeth' was for this woman connected to the wolf – an animal she had never seen other than on television, in the cinema and at the zoo.

I have met several other neo-shamans who had the wolf as their Power Animal. One of them was Mathilda (a pseudonym), an artist in her mid-forties. The wolf was her principal Power Animal, and her 'medicine name' was 'Wolf-Woman'.[3] The wolf was depicted on her drum and figured in her 'Power Songs' (ritual chants composed by neo-shamans for special ceremonial occasions). She had a wolf skin that she used as a Power Object in various rituals. Mathilda, a veteran, core figure in the neo-shamanic community in Stockholm (in my terms, a shaman of high engagement), had authored, initiated and led many ceremonies devoted to the conservation of the wolf population in Sweden, the protection of wolves against wolf diseases, and opposition to illegal wolf-hunts.

Mathilda's own wolf was a protector, a counsellor and a healer. It was clearly very important to her self-definition. As in the example with the polar bear, Mathilda's wolf did not represent any specific quality. Rather, it was chosen from the available pool of symbols and was constantly present in her consciousness as an abstract symbol of strength. However, the paradigmatic quality of the wolf, its fierceness, seemed to play an important role in Mathilda's identity. In her demeanour, she appeared to cultivate a certain 'fierceness'; she had crafted her social self in opposition to mainstream-valued stereotypical female qualities of 'pleasantness', 'niceness' or 'softness'. Mathilda was a fierce woman, much less approachable than the majority of other neo-shamans.

Neo-shamans themselves are aware of the fact that most Power Animals are wild predators. I once asked an informant, a shamanic teacher, to comment on this. His explanation was that 'the Universe' presents us with the images of power that we can understand. Our culture, he said, uses wild predators extensively, starting from children's books and animated cartoons, to designs on clothes, logos of industrial products and all kinds of advertising. Urban dwellers see live wild predators only in zoos where they go to entertain their children, but images of wild predators pop up everywhere, from alligators on LaCoste shirts and jaguars on luxury cars to the roaring lion of Hollywood film studios featured at the beginning and end of movies. Tigers, wolves and eagles are our culture's 'natural symbols'. They stand for certain recognizable qualities that we perceive as desirable and rare, like life-strength, physical harmony, freedom and survival amidst the cruel competition of modern life. When these animals become Spirit Helpers, the modern individual, disempowered by society and civilization, believes he or she can partake of these desirable qualities.

This way of using images of predators as metonymical representations, standing for one specific quality or characteristic that urbanites imagine wild animals to possess, has many examples in contemporary Western advertising. Recently, the Stockholm municipal transportation company, on launching a new monthly travel pass, put out an advertisement featuring a close-up shot of a resting lynx – an animal that is calm but poised, relaxed but ready for all the surprises and challenges that a predator's life throws up. The message, presumably, was that the owner of a new monthly travel pass can (by virtue of their new-found mobility) attain the same kind of poise and a lynx-like readiness to meet life's opportunities and challenges.

Here again, the advantages that the advertisement promises seem to have only the loosest of relations to the lynx as a predator species. The abstract image of lynx is made to stand for a certain quality of life that is supposed to be desirable for an urbanite. This quality is attached to the image of the lynx in a rather arbitrary way (the whim of the creator(s) of the advertisement). The connection between this state of life of an urban person and an animal totally abstracted from its real-life context can be made by the users of the advertisement because Swedish urbanites have no concrete experiences of encounters with live lynxes. But it is likely that if they were repeatedly confronted with corpses of reindeer that have been torn apart by lynxes or wolves, as the Swedish reindeer-herding Saami are, their images of these wild predators would be very different.

Saami and reindeer

The Saami are the native people of the area in northern Europe known earlier as Lapland. They have been in this area since long before the nations of Fennoscandia (Norway, Sweden and Finland) took the first steps to colonize it in the end of the first millennium. Due to the national borders forced upon them, the Saami have been parcelled into four separate countries. Now there are 35,000 Saami living in Norway, 17,000 in Sweden, 5,700 in Finland, and 2,000 in Russia. Unlike many other ethnic minorities, the Saami in the countries of Fennoscandia retain access to much of their land, despite numerous state regulations and ongoing debates concerning questions of legal ownership. Yet, in spite of the fundamental differences between the Saami minority and other non-indigenous minorities in these countries, the Saami have been treated in many respects like immigrants, being for many years subjected to assimilationist policies.

The Saami were hunters and gatherers long before some of them became reindeer-herding pastoralists. They have also farmed and herded together, and produced traditional handicrafts highly appreciated in Scandinavia. But access to resources for hunting and fishing, as well as to farming possibilities, have been heavily regulated by the nation states. Early on in the history of the Swedish nation-state, there were laws insisting on the separation of reindeer-herding and agriculture. A commitment to farming and a permanent house for Saami herders was strongly discouraged by the authorities who feared it might cause the herder to leave the nomadic life or neglect the reindeer and allow them to spread unattended and cause damage to settlers' property.

This policy led to the collapse of the combined economy. Many Saamis who were unable to sustain herding alone were driven away from herding, to join the poor Saami proletariat in the big cities. Now in Sweden Saami reindeer herders are a minority within a minority: out of the 17,000 Saami there are only 900 active herders, and together with their families they constitute a total population of 3,000 Saamis who live by herding. The second largest population of Saami is in Stockholm, and other cities of Sweden also have Saami communities who maintain their ethnic identity by voluntary self-ascription.

Even though the Saami practise a range of traditional subsistence styles and adopt modern livelihoods, reindeer-herding has long been their special expertise, for which they are well known. Already at the end of the nineteenth century, Saami were contracted as herding teachers among native groups in Canada and in Greenland. Until recently, the policies of the encompassing nation-states have commonly interpreted Saami resource rights (such as the right to hunt, now severely restricted, as will be seen below, and the right to use raw materials for handicrafts) as privileges reserved exclusively for the reindeer-herding Saami. But preoccupation with the reindeer stretches far beyond the resource rights practised by the herders alone. Herders or non-herders, Saami regard the reindeer as a basic guardian and the source of their culture, the flame that keeps their identity as Saami alive.

Before modern transportation linked the herders to a broader non-Saami market, and also provided them with the means to meet commercial demands for herding produce, herding was a subsistence activity involving few external transactions. Herding families practised mostly what is known as intensive herding; this involves keeping tight control of the reindeer, continually guarding them and preventing them from straying or mixing with other herds, and milking them daily for a large part of the year. When a reindeer was slaughtered there was little that was not used. Reindeer provided everything for Saami in the way of food and clothing, and a herder knew each individual reindeer.

Today reindeer are exploited primarily for meat which is sold on the market in competition with other husbandry products. This has led to bigger herds and more extensive herding, when reindeer graze free for the most of the year and are gathered by herders prior to the spring for calving and slaughter. Reindeer-herding in the circumpolar regions of Fennoscandia is a tough existence, involving frequent moves, physical risk and long separation from family members. While there are a few big herders with many head of reindeer, most have only enough to survive and the family income must be supplemented by part-time jobs. Yet reindeer-herding remains special, for it represents a way of life within a Saami community, as a Saami – it is a lifestyle and not just a job (Beach 1994).

In the past era of herding, herders individualized every single animal in the herd and had names for the most of them. Nowadays, it is only certain special animals in the herd which tend to have names and with which a herder can be said to maintain an affective long-term relationship. These are often the most beautiful or the smartest animals, or reindeer tamed by the herder to perform a specific task, such as to draw a sledge. Children of herders receive a reindeer when they are born, when they are baptized, when their first teeth emerge and on other important personal occasions. Such reindeer live close together with men and are like pets. They have names, and they are linked with their owners in an affective relationship. However, herders individualize and recognize all of their deer; a herder can see that 'the one with the pale nose and black hind leg' is missing. Such affective relationships were stronger in the past. Yet even in the past such emotions had their limits because reindeer were, and are, in the end slaughtered for meat (Beach, personal communication).

Saami herders are organized in so-called *samebys*. These are historically defined territorial grazing zones as well as social units. They comprise those people whose reindeer are permitted to graze these zones. A *sameby* is also a form of legal entity and economic cooperation. Only *sameby* members can herd and all herders are *sameby* members. The traditional rights of hunting and fishing are restricted to the members of a *sameby*. A Saami who leaves herding also loses his privileged right to resources. The *sameby* collective is responsible for the herding on its territory, but it is not allowed to engage in any economic activity other than herding. Each *sameby* is ascribed a specific (optimal) herd limit, the total number of reindeer maximally allowed to graze the territory, to avoid overgrazing. Reindeer meat sold on the market provides the main source of income for the herders' families, and so the herds limited by this number allow the herding Saamis just to get by in terms of living standards. It is against this economic background that to lose reindeer to contingencies such as sickness or wild predators is a serious disruption of their herders' livelihood (Beach 1994).

The five main wild predators of the reindeer are the wolf, the wolverine, the lynx, and, to a lesser extent, the bear and the eagle. Altogether these predators kill thousands of reindeer each year and constitute one of the main threats to the livelihood of the herding Saami. Even though the wolverine for many years topped the list of reindeer killers, and the lynx was not far behind, it is the wolf which is perceived by the Saami herders as the greatest danger. Wolf predations are known to be horrific. The wolf inflicts a slow and painful death on the reindeer by tearing apart its body or biting through its sinews. Wolf predation seems excessive and wasteful because wolves destroy many more animals than they can eat. A wolf also frightens and stampedes the herds which scatter far and wide, making the herders spend much time and effort gathering them up again.

The legal protection of the wolf means that reindeer herders cannot effectively protect their herds. The herder is not allowed to hunt or trail the wolf, except on skis. A herder is allowed to kill the wolf only if he comes upon it in the act of eating reindeer, 'red-toothed', as it were. The herder is not allowed to carry his rifle on his snowmobile; it must be packed down in the sled. Nor is he allowed to keep the rifle and the bullets in the same place. In other words, in his fight to protect his reindeer, the herder is legally incapacitated. His only real protection against predators lies in his ability to scare them off by his presence. This form of defence was inefficient even in the old days of intensive herding when herds were concentrated in fenced-off areas. In the present day conditions of the extensive herding, when herds are scattered over large grazing territories and gathered together only in spring for slaughter, a herder has neither physical nor legal means to protect his reindeer, and so he must be prepared to accept substantial loss (Beach 1981).

Even though the laws protecting predators came about only in the 1960s, fear of and resentment towards the wolf have long been a part of the Saami worldview. In Saami hunting stories the wolf invariably signifies threat, danger and anxiety. This attitude is different from the rather neutral one towards the lynx or the wolverine and the opposite of that towards the bear which, although traditionally hunted by Saami, has always enjoyed great respect and had central ritual significance in their culture. By contrast, many stories describe the wolf as a cannibal and an eater of human beings, especially children. Saami also carried out wolf-hunts in the past. The wolf-hunt was looked upon as a dangerous struggle, in which hunters risked their lives; it was often emphasized how important it was to kill the wolf with the first blow. A wounded wolf was believed to always get back at the hunter and take his life. This mysterious, frightening power of the wolf also appears in more recent folklore accounts in which, for example, the wolf is said to cast spells on the hunter's bullet so that it misses or on the rifle so that it fails to fire.

The wolf was ascribed the ability to read a man's mind; the wolf was said to have the strength of one man and the intelligence of ten. The meat of a reindeer killed by a wolf was considered to be contaminated and inedible. A man bitten by a wolf was believed to be doomed to death. The only way to save the life of such a person was to pour wolf's bile on the sore and bandage it with wolf membrane. The belief in the wolf's magical power is probably the reason why it is depicted on many Saami drums. The drum was the main instrument of Saami shamans, *nåjds*, who were considered to be the only people capable of confronting the wolf and steering it away from the herds by the use of magical power. It was believed that human transgressors, such as thieves and murderers, could be punished by *nåjds* by being turned into wolves. Shapeshifting into a wolf was a weapon of magical warfare between rival *nåjds* (see Larsson 1998).

Saami–wolf conflict

We can now return to the Saami protest of 1995. The incident in the Stora Torget appeared to be directed against the ban on hunting wild predators. But in fact the Saami demands were more complicated. Until 1995 the law stipulated financial compensation from the state for every reindeer killed by a wild animal. In practice, however, compensation was very difficult to obtain because of the requirements of proof that the reindeer was indeed a victim of a wild predator. Saami representatives, together with the National Authority for Nature Conservation (hereafter NANC), worked out an alternative proposal according to which every *sameby* would annually receive a set amount of money based on the number of predators inhabiting the grazing territories of their herds.[4] The incident in the Stora Torget was staged when other means of attracting the attention of Parliament to this proposal had failed. The law was formally adopted some time later, but it turned out to be a source of bitter disappointment among the Saami who saw it as a form of ethnic discrimination on the part of the government, since the allotted funds turned out to be about half of the amount agreed upon. The Saamis retained the right to kill some predators when they caught them in the act, but they were still not allowed to hunt wolves, mountain foxes, bears, lynxes and mountain eagles (all protected species in Sweden) as they deemed appropriate, for example by tracking them from the site of a recently killed reindeer.

At the end of 1994 another Saami–wildlife conflict came to the attention of the Swedish public. Its coverage in the Swedish media, unfolding in several successive newspaper articles almost like a detective story, illustrated a whole set of uneasy relationships in what is generally seen as a harmonious and conflict-free Swedish society – in particular, tension between the Saami and the state authorities, and between the Saami and environmentalists. It also revealed a strain between, on the one hand, popular representations of Saami as 'traditional' people ('our roots'), and, on the other, a less sympathetic image of them as modern entrepreneurs thoughtlessly exploiting nature, and even as ruthless environmental criminals.

Throughout 1994 the dwellers of a *sameby* called Svaipu in the Swedish province of Västerbotten complained that a new pack of wolves had settled in the woods around the village and had destroyed some fifty reindeer in a couple of weeks. According to press reports, villagers were particularly upset about the cruel way the wolves killed their prey: not in one blow like other predators do, but torturing the victims in a slow and painful death. Villagers were especially upset by wolf attacks on pregnant reindeer which had their stomachs ripped out and their foetuses torn from their wombs.

The appearance of the wolves coincided with the news that the government had drastically cut the predator payments previously agreed upon. In 1994 the state compensation for reindeer loss amounted to 14 million Swedish krona. In 1995 the Saami assessed their loss in reindeer livestock at 40 million krona, while the corresponding assessment of NANC was 25 million krona. The government allotted only 14 million in predator funds, saying that there was no more money. In response, according to press reports, three *sameby* applied for permission to hunt (in order to remove) all the predators in their areas. These were villages where the predators were not taken stock of, as the assessment took place only on grazing lands, not in the forest areas. The Saami appealed at various levels of the Swedish legal system, but the application was rejected again and again.

At the end of December 1994 two Svaipu villagers were arrested in connection with the shooting of a wolf. This was a criminal offence because the wolf is totally protected in Sweden (the population of wolves at that time was reported to stand at around forty animals), and because the men shot from snowmobiles, which is also illegal in Sweden. There was a witness to the shooting, and, even though no wolf remains were found, the two Saami men from the village were easily identified (there were traces of wolf blood inside one of the snowmobiles and on the sledge runners of the other). Both men were convicted and sentenced to a year in prison and fined 50,000 krona. Together with legal fees of 100,000 krona, the total sum far exceeded the commercial value of the entire reindeer herd owned by the whole village. The local Saami community was insulted and enraged. A spokesman compared the convicted men with shopkeepers who, after being repeatedly tormented by a thief while the police do nothing, finally take the matter into their own hands and kill the thief. A villager commented bitterly that in the old days such a deed would have been a feat, but now it is considered a crime. 'Lapps and reindeer don't count in your Swedish society. When wolves rip off the flesh of our reindeer, the friends of animals and the bureaucrats say nothing!'

In an attempt to explain to readers the Saami way of thinking, a journalist noted that 'a Saami village is an economic enterprise, not an old-fashioned settlement with *kåtas*'.[5] (All quotations are from *Expressen* 14 January 1995.) On a romantic note, he described the Saami land as a 'landscape to be seduced by: enormous expanses, one feels oneself so small in the shadow of the mountains. Everything is so exotic.' And he concludes: 'Would some wolves not be at home here? Everybody should have a right to live.' Finally, the reader is informed that the slain wolf was indeed the leader of the pack, 'with a right to generate offspring', and that it might have helped to regenerate the population of Swedish wolves.

In this text, both the wolves and the Saami are presented as the Other, but bearing opposing connotations. The Saami presentation of their reindeer as victims is brushed off as 'demonization' of the wolf. For the reader, the Saami image of the wolf as a brutal killer is overshadowed by the journalist's image of the wolf as a noble victim, a source of renewal, a leader, 'the male with new blood with the right to generate offspring'. What is represented as an incarnation of evil by the Saami becomes for the reader the incarnation of good, the reviving, invigorating force of nature, brutalized by the industrial rationality of modern man who appears as the product of inhuman and unnatural civilization. Concurrently, the Saami, from being the Noble Other, the 'traditional' man living in the picturesque *kåtas* in harmony with nature, is transformed into a mercenary entrepreneur. The Saami has fallen from grace, no longer linked with the wisdom of nature, but still unsalvaged by post-modern environmental wisdom.

In these representations, the image of the Saami as 'our roots', the authentic Other for the Western self, is hinted at as an option but rejected as invalid. Wild nature in the image of the victimized wolf is offered instead. This suggests that in the view of the Saami the idealized Other may be largely confined to neo-shamans (and probably some other groups of Scandinavian intellectuals) and has not really reached into popular culture. This distinguishes Scandinavia from the USA, where the image of the Noble Native American as the authentic Other has firmly taken root in popular culture, both in ideology and in aesthetics, and often much to the irritation of the Native Americans themselves. The reason, as suggested by the Swedish anthropologist Hugh Beach (personal communication), might lie in the fact that in the USA Native Americans were divested of resources on such a large scale that they ceased to represent a real threat to the white domination. In Sweden, however, the Saami are still in possession of such resources and represent a challenge to the power of the dominant culture.

But there seems to be more to the Saami's resentment of the wolf, which in the exchange rendered above is presented as 'rational' by the

Saami themselves, and stamped as 'irrational' by the mainstream journalistic comment. The question of why the wolf, rather than the wolverine, occupies such an important place in Saami symbolism, given that the latter also inflicts considerable damage on reindeer herds, is not within the scope of this chapter. It may be, however, that it is precisely its special importance to Swedes that gives the wolf such potency.

The construction of the authentic Other

The clash of the Saami and the wolf poses a problem for the neo-shaman back in Stockholm. For the indigenous people of Scandinavia are powerful symbols of authenticity, as is the wolf. When the proponents of sacralized environmentalism are forced to take sides, which of the two images of the Other – wolf or Saami – will they opt for? This is an empirical question, and the answer can help elucidate the problem at the core of the process of cultural creation in which neo-shamans (and many similar groups) are engaged – the construction of authenticity.

I cannot claim to have done an exhaustive survey among the neo-shamans I knew as to which side they took in this conflict. Several neo-shamans to whom I talked knew nothing about the details, and were not particularly interested. But when pressed, some would admit that their sympathies were by and large with the wolf.

> The original Saami culture was so much wiped out by Christianization and urbanization [that] they have lost connection with their own roots. They are reconnecting now, but this is a difficult process. Their shamanic traditions are in fact destroyed and need to be revived just like many other tribal and traditional cultures. They don't know what they are doing.

The wild predator and the domestic native in neo-shamanism reflect two ways of constructing authenticity. One of them is expressed in the quest outside the Western confines of time and space, for the Tribal, the Authentic Savage, which Westerners have traditionally seen as representing their origins and roots (Handler 1986; Bauman 1992). On another plane, we find the quest within – that is, the quest to get in touch with one's real self and its potentialities, to which end various therapies have been developed (such as the drum journey). In the first case, the quest for authenticity occurs with reference to the distant Other, never encountered in reality but rather mediated by culture. In the second case, authentication is achieved with reference to the Self as a source of ultimate truth. In the tradition of New Age spirituality, to which neo-shamanism belongs, the Self is conceived as the source of moral authority, the source of authenticity (Heelas 1996). At the same time, in the construction of such New Age practices as neo-shamanism, extensive use is made of traits and models borrowed from the Other distant in time and space.

Which of these authentication strategies is pursued in each particular case is always a matter of choice and is open to challenge. Certainly, there are neo-shamans who take the Saami side in the wildlife controversy described above, although they would seem to be few in number. The New Age quest is always the quest within, to the Holy Grail of the Self. The chosen authentic Other can be abstract Nature, represented by culturally recycled symbols of wild predators; or it can be an abstract Native Other who represents the wisdom of nature and tradition. Whichever is chosen, it will work only as long as it resonates with the truths of the Self. So it is likely that the attitude of this society to the domestic native will taint, if not completely determine, the corresponding attitude with respect to matters of authentication. From the argument above, it is likely, for example, that more neo-shamans in the USA would identify with the real-life struggle of Native Americans than would the Swedish neo-shamans with respect to the Saamis.

In general, however, it is unlikely that the real-life 'Natives' enmeshed in national and global economies, politics and bureaucracies will always manage to serve as an iconic image of the Other for urban spiritual seekers. Living side by side in a complex world, they are in reality much less an authentic Other and much more a social counterpart, rival or opponent. In the absence of mediation by subcultural ideologies and popular imagery, they are confronted not as an idealized icon of the Self as the spiritual seeker wants to conceive it, but as social actors, competing for limited material and cultural resources.

Were Swedish politics to be built on the Christian moral premises of the unconditional primacy of the human being over the beast, the outcome of the Saami–wildlife controversy might have been to the advantage of the Saami. Within the framework of new, post-Christian folk models of the world, the primacy of the human being over the beast is no longer evident. The premises of new spirituality, such as equality between all living beings and the need to protect the weak in Nature, also seem evident in folk models of the world and even in state legislation. For an increasing number of environmentally-minded urban dwellers, the place of this exposed Other is occupied by Nature, and specifically by wild predators.

In the ideology of the new spirituality, the existing Native peoples are icons only if seen as pre-modern. The Saami strive to survive in the modern world, maintaining their traditional (pre-modern) occupations like reindeer-herding. It is this occupation in the first place that serves as the basis of their self-definition as traditional. But Saami occupations may prove incompatible with the Saami status as 'Traditional People' in modern society. Their iconicity dissolves as these peoples try to come out and assert themselves as equal actors in the modern political economy. Ironically, the peoples who are made into modern icons can easily become victims of modern realities.

Conclusion

This chapter has compared two groups in contemporary Swedish society in terms of their relations to wild predators and, more specifically, to the wolf. The wolf is used by neo-shamans as an abstract symbol in their search for spiritual truths and an authentic self. This stands in sharp contrast to the Saami, for whom real-life wolves are livestock pests which threaten their livelihood.

The neoshamanic wolf seems a very different animal from the reindeer-mauling wolf of which the Saami complain. For the neo-shamans of Stockholm, the wolf is a favoured Power Animal – a spiritual guide in the nebulous land that is our inner space. A Saami would no doubt argue that it is their very distance from the wolf that allows these urbanites to so admire it. Clearly, this employment of the wolf as a Power Animal separates the neo-shaman from the wider Swedish society. But, in their reverence for the wolf, the neo-shamans can be seen as manifesting in extreme form a sentiment that is widespread in modern Sweden.

The comparison of wolf symbolism in these two groups illustrates the remarkable versatility of wild animals as symbols. These two groups of people, both of which have a critical attitude to mainstream society, converge on the use of the wolf as an important element in their symbolic universe. One and the same signifier, the wolf, has two different ranges of signification that converge at one point of reference but then diverge so much as to acquire totally opposite meanings. For the neo-shamans, the wolf is a symbol of wild nature that also signifies the authentic self free from the shackles of bureaucratic industrial society. While the neo-shamans identify with the wolf, the Saami see this animal as a threat to their way of life. The persistence of the wolf as an unambiguous symbol of evil in Saami culture shows that this predator threatens not only their livelihood, but the very foundations of their cultural identity.

It is tempting to relate the contemporary anger towards the wolf among the Saami to Saami anxiety towards Swedish society. In their loss of reindeer to wolves, the Saami have obvious practical reasons to resent the wolf, and it might therefore seem unnecessary to ascribe a symbolic dimension to their antipathy to the wolf and to wolf conservation. But the Saami–wolf conflict can be compared to similar ethnographic cases in other geographic regions. Here, for example, one recalls the argument made by Moore (1994) in relation to another group of European livestockers, Greek shepherds. For the shepherds, he argues, the wolf which threatens their sheep has come to be associated with the wider forces of European modernity which threaten their way of life. Again, the association is triggered by wolf conservation demands – this time, on the part of the European Community. In other words, in the context of an increasingly aggressive trend towards European integration, the wolf becomes a ready 'metaphor of encroachment' in this remote part of Greece (ibid.).

The contrast between the two views of the wolf described in this chapter points to a more general divide between different views of nature in modern societies, one that pits rural dwellers against the larger urban-dominated society. This is evident in the much-publicized battles over wolf reintroduction in North America. Arguably, as actual wildernesses recede, this symbolic pressure on the remaining wild lands and 'celebrity' wild animals such as large predators will only increase, and with it conflicts with the remaining human inhabitants of this wild periphery.

Acknowledgements

I am greatly indebted to the anthropologist Hugh Beach who has generously shared with me his knowledge and expertise on the Saami.

Notes

1 In New Age practice, dolphins are considered to be representatives of higher civilizations and they sometimes make their wisdom heard to the New Age seekers through various channellers.
2 It should be added that, as might be expected from the above exposition of the neo-shamanic Other, the Spiritual Teachers that Scandinavian neo-shamans meet on their journeys are represented by the figures of Native or Traditional Peoples, like Native American medicine men, Saami *nåjds* (shamans), Maori warriors etc.
3 'Medicine name' is a name that is 'given', that comes from the Non-Ordinary Reality in one way or another, just like Power Animals do. Usually people are 'given' a medicine name in trance-like states like journeys, or under vision

quests; they can also be uttered by a shaman-in-action at times of divination. These medicine names are seen to contain some Non-Ordinary power and also to reflect their owners' Non-Ordinary or hidden aspects, their personal gifts. Usually, people introduce themselves by their medicine names in closed ceremonial contexts. For more on the term 'medicine', see Lindquist (1997: 235).

4 This figure for the number of predators was based on data provided by the local Nature Conservation wards in co-operation with the Saami, and derived from the number of animal dens in the grazing areas. The monetary figures were reached by working out the equation of the number of predators in the area times the amount agreed to be paid per predator. The latter in turn was based upon the agreed compensation value of different reindeer categories (male, female, calf) averaged together (Hugh Beach, personal communication).

5 *Kåta* is a tent of reindeer hide traditionally used by nomadic Saami herders.

References

Bauman, Z. (1992) *Intimations of Post-Modernity*, London and New York: Routledge.

Beach, H. (1981) *Reindeer-Herd Management in Transition*, Uppsala Studies in Cultural Anthopology, Uppsala, Sweden.

Beach, H. (1994) The Saami of Lapland, in *Polar Peoples: Self-Determination and Development*, London: Minority Rights Group Publication.

Eliade, M. (1964 [1951]) *Shamanism: Archaic Techniques of Esctasy*, Princeton: Princeton University Press.

Handler, R. (1986) Authenticity, *Anthropology Today* 2(1): 2–4.

Harner, M. (1982) *The Way of the Shaman: A Guide to Power and Healing*, New York: Bantam Books.

Heelas, P. (1996) *The New Age Movement*, Oxford: Blackwell Publishers.

Larsson, T. (1998) Samiska trosföreställningar om vargen, in E. Olofsson (ed.) *Trolldomsprocesser, Myter, Helande och Modern Samisk Identitet*, Lund: IWGIA.

Lindquist, G. (1997) *Shamanic Performances on the Urban Scene: Neo-Shamanism in Contemporary Sweden*, Stockholm: Stockholm Studies in Social Anthropology.

Lindquist, G. (1998) Andliga anarkister och magiska aktivister: Nyschamanism i dagens Sverige, in *Svensk Religionshistorisk Årsskrift*, Uppsala.

Mead, G. H. (1972 [1934]) *Mind, Self, and Society from the Standpoint of a Social Behaviorist*, Chicago: Chicago University Press.

Moore, R. S. (1994) Metaphors of encroachment: hunting for wolves on a Central Greek Mountain, *Anthropological Quarterly* 67(2): 81–88.

Spooner, B. (1986) Weavers and dealers: the authenticity of an oriental carpet, in A. Appadurai (ed.) *The Social Life of Things: Commodities in Cultural Perspective*, Cambridge: Cambridge University Press.

Chapter 9

The problem of foxes
Legitimate and illegitimate killing in the English countryside

Garry Marvin

Introduction

This chapter is an attempt to understand and explore some of the cultural meanings that underpin foxhunting in the English countryside.[1] A fox-hunt involves the search for and pursuit of a fox by a trained pack of hounds followed by a group of horse riders. I shall argue that this event cannot be fully understood by focusing exclusively on the immediate relationships between the animals and humans involved in the hunt. In order to understand the cultural sense of the event for those who participate, to understand the acceptability and legitimacy of this form of killing a wild animal, the structure of the event and the emotional responses of the participants, it is necessary to set the analysis in the context of other human–animal relations and other animal–animal relationships in English rural space.

It will be argued in this chapter that the fox is hunted because it kills animals – game birds and domesticated livestock – which should only be killed by human beings. The fox is a rival which competes with human interests. In terms of these legitimations the fox is perceived as a pest or vermin which needs to be controlled. But such legitimations for *hunting* foxes, rather than killing them as vermin, have developed since fox-hunting became an organized country sport. In recent years there has emerged strong opposition to fox-hunting in Britain from a variety of animal rights and welfare groups which regard it as immoral, barbaric, cruel and unnecessary. There are growing calls for fox-hunting to be banned. In response, those who organize, participate in and support fox-hunting have been forced to offer a legitimation for it beyond that of mere pleasure.

This chapter does not examine this political aspect of the contested relationships of hunting. Rather, it focuses on some of the processes and practices internal to hunting itself and explores the various animal–human relationships from the perspectives of those involved in the sport. While hunting has been examined in great depth by anthropologists interested in what are loosely called 'hunting and gathering' societies, hunting for sport has scarcely been touched. I suspect that this is because it is regarded as unworthy of academic consideration, and also perhaps because it is perceived to be disagreeable and morally unacceptable. My own research suggests that hunting as sport can be interpreted as a complex social and symbolic practice and hence a rich area for anthropological enquiry.

Images of the fox

The organized and formally structured hunting of foxes in England does not have a very long history compared with the hunting of other animals. Although forms of fox-hunting as a country sport were practised from the second half of the seventeenth century (see Ridley 1990:2; Carr 1986: 26–30), it was not until the second half of the eighteenth century that the fox was perceived as a suitable beast of the chase. Before that time, foxes were simply perceived as vermin or pests which were unceremoniously killed when necessary or when the opportunity arose. Oliver St John, writing in 1641, indicates the difference between the special treatment due to game animals and the lack of respect owed to others:

> We give law to hares and deer, because they are beasts of the chase; it was never accounted either cruelty or foul play to knock foxes and wolves on the head as they can be found, because they are beasts of prey.
>
> (quoted in Itzkowitz 1977: 6)

The problematic character and image of the fox in European culture have developed over many centuries in folk-tales, popular lyric traditions and literature (for a survey, see Rowland 1974). As a character, the fox appears in works such as Aesop's Fables, the medieval Beast Epics (particularly in the stories of the *Roman de Renart* – see, for example, Terry 1992; Varty 1967 and Varty *et al.* forthcoming) and later in the works of authors such as the Brothers Grimm and Beatrix Potter. According to this image, the fox is a sly, amoral, wily, cowardly and self-seeking creature, but was also viewed as a not unsympathetic rogue that survives by cunning. It was regarded as a pest because it killed poultry and lambs and thus impinged on human livelihoods. Because of the manner of this intrusion into the human world, it was also perceived as crafty, dissimulating, and a ruthless killer. Chaucer, in *The Nun's Priest's Tale* refers to the fox lying in wait for a cock as an 'iniquitous' and 'sly' creature and compares it with a 'treacherous assassin' and a 'murderer' – unacceptable killers. William Somerville, writing in 1735, represents the pursuit of such pests as part-battle, part-morality play:

> For these nocturnal thieves, huntsman, prepare
> Thy sharpest vengeance. Oh! How glorious 'tis
> To right th'oppress'd and bring the villain vile
> To just disgrace!
> (quoted in Thomas 1984:163)

Anyone was allowed to kill foxes and parish authorities made payments to those who produced the dead bodies of foxes.

In early modern times it was deer and hare that were hunted with hounds. But, for a variety of reasons, at the beginning of the eighteenth century there were not enough deer for those who wished to hunt (see Carr 1986: 22–24). A small number of owners of packs of hunting hounds discovered that the fox offered good sport when pursued and this quarry quickly became the focus for a new form of hunting. As a result, a set of practices supported by a new hunting ideology had to be developed. The fox was therefore a substitute for 'ideal' or 'noble' species. As one of the few anthropologists to write on fox-hunting has put it:

> the fox appears not as the star of a ritual drama specifically written to his personal qualities, but rather as a second-rate substitute, an understudy drafted into the central role after the lead came down with a lingering terminal illness. While only the fox can lead riders on a chase suitable as a ritual of nobility, the riders have not been keen to transfer the fox's qualities to themselves.
> (Howe 1981: 295)

Hares and deer had long been viewed as 'noble' creatures, whereas the fox came to be an important animal of the chase tainted with a much earlier image as vermin. Although those who hunted did not attempt to transfer the perceived qualities of the fox to themselves, its image became more nuanced as the quality of the attention paid to it changed. When fox-hunting became established as a country sport of the rural elite in the eighteenth century, the animal was still perceived as a rural pest, but the elite wanted to make sure that it was only they who ceremoniously hunted and killed it. As it came to be the most popular hunted animal in the countryside, those who participated in the event conferred a different status on it. The fox was, in some new sense, worthy of the attention of those who hunted, and deserved to be killed *only* through the hunt. Death by hounds was the *appropriate* form of death. Hunting with hounds was regarded as an essentially noble enterprise; for the quarry to have been a contemptible creature would have been discordant with this image. The fox had to be redefined as worthy of being hunted and as offering a worthy challenge within what was becoming an elite sport. It was still regarded as a thief and a villain, but the distasteful and disagreeable associations of vermin were tempered by the view of the fox as an 'artful rogue'. The fox was praised, and continues to be praised, for its its cunning, its courage, and its strong spirit when hunted. For those involved in the practice, the pursuit of the fox offers a complex series of challenges which make the animal worthy of hunting.

From the very beginning of fox-hunting as an organized event the fox has carried a set of contradictory images and such contradictory images continue. Today those who participate in hunting publicly defend the practice as an efficient and appropriate method of pest control but the highly elaborate nature of the event suggests a more complex cultural practice being enacted – a point which will be developed more fully later in this chapter.

The fox-hunt

At present there are some 200 registered fox-hunts in the United Kingdom,[2] each with its defined area, and approximately 250,000 people regularly participate, either on foot or on horseback, in the event. Hunting takes place during a season which runs roughly from early autumn to early spring and during this time Hunts[3] will go out at least twice a week, once on a weekday and once on a Saturday. Some of the larger Hunts may go out three or four times a week. I will leave aside the social organization of the Hunt and instead give a short outline of the key elements of the hunting itself.

Foxes are hunted by scent by specially bred and trained hounds under the direction of a Huntsman.[4] A hunting day is planned in advance in terms of the area to be hunted, and farmers and other landowners are contacted to obtain their permission to cross and hunt on their land. Around mid-morning the hounds, officials and participants meet at a predetermined place, and after light refreshments move off to the hunting area. The Huntsman and his hounds always precede the mounted participants, and he will encourage the hounds into the first wood, field or hedgerow of his planned route. The mounted followers are held well back to allow the Huntsman and hounds to work. This process is referred to as 'drawing a covert'. The Huntsman allows the hounds some time to see if they can pick up the scent of a fox – all the time encouraging them with his voice and his horn. If no scent is found he will call the hounds to him and the whole Hunt will move off to the next point where he hopes to find a fox.

When one or a few hounds do find a scent, this is communicated to the other hounds by an excited change of 'voice' between them and they will quickly group together. The fox may have left the wood sometime before and the hounds attempt to follow its scent. It may still be in the wood and be forced to flee by the intrusion of the hounds. If it leaves ahead of them, the hounds will still follow it by scent rather than sight. Once the hounds have raced away, the Huntsman blows the signal 'Gone Away' and the mounted riders prepare to follow. Nowadays, these riders are not free to ride across the countryside in any direction they choose – they are controlled by a Field Master who leads them in pursuit of the hounds.

The hunted fox attempts to avoid capture in several ways – by outrunning the hounds, by taking a route on which its scent will be disguised, by running through terrain where it is difficult to follow, or by seeking shelter in a place inaccessible to hounds. Hounds often have difficulty following the scent and the fox may well escape while they try to work out where it has gone. When they are able to closely follow the scent, there will come a moment when they lift up their heads, see the fox, and race on to kill it as it is still running. All the hounds will then tear at the dead animal, and the Huntsman, if he is close to them, will blow 'The Kill' on his horn to signal to other members of the Hunt that the hounds have killed.[5] Following a short pause while the riders regroup, they proceed to the next point to start the procedure over again. Hunting usually continues late into the afternoon or even until sunset.

A 'good hunt' from the point of view of the participants is one where the hounds have worked hard to find the scent; where the hounds have worked well as a pack to keep on the scent and have killed the foxes they pursued; where most of the hunt has been visible; and where the fox has run long enough and fast enough that those on horseback have had an exciting gallop across the countryside and have jumped some challenging obstacles. Not all those who go hunting participate on horseback;

from the foot-followers' perspective an entertaining day is one in which they have been able to see the key moments in the relationship between fox and hounds. It is the attempt to discover the scent and to keep the scent and the pursuit of the fox in difficult circumstances that are the key elements here – the actual killing of the fox is not the focus of the pleasure of hunting, nor is it culturally elaborated.

Opponents of the event characterize the participants as being motivated by 'bloodlust' or a desire to see foxes killed. But I have never heard anyone speak of the pleasures of killing, express the wish to be present at the kill, or judge the event in terms of a 'good kill'. What is celebrated is the process that leads to that. It is spoken of in terms of 'performance' – what the fox did; the challenges it posed; what it made the hounds do; their initiative in the search and pursuit; whether the Huntsman read the developing drama accurately; and whether his skill or lack of it increased or decreased the sport that day. The death of the fox by hounds is merely the appropriate conclusion to a hunting event. As the Spanish philosopher José Ortega y Gasset elliptically comments in his essay on hunting, '[o]ne does not hunt in order to kill, rather the opposite, one kills in order to have hunted' (1968: 94).

There is one common end to the hunting of a particular fox during the day that must be mentioned because it is related to the discourse on the necessity of killing foxes and the image of the fox as a pest that must be controlled. If the fox takes shelter in a place that the hounds find but which they cannot enter, then decisions have to be made about what to do with it. The technical term for this is that the fox has 'gone to ground'. Those in charge of the hunt can decide to leave it where it is and simply move on in search of another fox. They can, however, decide to hold up the hunting and deal with it – especially if the farmer or landowner has told them to kill all foxes they put to ground. This requires the services of another member of the Hunt – the Terrierman – who works not with hounds but with small terriers. If the fox has taken refuge in what is called an 'artificial earth' – a building, drainage pipe, straw bales, a pile of rubbish or whatever, then it is acceptable to 'bolt' the fox. The hounds are taken out of sight of the activity and a terrier is put into the refuge and will attempt to force the fox out. The animal is allowed to get on its way and then the hounds are brought back to attempt to pick up the scent and hunt it once more. If, however, the fox shelters in a 'natural earth' – often another fox hole or badger sett – then exits from the earth or sett are blocked and a terrier, wearing an electronic collar, is put into the hole. The Terriermen have a device which emits a sound which allows them to track the terrier underground. When the sound becomes stationary at a point on the surface this normally indicates that the terrier has forced the fox to a position where it cannot escape. The receiver also indicates the depth at which the terrier and the fox are underground. The men dig down to this point, the terrier is removed and the fox is shot with a pistol.

The members of the mounted Field, the foot-followers and the hounds take no part in this process. Apart from the Terrierman and one or two assistants, all other people are kept away and the hounds must be taken out of sight and hearing of the activity. If it is decided in discussion between the Terrierman, Huntsman and Master that the digging and killing will not be a prolonged process, the hunt is often held up until the fox is found and disposed of. If the Terrierman judges that the dig will be long and complex then he and his assistants are often left on their own and the Huntsman will begin a new hunt. In terms of the observations made during this research, no hunt participants ever took any interest in the digging out of the fox, unless it was to complain that it was taking too long and to express a wish to leave it to the Terriermen and to start looking for a fresh fox. During this time they would talk among themselves, rest their horses, some would have a drink from a hip flask and others would have a cigarette. If the entire hunt has been held up for this process, when the fox has been killed, the hounds will be called for so that they can tear at the carcass – a process referred to as 'breaking' the fox and explained in terms of giving the hounds a reward for successfully hunting it.

At this point hunting has ceased and vermin control takes over. It should be noted that the Terrierman wears no special costume and here operates as a skilled and efficient rural workman. The digging and shooting normally take place because the landowner has decided that there are too many foxes on his or her land and wants them destroyed. The event can be classified as an efficient pest control operation in which the fox is not allowed any chance of escape. There is no aesthetic here, no one comes to watch (indeed, according to the rules of the governing body of fox-hunting, those out hunting may not participate), there is no 'performance'[6] and, unlike the *hunting* of the fox, death is administered by humans using a weapon as is the case in many forms of pest control. There are, however, landowners who do not allow digging to occur – either because, while accepting the legitimacy of hunting, they do not object to having foxes on their land, or because they feel that in terms of 'fair play' a fox that has outrun or outwitted the hounds has, in a sense, 'won' and should be left alone.

Structures of pursuit

All hunting, whether between animals, or between humans and animals, involves a central contest – that of the predator's desire to obtain its prey and the prey's attempt to escape. Some writers have been tempted to draw analogies between human hunters and animal predators, but, as Ingold has shown (see, for example, Ingold 1986, 1996), this produces superficial analyses. From a social anthropological perspective, there are important differences between human hunting and animal predation. Human hunting is a form of social action and must be explored in social and cultural terms. Here there is no space to comment on the place of hunting in societies where the activity is important for procuring meat; suffice to say that, in contrast to hunting for sport, where hunting is a livelihood activity the hunted animal should be given as few chances to escape as possible.

In sports hunting, however, humans must voluntarily reduce or restrict their ability to kill animals if there is to be sport rather than slaughter. If the animal to be hunted does not have to be found, if it is not able to flee, if there is not some doubt about whether the hunter will be able to kill it – then there is no challenge, no sport and no hunting. For example, if deer were driven from a wood and into a fenced enclosure where they could be shot at, this would not be hunting but simple slaughter. Equally, huntsmen have said to me, when questioned about the basis of their sport, that, for example, when men shoot at polar bears with high velocity rifles from a helicopter this is not hunting, and neither is killing a sleeping animal. There are, within sports hunting, rules (some of which are actually codified as written regulations) which are integral to each form of it and which allow it to be hunting as distinct from any other killing of animals.

Although few anthropologists have taken an interest in hunting as sport, a notable exception is Matt Cartmill's *A View to a Death in the Morning* (1993). In this major work, which looks mainly at hunting in present-day North America, Cartmill carefully explores hunting as symbolic behaviour. The elements he builds into his general definition are essential for understanding any form of sports hunting. His fundamental point is that:

> hunting in the modern world is not to be understood as a practical means of latching onto some cheap protein. It is intelligible only as symbolic behaviour, like a game or a religious ceremony, and the emotions that the hunt arouses can be understood only in symbolic

terms. . . . Hunting is not just a matter of going out and killing any old animal; in fact very little animal-killing qualifies as hunting. A successful hunt ends in the killing of an animal, but it must be a *special* sort of animal that is killed in a *specific* way for a *particular* reason.

(1993: 29, emphasis added)

Other essential elements that he builds into his definition are that the quarry must be a wild animal, that hunting must involve violence (one may hunt an elephant with poisoned arrows but putting out poisoned hay is not hunting), that this violence must be inflicted directly and that the hunter's assault on the quarry must be premeditated (running animals over on the road is not hunting, even if the person does it deliberately). This ties in very closely with the view of Ingold when he writes of hunting being different from predation in that 'the essence of hunting lies in the prior intention that motivates the search for game', whereas the essence of predation lies in 'the behavioural events of pursuit and capture, sparked off by the presence, in the immediate environment, of a target animal or its signs' (1986: 91). Hunting is something which an individual or a group of individuals deliberately set out to do – it is not simply the killing of wild animals they happen to come across while doing something else.

English fox-hunting has all of these elements. People come together with the deliberate intention of finding, pursuing, and attempting to kill particular wild animals – foxes – during the course of a hunt. It should be emphasized that they are *only* interested in foxes on these occasions. Even if the hounds put rabbits, hare, deer or other animals to flight during the hunt, these other animals should not be pursued, and a Huntsman will soon punish hounds that divert their attention to them. The animal must be given a chance to escape – it is never in any way held up or restrained so that the hounds can catch up with it and have the certainty of killing it. Although the event involves direct violence, this violence is not administered by a weapon controlled by an individual hunter, but by means of other animals (the hounds) under the control of the Huntsman.

An understanding of the internal construction of the event requires a close analysis of the relationships involved. Who or what is doing the hunting? What or who is the focus of that activity? In forms of hunting in which use is made of, for example, rifles and shotguns, all who go out to hunt will have these weapons and all will be 'hunters'. This is not so when hunting solely with a pack of hounds. The hounds are certainly hunting – they search for, pursue and attempt to kill foxes – and are the only members of the Hunt who are doing this in any direct way. In a sense, the Huntsman is also hunting the fox. He attempts to find and pursue the fox – and in a limited way he could do so on his own on his horse – but it would be difficult to kill it without a weapon. Realistically, though, he is hunting with and through his hounds – they act as a team and only make sense as a team. Foxhounds can hunt without a Huntsman but they only exist as a pack because they have been created by human will – their 'natural' instincts have been shaped by human effort. The Huntsman cannot actually find and follow the scent, but he can help and encourage the hounds to do so. When they are having difficulties in locating a scent he can encourage them, move them along, give them more time or decide to go elsewhere. If they have started on a scent and then lost it he should try to understand what has happened and suggest a new approach to them. In short, he should use all his experience to think like a fox and also know both how to read the behaviour of the hounds and how to communicate with them.

What of the other humans – whether mounted or on foot? If asked what they are doing on Saturday morning a person may well say 'I am going hunting' or 'I am hunting with the Blankshires'. They would never, however, identify themselves as 'a hunter' (which is the name for a type of horse) and certainly not as 'a huntsman/woman' (the name for a very particular person in the Hunt). The collective name for the mounted riders on a hunting day is 'the Field'. They participate in the activity of hunting but they are not, strictly speaking, hunters themselves. They follow the action of the hunt either slowly on foot or more directly on horseback. It is important that they can *only* follow – they do not attempt to find foxes, they are not permitted to be close to the hounds when they are working, and they must certainly never get ahead of them or directly pursue the hunted fox. They would be severely reprimanded if they attempted to engage in any of these activities.

As mentioned earlier, central to any form of hunting are a series of challenges and contested relations. Will the hunter be able to discover the prey? Will the prey elude the hunter? Will the skills of the hunter overcome the skill of the prey attempting to evade capture? Within foxhunting these are structured in various ways. The central challenge is that of the hounds attempting to find the scent of a fox, which may or may not be there. The subsequent contest is that between the fox trying to evade capture and the hounds intent on pursuing and killing it. Intimately connected with this is the will, desire and intention of the Huntsman who is directing them. The fox presents both a challenge and contest for the Huntsman, but this has to be mediated through other animals. Although fixed, the landscape also presents a challenge to all members of the Hunt. When the hounds are pursuing a fox, the mounted participants attempt to keep up with the action, which involves galloping across fields, jumping hedges or other obstacles, and getting across streams and ditches – all of which are highly dangerous activities on horseback. In these circumstances, maintaining the proper relationship with the horse is fundamental for each rider. In addition to the challenge of the landscape, for the rider each jump might be an emotional and psychological challenge. Riders may well compete against each other in terms of who dares or does not dare to jump certain obstacles.

The landscape and the way the hunt develops as a drama in this space are also a challenge for those who follow in motorized vehicles or on foot. The central concern of these followers is to get to a location where they can see the most significant aspects of the hunt as it develops. For the majority this means being in sight of hounds working or where they might see the fox in flight. As they cannot take their vehicles across the countryside, they must have an intimate knowledge of the public and private roads that will get them close to where they predict the next stage of the hunt will occur. Their choice of routes and their decisions about where to position themselves also require a fine knowledge of how and where the hunt itself is likely to develop.

Each hunt develops with a particular rhythm dictated by the relationship between the present or absent fox and the hounds. Ideally, there ought to be time for a certain flow and an excited interest to develop. There is no interest in hounds quickly finding a fox in a wood and killing it before it has time to escape. This might be efficient pest control, but it does not generate the heightened excitement looked for in hunting. From the initial search for a scent to the flight of the fox, the event should build to a crescendo with the hounds in full pursuit of the fox and the riders galloping fast behind them. This is the peak of the event where aesthetic and emotional satisfaction is completely fused with purpose. The death of the fox brings this to an abrupt end. There are many moments in hunting that give the participants satisfaction or create a situation for reflection and comment on human and animal relations, but it is this combination of fox, hounds, horses and riders moving at speed to which it should all ideally build. At this point of heightened emotions it is difficult to interpret the fox-hunt as a pest control operation.

Ritual or pest control?

Fox-hunting can be interpreted as a ceremonial event and a symbolic practice. It is an event in which the expressive and communicative qualities of the actions involved are more important than their instrumental qualities. Here I follow Gilbert Lewis's (1980:19ff) points about the 'alerting quality' of events which might lead an anthropologist to interpret an event or a series of events as being a ritual practice. He suggests that the key elements of ritual include pageantry and ceremony, its highly regulated and formal nature, its direction by specialists, the attention paid to elaborate dress codes, a complex lexicon not easily understood by outsiders, archaic forms of address between human participants, the continual internal reference to notions of tradition, and the use of a specific form of music. These qualities, he suggests, leads the observer to think that there is something more going on than meets the eye. Fox-hunting has such elaborations – special dress; codes of practice and etiquette; a complex lexicon not easily understood by outsiders; specialists such as the Huntsman with (what is regarded as) a quasi-sacred knowledge and a mysterious relationship with hounds and foxes; a cultural elaboration of hounds and foxes; highly valued 'music' in the form of the baying of hounds and the horn calls; and a central concern with tradition.

In response to outside criticism, supporters of fox-hunting attempt to legitimate this event by arguing that it is the most efficient and acceptable means of culling an animal pest. But a striking feature of fox-hunting is its over-elaboration of means compared with ends and the ways in which the means are enacted in a ceremonial form. Foxes can be culled simply by shooting, snaring, trapping, poisoning or gassing them. There is a debate about these means of killing and the pro-hunting lobby has strong arguments against them. Part of their argument is that hunting foxes with hounds is a 'natural' process, with the foxes being killed by a predator, and that even though hounds are not the natural predators of foxes, they are the closest equivalent, and the event the closest to a natural (and therefore acceptable) hunting relationship between predator and prey. Yet the hunt is clearly a culturally constructed rather than naturally occurring event. In terms of practicality, it is also an enormously complex, expensive, and time-consuming way of killing foxes – usually accounting for no more than one or two foxes each day. As well as the expense of the subscription to be a member of a Hunt, those who participate as riders must have the financial resources to own and maintain or to rent horses, they must invest in the appropriate clothing, and, if they are to make the most of their membership, they must be willing to devote many days a year to hunting. I would maintain that this investment in time and money is dedicated to something more than a simple pest control operation.

The idea that the fox is a pest is a contested one in the modern English countryside and three recent reports highlight contrasting views. In 1993, 1,009 farmers were interviewed for a survey on fox damage commissioned by the field sports journal *The Field*. According to the survey, sheep farmers felt they lost, on average, only 1 per cent of lambs to foxes. Of those interviewed, 33 per cent reported having seen foxes killing lambs and 70 per cent had seen foxes among their sheep; 53 per cent felt that fox control had a significant impact on livestock predation, 64 per cent of those interviewed supported foxhunting and 55 per cent allowed the Hunt on their land (see *Survey on Fox Damage* 1993). In 1995 The British Field Sports Society commissioned a study of farmers' attitudes to fox control. A total of 831 farmers were interviewed as part of this study. Most of those who considered the fox to be a problem were sheep farmers (34 per cent said the creature was a serious problem, 37 per cent a moderate problem, 25 per cent a slight problem). At least 69 per cent of those interviewed (including those who did not consider foxes a problem) used some method of fox control (*Farmer Attitudes to Fox Control* 1995).

The last report was published in 1997 and is based on research carried out by members of the School of Biological Sciences at Bristol University (see McDonald *et al.* 1997). This report summarizes the available scientific information on the problems caused by foxes in the United Kingdom. It suggests that foxes do not warrant their reputation as major pests of agriculture. One of the main findings is that between 0.5 per cent and 3 per cent of otherwise viable lambs may be taken by foxes, but that the economic losses as a result of this level of predation are low compared with other causes of mortality. The authors quote a survey of 892 farmers in which 70 per cent thought that the numbers of foxes on their farms was not harmful, 64 per cent suffered no financial loss from damage proved to have been caused by foxes and only 2 per cent claimed losses of more than £100 per year from damage attributed to foxes. They go on to suggest that the damage caused by fox predation on young pigs and poultry is also negligible. The only animal raised by humans which suffers significant fox predation is the pheasant raised for shooting. Of the 20 million birds reared for release each year, only 12 million of these are shot and, while the remainder die in a variety of ways, the major cause of death is fox predation.[7]

The *image* of fox as a pest continues to be an important one for some rural dwellers. There is serious concern about the damage done by foxes. Farmers and landowners I spoke with claimed to have lost lambs, poultry and young game birds to foxes. They believe that the numbers of foxes have to be controlled because the fox has no natural predators in the countryside. Part of the difficulty in understanding farmers' and landowners' attitudes to foxes and their classification of them as 'pests' or 'vermin' is that the nature of the occasion on which they express or do not express such a view, and the perceived position of the questioner, determine, at least in part, how they express their views. The terms 'pest' and 'vermin' seem to be most often given when they are directly questioned about whether foxes are really a nuisance. In other words, it is when they feel the need to justify fox-hunting that they talk of foxes as 'pests' that ought to be controlled.

Those outside the hunting world are usually given this set of views because the argument that hunting is the most efficient and acceptable form of fox control is central to the pro-hunting lobby. On occasions, such as social events, when they do not feel they are being forced to justify hunting, many farmers and landowners will talk about foxes in different terms. Some complain about losses of animals to foxes, and refer to foxes as a nuisance, or complain that there are too many on their land. But the terms 'pest' and 'vermin', especially in the sense of loathsome or noxious animals, are rarely used about the fox. The fox is not spoken about as a hated and despised creature. Many would discuss in a neutral way where they thought foxes were living on their land, where they had seen them that day, or what luck they thought the Hunt would have in finding them. They might even express grudging respect for the wily or artful 'rogues' which had the cheek to come close to human habitation. There is, in short, an ambivalence in attitudes to the fox. Although sometimes labelled as 'pest', the fox equally elicits positive aesthetic references. Indeed, many of the people directly involved in hunting talk of the pleasures of seeing foxes in the countryside.

Those who express the view that foxes must be killed do not suggest that the fox, as a species, has to be eradicated as is often the case for other species classified as vermin. Many landowners are happy to leave fox-killing to the local Hunt to which they allow access to their land. But again, this is not purely instrumental, but rather a positive response to hunting as a rural tradition that also serves a useful purpose. However, not all farmers and landowners are in favour of hunting. Others are not prepared to leave fox control to hunting, and will simply shoot the animals or use other methods to control them.[8] Hunt supporters regard this as an unacceptable and unworthy practice and often refer to it as 'vulpicide' – the illegitimate killing of foxes. In some parts of the country – particularly where landowners have invested in game shooting – there is antagonism between fox-hunters and shooters and gamekeepers. Gamekeepers have even been known to display the bodies of shot foxes in highly visible places to show the fox-hunters what they have done!

Until recently fox-hunters did not feel the need to justify their sport. This was in part because they were members of the rural political, social and economic elite or urban equivalents who visited the countryside for this purpose. In general, they either took no notice of attacks on the practice or were immune from such attacks. But in recent decades there has emerged in Britain a widespread popular concern with animal welfare and vociferous public campaigns for animal rights. As a result of this, proponents of hunting have had to resort to an elaboration of the pest status of the fox as a key element in the process of legitimation. But in my experience, this fox-as-pest discourse is heard very little in the everyday talk of those involved in fox-hunting. Rather, talk about foxes has to do with their place in hunting *per se* as one the central performers in a complex drama set in a rural landscape. Such talk centres on where foxes have been seen, the skill and intelligence of foxes in avoiding capture, the challenge an individual fox presented to hounds and Huntsman on a particular hunting day, the distance a particular fox ran and the sport it showed, and more generally the part played by the fox in the success or failure of any day's hunting.

There is thus a rather interesting situation in terms of the practice of fox-hunting. Those who participate claim, as part of a moral justification, that they are involved in the necessary culling of a pest. Animal pests, though, are normally killed as efficiently as possible to eradicate the problem they pose. They might be, in the loose sense of the term, hunted down but this is simply to find them and destroy them. In pest control there is no notion that one should pursue only one particular individual until it is dead before moving on to find and pursue the next. They are rarely offered a sporting chance of escape or treated in terms of notions of fair play. They are not generally the objects of ceremonial practice with complex rules of engagement, nor is the pursuit and subsequent death of one individual animal celebrated in conversations and written accounts. This is exactly what happens in the fox-hunt and suggests that the fox is, in some ways, an ambiguous creature. To explore this more fully, I now examine how the fox fits into a series of human–animal relations in the English countryside that have, as their focus, the human killing of animals.

Animals in English rural space

Edmund Leach's famous essay, 'Anthropological aspects of language: animal categories and verbal abuse' was first published in 1964 and subsequently republished several times (Leach 1972). The essay offers temptingly elegant structural arguments about English animal–human relations. But it has been much criticized by anthropologists who have shown that its brilliance was superficial, and that the essay rested, in the main, on 'unsupported assertions, inconsistencies, and factual errors' (Howe 1981: 279; see also Halverson 1977). There is, however, a section of his analysis, that is useful for understanding the place of foxes and fox-hunting in English rural culture. Part of Leach's argument concerns the edibility or otherwise of different species of animals, which he relates to ideas of social and cultural distance between them and humans. The 'ideal' food source are animals which are domesticated but which are not socially close to humans. Pets, such as dogs and cats, are never regarded as potential food because they are too close to humans and share an intimate life with them. Most wild animals are remote from humans and are rarely eaten. Field or game animals constitute an intermediary category – they are usually raised by humans or protected by them but they should act like wild animals. They are edible but must be killed according to certain ritual practices.

I will not rehearse all Leach's arguments here, and there are certainly problems when he tries to fit rabbits and pigeons as 'pests' into this model. The following comment should, however, be noted: 'the fox occupies the borderline between edible field and inedible wild animals. In England the hunting and killing of foxes is a barbarous ritual surrounded by extraordinary and fantastic taboos' (Leach 1972: 59). Leach wants to claim that the fox is an ambiguous creature, but this seems to be too strong a term. One sense of ambiguity that is expressed is when an urban dweller comments on how strange, confusing and sometimes threatening it is to see a fox walking along a city street at night. But otherwise the unusual status of foxes derives from the fact that they are, at different times and sometimes simultaneously, both vermin and a creature suitable for hunting. Even within the normal structure and meaning system of sports hunting they are unusual in that they have never been hunted for food, nor have they been hunted as a trophy animal.[9]

One of the problems for those who hunt is that the fox is a creature with a highly elaborated character that has, in part, come about because it is the focus of ritual attention within hunting. Its character, attitudes to it and ideas about how it should be treated have developed *because* it is hunted and this hunting has a long tradition and a deep cultural resonance for many. As mentioned above, the difficulty for those who hunt is that they can no longer justify the event in terms of the dynamics, relationships and cultural attitudes that are internal to hunting itself. It is no longer enough to say that the fox is hunted because foxes are good to hunt, and it is certainly not possible to talk about the pleasures of hunting because this is immediately equated with the pleasures of killing. In terms of public discourse, which turns on contested notions of justification, they must, as it were, play down the expressive, emotional, aesthetic and ritual aspects of hunting and emphasize it as purposive action that has a particular utility.

Although fox-hunting does not lead to the production of meat for humans or hounds (the hounds tear up the dead body, but it is not regarded as food for them), there is, I believe, a connection between fox-hunting and meat eating which situates the event in terms of human attitudes towards animals in the countryside. Elias and Dunning, in their essay on sport and violence that in part examines the development of fox-hunting in terms of Elias's concept of 'the civilising process', note that:

> In earlier days the pleasurable excitement of the hunt [i.e. hunting in general] had been a kind of fore-pleasure experienced in anticipation of the real pleasures, the pleasures of killing and eating. The pleasure of killing animals was enhanced by its utility.
>
> (1986: 161)

Here the 'utility' is not pest control but the production of meat, a much prized addition to the table. They go on, however, to note this other sense of 'utility': '[m]any of the hunted animals threatened the fruits of people's labour' (ibid.), and it is in this sense that the fox is a problem in the countryside. It is not that foxes directly threaten human life as other predators do, but that they pose a threat to that which belongs to humans – reared game and livestock. The fox kills animals that should only be killed by humans.

In comparison with urban societies, human–animal relations in rural space are complex, proximate, wide-ranging and engaged. One of the key strands of these relationships is that of the right and necessity of humans to inflict death on animals. In some cases the need to inflict death is a necessity which is shared by urban dwellers. For example, people in cities and in the countryside both keep pets and these sometimes have to be killed when injured or sick. In the countryside, though, there are animals that are there in order (ultimately) to be killed – domesticated livestock such as cattle, sheep, pigs and poultry. It is regarded as legitimate for certain humans to kill them – that is, as owners of the animals or as an agent of the owner (this ownership will be transferred several times during the course of the life of the animals). They are not usually killed in the countryside but taken alive to a specialist establishment, a slaughterhouse, where they are killed in accordance with a set of regulations governing welfare and hygiene. There are also wild animals whose 'natural' environment is the countryside. They are not owned by anyone, but wild animals that enter land owned by an individual may be killed (unless protected by special laws) by that landowner or his/her agent. Between these two categories are animals which are classified as 'game' – wild animals which receive more attention from humans than other wild animals. They are protected in a way that wild animals are not but they do not have the close protection and control that domesticated livestock do. This ambiguity is seen most clearly in the case of game birds such as pheasants, which, during the early part of their life, are raised by humans in the uncultivated zone of the countryside, but are subsequently expected to live and behave as wild animals. These are 'culturally wild' creatures and they are subject to human ownership. Only those who own them (or those who obtain permission from the owner) may kill them.

There is therefore a discernible set of ideas about who can legitimately kill what in the English countryside. I am leaving aside here the moral and philosophical debate about whether the killing of any animal is legitimate. The fox is an animal that regularly threatens, or is perceived to threaten, this order. So long as the fox, a wild animal, kills only its own kind, other wild animals, it is not a problem. That is perfectly legitimate and natural. Wild animals do not belong to humans and there is no threat to them if foxes eat rabbits, voles, mice or other wild creatures. The problem occurs because foxes kill lambs, poultry and game birds that belong to humans and should be killed only by humans. This is illegitimate killing and must be dealt with.

One of the key popular images of the fox is that of 'poacher' – the animal analogue of the human who kills animals which he should not kill or in ways he should not kill them. As the *Oxford English Dictionary* puts it, the poacher is 'one who poaches or trespasses in pursuit of game: one who takes and kills game unlawfully'. The word 'poaching' derives from the French *pocher*, to encroach, and although the word appears in some Acts it has never been judicially defined (Parkes and Thornley 1997: 35).

The issues of encroachment, contested ownership and killing are related in complex ways here. In their comprehensive study of the laws relating to killing for sport and for culling and pest control in the countryside, Parkes and Thornley offer this commentary:

> where wild animals and birds are free to roam from one person's land to another they are ownerless and not capable of being stolen. The poaching laws of today still reflect these attitudes. Poaching is not theft, nor even a particular kind of theft. Poaching is the *unlawful taking or killing of game*, whereas theft is the *dishonest taking of property belonging to another*. Wild animals at liberty are ownerless and cannot be deemed *property*: they can be poached, but not stolen.
>
> (ibid.: 19, emphasis in original)

The authors above are talking about the legality of ownership of game animals and birds and the right to kill them. Many landowners certainly feel that they are, morally, the owners of the pheasants they raise and release. Not only is the notion of ownership involved in the image of poaching, but so are the ideas of encroachment into areas where the poacher does not belong, and of taking something unfairly, in an unsportsmanlike way, at an improper time and by stealth. Game should be killed in daylight in a ritual manner and not taken secretly at night with gun, snare, trap or teeth. Such contested issues do not apply to domestic livestock which is owned. Although the fox is rarely referred to in a direct way as a poacher when it takes lambs in the field, it certainly is when it comes into the farmyard to take chickens. In the literary references quoted earlier, Chaucer clearly describes the fox as an encroacher who gets through the stockade and hedges around the farmyard and then lies in wait for its prey. Despite contested notions of ownership, trespass and rights to kill, the poacher, whether human or animal, is perceived as a criminal by those who claim ownership of animals. Just as the poacher ought to be hunted down for his crimes, so should the fox.

The fox as illegitimate killer is an image further developed in terms of the supposed motivations of the killing, particularly what is perceived to be unnecessary killing. A fox that gets into an enclosure with poultry will often kill a large number of birds but take only one to eat. This is interpreted in moral terms as viciousness and greed, rather than in animal behavioural terms (which would suggest that the fox, as predator, when confronted with so much prey is confused and merely following its instinct to kill in a supersaturated situation). Similar comments are made about foxes which attack very young lambs and kill and tear at several without eating them completely. Farmers often comment that they could understand the fox taking one lamb as a meal but not the overkill. This general and apparently 'senseless' killing suggests to them that the fox has an innately vicious character.

Conclusion

The perspectives and interpretations developed in this chapter have come about as a result of fieldwork among a particular set of people and interest groups in English rural space – members and followers of Hunts, Huntsmen, Masters of Foxhounds, gamekeepers, a wide variety of farmers and landowners and others who have no particular involvement in the event but who are not opposed to it either. Out of these comments, opinions and perspectives, I have constructed an interpretation which captures the cultural sense and significance of fox-hunting in the English countryside. For them, the fox is regarded as a pest and vermin because it is an illegitimate killer. It interjects itself into a set of animal–human relations and subverts the human part. It is a problem because it is subversive. In my research I never heard the fox being spoken about as verminous in the sense of carrying disease or being unclean, nor causing a sense of unease in the way that rats and mice do because of their invasion of domestic space. In conversation people speak positively and often poetically about the physical body of the fox. It is always perceived as an attractive animal and certainly never provokes disgust or repulsion as many vermin do.

In common with most pests, or perhaps as with all pests, the fox is a problem because of what it does rather than what it is. What this means in this particular case is that the illegitimate killer becomes an object of legitimate killing. Although foxes might be perceived as a problem by some in the English countryside, the method of dealing with them by the formal fox-hunt must be understood in terms of how this creature is located within a long-established symbolic practice and tradition which makes cultural sense to those involved. It must also be understood in terms of how the event is embedded within structures of social and cultural identity in rural communities.

There is, of course, an alternative view of the fox. For many people, especially in urban Britain, the fox is seen not as a villain but as a victim of an immoral practice. Fox-hunting is widely perceived as an activity in which human beings derive pleasure from subjecting an innocent creature to gratuitous cruelty and violence. The contested images of the fox and the relationships which humans have with it through hunting are the subject of vociferous and passionate debate in the media and Parliament as plans are made to consider banning all hunting with hounds.[10] The fox is the central character in a social and political drama concerned with forms of legitimate or illegitimate killing by humans in rural space and the appropriate or inappropriate relations humans have with wild animals.

Acknowledgements

I would like to thank John Knight for giving me the opportunity to develop this piece by inviting me to participate in his panel at EASA in 1998 and for his patience in the revisions of this piece. I would also like to thank Stephanie Schwandner-Sievers, Maria Pia Di Bella and Bob Davis for their comments. Finally I would like to thank the anonymous reviewer at Routledge who carefully outlined all the weaknesses of the first version of the chapter – whose comments were invaluable.

Notes

1 Although fox-hunting exists in most parts of Britain, my fieldwork, which is part of a much wider study of the event, has been conducted with Hunts in southern, south-western, central and eastern England, and has been concerned with the form of fox-hunting which features horse-mounted participants. It is important to note that my research, which began in the early 1990s, has been conducted solely among those who participate in fox-hunting. No research has been conducted with those opposed to it. During this time my research has taken the form of participant observation with three Hunts. Although I did not ride with the mounted Field, I was allowed to follow with a variety of other participants and I spent much of my time with the Terriermen who liased closely with the Huntsman during hunting itself. With each of these Hunts I regularly attended their formal and informal social events and was a regular guest of one Master of Foxhounds. In addition to this aspect of my research, I conducted a large number of interviews with Huntsmen and Masters of Foxhounds in many parts of the country.
2 These are named, associated with a specific area, and registered with the Masters of Foxhounds Association.
3 Throughout this chapter the use of the word Hunt with a capital letter refers to the fox-hunt as a social entity rather than to the activities which constitute hunting itself.
4 The Huntsman can either be a professional (paid by the Hunt) or an amateur but there is only ever one Huntsman per Hunt.
5 After the hounds have torn at the dead fox the carcass is usually picked up by someone from the Hunt. It is usually incinerated at the Hunt kennels so that the mutilated body cannot be used by anti-hunt forces for publicity pictures.
6 This is actually more complex than I allow here. Terriermen and their assistants are extremely proud of the part they play in the event and there are

important elements of craftsmanship and sport in it for them. But setting the terrier to find the fox and the digging out are never referred to as hunting.
7 A full understanding of these reports needs a much more careful analysis and a consideration of who is asking what questions of whom and on behalf of whom. The 'findings' are also challenged or accepted in terms of different positions for or against hunting. For example, the anti-hunting lobby is suspicious of reports which claim to be unbiased but which are commissioned by a country sports magazine and a field sports society. Equally, the pro-hunting lobby is sceptical of the Bristol study where it is felt that one of the authors is openly opposed to hunting. Such reports do not 'prove' that foxes are or are not pests but rather that, depending on other factors, such as being for or against hunting, foxes are *perceived* or *not perceived* as pests.
8 The 1993 *Survey on Fox Damage* study showed that 67 per cent of the respondents shot foxes, 21 per cent trapped them, 7 per cent gassed them and 55 per cent allowed the Hunt on to the land. What these figures do not show is that many farmers who approve of hunting and allow the Hunt on to their land will also use other methods of fox control if they feel it necessary.
9 Leach suggests that the head and tail are taken as trophies – in fact this rarely happens. The head and tail (sometimes the feet as well) are occasionally taken to be mounted by a taxidermist but this tends to be only to mark a special occasion for someone within the Hunt. For example, they might be taken if someone is retiring or moving away from the area.
10 Deerhunting with hounds too has become the object of a similar public controversy to fox hunting.

References

Carr, R. (1986) *English Foxhunting*, London: Weidenfeld and Nicolson.
Cartmill, M. (1993) *A View to a Death in the Morning: Hunting and Nature Through History*, Cambridge, MA: Harvard University Press.
Chaucer, G. (1985) *The Canterbury Tales*, Oxford: Oxford University Press.
Elias, N. and Dunning, E. (1986) *Quest for Excitement: Sport and Leisure in the Civilizing Process*, Oxford: Basil Blackwell.
Farmer Attitudes to Fox Control (1995) Report prepared for the British Field Sports Society by Produce Studies Limited.
Halverson, J. (1977) Animal categories and terms of abuse, *Man* (n.s). 11: 505–516.
Howe, J. (1981) Fox hunting as ritual, *American Ethnologist* 18(2): 278–300.
Ingold, T. (1986) *The Appropriation of Nature: Essays on Human Ecology and Social Relations*, Manchester: Manchester University Press.
—— (1996) Hunting and gathering as ways of perceiving the environment, in R. Ellen and K. Fukui (eds) *Redefining Nature: Ecology, Culture and Domestication*, Oxford: Berg.
Itzkowitz, D. (1977) *Peculiar Privilege: A Social History of English Foxhunting 1753–1885*, Hassocks, Sussex: Harvester Press.

Leach, E. (1972) Anthropological aspects of language: animal categories and verbal abuse, in P. Maranda (ed.) *Mythology*, Harmondsworth; Penguin.
Lewis, G. (1980) *Day of Shining Red: An Essay on Understanding Ritual*, Cambridge: Cambridge University Press.
McDonald, R., Baker, P., and Harris, S. (1997) *Is the Fox a Pest? The Ecological and Economic Impact of Foxes in Britain*, Bristol: School of Biological Sciences, University of Bristol.
Ortega y Gasset, J. (1968) *La Caza y Los Toros*, Madrid: Ediciones de Occidente.
Parkes, C. and Thornley, J. (1997) *Fair Game – The Law of Country Sports and the Protection of Wildlife*, London: Pelham Books.
Ridley, J. (1990) *Fox Hunting*, London: Collins.
Rowland, B. (1974) *Animals With Human Faces: A Guide to Animal Symbolism*, London: George Allen and Unwin.
Survey on Fox Damage (1993) The Oxford Research Agency prepared for the Burlington Publishing Company, London.
Terry, P. (1992) *Renard the Fox*, Berkeley and Los Angeles: University of California Press.
Thomas, K. (1984) *Man and the Natural World: Changing Attitudes in England 1500–1800*, Harmondsworth: Penguin.
Varty, K. (1967) *Reynard the Fox*, Leicester: Leicester University Press.
—— et al. (eds) (forthcoming) *Reynard the Euro-Fox*, Oxford and New York: Berghahn Books.

Chapter 10

The Great Pigeon Massacre in a deindustrializing American region

S. Hoon Song

Introduction

> On one Labor Day afternoon, I fell into gawking at an old man crossing the sparsely peopled part of Hegins Community Park, so abnormally laborious and faltering was his trudge. He was pulling his feeble body along in tiny steps with a grotesquely stooped gaze fixed on the ground, a few feet away from a wounded pigeon fluttering in the dust. Then, out of nowhere appeared several animal rights 'rescuers', closing in at full speed. The old man, spotting the storming pack through the corner of his eyes, instantly came to his senses. He sprang forth on swift feet and stomped on the bird over and over, until its body got limp, trails of intestines exuded, and an eye popped out. Then, spent and out of breath, he stood pale a while before going back to his ever so laborious walk as though nothing had happened, heedless of the cheers of the belatedly gathering onlookers and the rescuers' cries of protest.
>
> (Fieldnotes, The Labor Day Pigeon Shoot, Hegins, PA, 1994)

In August 1999, the closing of an obscure small town's 65-year-old tradition of pigeon shooting by the Pennsylvania Supreme Court made headlines in the American news media. This chapter explores the origin of the passions that had been fuelling this small town's crusade against pigeons in the face of more than a decade of legal challenges by powerful animal rights organizations. 'Pest control' is the most frequently articulated reason for the shoot. But pest control turns out to be, upon closer inspection, neither a utilitarian explanation nor a mere justification, but a layered commentary on the region's embattled social history.

The place and the shoot

Hegins, the home of the annual Labor Day Pigeon Shoot, is a small town of about 3,690 residents, located in the Appalachian Mountains of central Pennsylvania. The town is seated at the southwest fringe of Schuylkill County (70 kilometres northeast of Harrisburg), once the nation's anthracite coal-mining capital and a hotbed of early Labour movements (Wallace 1987; Palladino 1991; Blatz 1994). Since coal's decline as the nation's energy source in the postwar period, the region has been going through a steady deindustrialization and population loss, the turbulent social effects of which are felt to this day (Marcus 1985). The county's population dropped from 235,505 to 156,400 people between 1930 and 1986. During the same period, employment in anthracite mining dropped from 45,800 to 8,500 people (Schuylkill Economic Development Co.).[1]

In 1985 a notable local Jewish family complained about the pigeon-shoot, condemning it as a 'blood sport' (*New York Times*, 3 September 1991). At this time nobody would have thought that the obscure Labor Day Pigeon Shoot would turn into an internationally notorious event.[2] When word about the first protest travelled through the local media, more than five thousand blue-collar residents (predominantly working miners, ex-miners, or descendants of miners) from surrounding areas of the county turned up to support the shoot. In subsequent years, phalanxes of activists fortified the animal rights contingent, while on the other side, an assortment of nationwide conservative advocacy groups (for gun-rights, hunting-rights, white supremacy, paramilitary-survivalism and anti-abortion) rushed to the pigeon shoot's defence, deeming the heritage of pigeon shooting a bastion of conservative values. In front of the mass media, annual battles have gone on ever since between those who support the shoot and those who protest.

Having read and seen media reports, I arrived at my first Hegins shoot in 1993, expecting to find a carnivalesque blood sport with an engaged crowd and a sharply divided battle between 'urban protesters' and 'rural supporters' on the sidelines. The shoot itself was bloody enough, with some 10,000 birds released from shoe box-size traps at the pull of a string and shot at 30 metres away, continuing from dawn to dusk. But the crowd paid only intermittent and languid attention to the shoot and was more interested in the disturbances in the spectator area behind the firing range.

Only a few people could explain the rules of the shooting game to me and these accounts were often inconsistent with each other. My question about the 'tradition' of pigeon shooting elicited answers that were either direct, cliché quotes from the shoot organizers' media-directed propaganda – of the shoot as a bulwark of modern-day conservative values, such as support for the family, local community heritage, patriotism and the defence of the right to bear arms – or references to other kinds of 'pigeon shootings' that did not seem to have anything to do with the Hegins shoot.

In the eighty-acre Hegins Community Park, six shooting games go on simultaneously – three single-barrel games facing north and three double-barrel games facing south – among some two hundred registered shooting contestants (who pay up to $400 to compete). Between the two stretches of games stand food vendors, picnic facilities and a playground, where some ten thousand shoot supporters mingle with one or two hundred animal rights protesters, fifty or so media personnel and a platoon of state troopers. All day long, the shoot supporters, young and old, wrestle with the animal rights activists and compete to get to the wounded birds that fall into the spectator area.

According to the estimate by the Fund for Animals, a Maryland-based animal rights organization, of the 5,106 birds counted in the 1995 shoot, only 13 per cent were killed outright. Of the rest, 10 per cent escaped harm and the remaining 77 per cent were wounded and returned to the park ground. This, I later learned, was due to the birds' instinct to flock and nurse their wounds upon the first available landing. They fall or fly down randomly and indiscriminately, anywhere, at any moment, regardless of prescribed boundaries and battle lines. They land near the inviolable demarcation of the firing range, often near loudspeakers set up for singing the national anthem at the opening ceremony, or on to patriotic emblems displayed by the advocacy groups, pursued by a mob of aspiring pigeon catchers. It is these 'ancillary' activities, rather than the shoot itself, that command the central attention of the event, and in fact claim the majority of pigeon lives on Labor Day.

If caught by an animal rights protester, the pigeon receives care from veterinarians and, most likely, a compassionate euthanasia at the Wounded Bird First Aid Station (a makeshift veterinary care unit at the parking lot).[3] But caught by a shoot supporter, the pigeon is lynched. Shoot supporters display an impressive familiarity with the pigeons. The favoured method of killing is decapitation, either by mouth or fingers. These tend to be highly theatrical acts before a baying crowd. There is much shouting of slogans and verbal abuse of the birds, followed by the decapitation of the bird with one's bare hands, which occurs at lightning speed, as if nothing could be easier. The head and the body, with a stem of bloodied spine quivering slightly at the missing head, are tossed their separate ways, although some people pocket the heads. The discarded body, still fluttering, is finished off by hands and feet. Some people get carried away: they call their children over to join in and lovingly smear pigeon blood over the child's face.

One shoot supporter notorious for his hell-raising ventures at the shoot was a man called Shally.[4] Shally was a tough-looking man in his late thirties, with a soiled pair of jeans, a check flannel shirt and a grimy cap as his uniform. He was an owner of a plot of fruit trees and a part-time independent miner.[5] One Labor Day episode involving Shally stands out in my memory. A wounded pigeon had fallen in an area fenced in with 'No Trespassing' signs. Several animal rights activists rushed up and desperately hung on to the fence, helplessly watching the suffering bird flapping its broken wings. One of the activists slowly lowered a net-cage device, which was inched gradually towards the bird. Watching all this some distance away was a bemused Shally, his arms folded on his broad chest and a smug look on his face. Just as the rescuer's cage was about to reach the bird, Shally walked over, picked up the bird, and popped its head off. Then, turning towards the stunned protesters, he threw the quivering bloody remains of the pigeon over the fence to them, with the words, 'Now, fix it'.

Pigeon as 'pest'

In large cities and towns, feral pigeons typically use the nooks and crannies in human dwellings and commercial buildings for nesting and roosting, as well as parks and garbage dumps for foraging. In rural areas they nest and roost in or near barns, feed in barnyards or feedlots, and thus can be important agricultural pests. Their droppings are voluminous because pigeons eat seeds without husking them. In built-up areas pigeon droppings are unsightly. Pigeons also cause structural damage to buildings by plugging rainstorm drains. Throughout the world, pigeons are accordingly the objects of pest control operations (Johnston and Janiga 1995). In North America too, pigeons have been an agricultural pest. In the Hegins area, row-crops, newly planted seeds and just-sprouted plants are all vulnerable to pigeons. But the pigeon is not a major pest. A major American review of avian pest control excludes feral pigeons from a list of 'the most common major bird pest species in the world' (Dyer and Ward 1977). Other specialists have similarly pointed out that 'feral pigeons are no longer agriculturally consequential in North America' (Johnston and Janiga 1995: 265). Nonetheless, in Schuylkill County today, pigeons are considered an abominable pest.

On one scorching Labor Day afternoon, under the shade of a tree near the entrance of Hegins Community Park, I learnt about all the different aspects of 'pest control' rhetoric in one sitting. Fats Hartman rapidly fired off a string of condemnations: 'pigeons are rats with wings'; 'they don't belong in the countryside'; 'they live off grain yards and make hay go mouldy'. Seeing my surprise, he repeated the point: 'rats with wings . . . that's what they are, flying rats', he intoned with a look of disgust at this imaginary monster with the body of a rat and the wings of a bird. He then recited part of the 'Letter to the Editor' he had sent to *The Citizen Standard* (the major newspaper within the Hegins Valley area) the previous day. 'Pigeons are birds of fouls [*sic*], not animals. Maybe Mr. Cave [the president of Trans-Species Unlimited Inc., the first national animal rights organization to protest against the shoot] should read Genesis 1:28.'

I was to hear these denunciations countless times after that from different informants, but none with the flair and authority of Fats Hartman. A retired miner frequently interviewed by the media on the Labor Day Shoot, he was especially compelling in making the case for pest control. 'Tradition' and pest control were inseparable for him. 'The shoot is a time-honored tradition that helps get rid of pests that would otherwise be poisoned for befouling property with their droppings and living off farmers' grain yards.' For him, the 'pest' was a threat to the very survival and continuation of the community and of tradition – narrowly the 'tradition' of the Labor Day Shoot, but frequently 'tradition' in a more general sense. His denunciation of pigeons as 'rats with wings' merged two requirements for the survival of the rural community: the vitality of tradition and agricultural utilitarianism. In this way, the sacredness of the pigeon shoot tradition was connected to subsistence.

Fats was adept at sound bites. But detail was not his strong point. He often sounded too 'studied' to be a sufferer of the problems he so well articulated. Some questions welled up in my mind. How 'traditional' and endemic was the pigeon as a pest? Has it really been a threat to the region?

Agriculture is not that important in the area. It was not agriculture but the garment industry that filled the vacuum left by the waning coal industry. The total number of agricultural employees in Schuylkill County has not been more than one hundred since 1953. Employees in the textile industry reached twice that of mining by 1962, roughly one-quarter of the county's total labour force – though the trend began to abate a little in the 1980s (*County Business Patterns*, US Department of Commerce, Bureau of the Census, CBP–74–40). The rest of the labour force has been largely absorbed by jobs at textile mills and appliance manufacturing.

Again and again, I brought up this point with other local residents, as well as with Fats Hartman. Responses struck roughly the same chord:

HS: You said pigeon shooting started largely to protect farming, but there haven't been a whole lot of farms around here, right?

FH: You are from the city. You cannot imagine how badly farmers hate them disease-carrying pigeons in their barns.

HS: Have you farmed yourself?

FH: No, I am a retired miner. I got the black lung and still get pension for that. (*Impatiently*) You see, the shoot is a good alternative to getting rid of them disease-carrying pigeons that are a nuisance to farmers and cities.

CF: (Chick Fetteroff): And with where them pigeons come, the cities. (Inaudible) . . . and our historical places that are defaced . . .

HS: Disease?

FH: Yeeesss. In Pittsburgh, Washington and Philadelphia, they spend hundreds of thousands of dollars to gas and poison them pigeons. This [the Labor Day Shoot] is a nice family affair. You don't see people who shoot pigeons shooting drugs.

(Interview, Labor Day 1995)

When pressed, men such as Fats Hartman accept that pigeons are not such a great farm pest, after all. But they then immediately point to the city origin of the bird and the threat of contagious disease, and even invoke the theme of urban moral degradation. The reference to drugs is a recurring one. Thus in the 1990 Labor Day Shoot the logo of the official T-shirt was 'shoot pigeons, not drugs'. There is a belief among shoot supporters that the animal rights protesters are predominantly drug addicts and homosexuals, and indeed one year they were actually nicknamed HIV. (A false rumour and panic spread in 1996 that an animal rights activist, infected with the HIV virus and who had only six months to live, was coming to the shoot strapped in a bomb.) 'Pest' here suddenly comes to be defined not simply in terms of damage to farms and buildings, but as an outside threat to the local community.

This led me to wonder if local pigeon 'pests' were in fact city pigeons, as some people seemed to suggest. Are the pigeons in the Hegins area migrants from nearby metropolitan areas such as Harrisburg? No informant was sure of this, nor were they much interested in the question. Feral pigeons are known to regularly fly considerable distances beyond city limits to farms or ranches at which feeding is possible (Johnston and Janiga 1995: 274). But feral pigeons are not migrants but 'commuters' which move between nesting (and breeding) and feeding sites. The known maximum round-trip distance they commute does not exceed 50 kilometres; Harrisburg, which is roughly 70 kilometres from Hegins one-way, is therefore beyond 'striking distance' (see Goodwin 1983). Moreover, such a phenomenon has been shown to be relatively infrequent in the United States (Glitz 1959; McDowell and Pillsbury 1959). Another factor is that, in Schuylkill County, there are not that many farms and ranches. This is more so as one looks back in time, into the active coal mining eras. I have looked through microfilms of *The Citizen Standard* and *The Pottsville Republican* (the county's largest newspaper) for coverage of early pigeon shoots beginning in the 1920s, but I did not find a single mention of pigeon pests – that is, until the start of the protest. The rather uneventful coverage of the first Labor Day Shoot in 1934 was no exception.

Exogenous 'pests'

Shoot supporters do not bother trying to hide the no-farm-but-farm-pest contradiction. This fact requires us to see beyond their seemingly utilitarian claims. Even to the untrained eye, the birds shot at the Labor Day Shoot are normal ferals, 'street pigeons' or 'city pigeons' in common parlance (scientific name: *Columba livia*). In fact, about 90 per cent of these birds are trapped in the train yards of Philadelphia and Pittsburgh and the rest at the farms of Lancaster and Manheim Counties. In other words, pigeons are actually brought in for the shoot.

Consequently, there are more pigeons after this alleged 'pest control' operation than before it. For at least a week after the Labor Day Shoot, pigeons are visibly numerous in the Hegins Valley area, though I lack the benefit of a scientific census.[6] Besides the intuitive 'feel' for the dramatic increase in number, there are other behavioural indications of the non-local status of many of the pigeons. Most pigeons spotted after Labor Day come in small flocks (fifteen at most) or as individuals. They are extremely jumpy and move about a great deal, though they never seem to fly at great speed or any distance. Pigeons are famous for their keen sense of direction and their territoriality. The fast flight of ferals indicates confidence in their environment, which links the nesting and breeding sites with a stable feeding source. But low speed of flight is an indication of their unfamiliarity with the territory.

The fact that the post-Labor Day population lacks such a source is evident also in their flock formation, since a stable and lasting social formation of a pigeon group of any size depends on the existence of predictable feeding sites. For a better observation, I took a bagful of peas – feral pigeons' favourite diet – to Hegins Community Park one day and spread them underneath a shack. It took an unusually long time (compared to my experience in Chicago's Hyde Park) for a flock-sized group to form for feeding. While stuffing hungry stomachs, the pigeons seemed to be on their own, having little to do with each other. There was no apparent peck-dominance; no sign of heavier-looking birds occupying the central position of the feed spread. This meant an unstable and an improvised social formation, perhaps the result of seeking the company of other pigeons out of alarm and fear. While this was going on, a child on a bicycle appeared and darted towards the middle of the pecking congregation, with a gurgling imitation of shotgun blasts. The birds jumped simultaneously but scattered in every direction, without a hint of that famous patterned manoeuvre against a predator – another sign of their unfamiliarity with each other (see Davis 1975). These were clearly displaced birds.

Pigeon as culprit and victim

There were more contradictions coming as I traced this elusive 'tradition' orally. When I questioned elderly members of the community about the first shoots (outside the context of the current controversy), they recalled not the tradition of pest control but the earlier consumption of pigeons. It was fondly recalled that wealthy members of the community inaugurated the shoot in the depths of the Great Depression in order to allow hungry people to collect pigeon carcasses after the shoot for consumption. The recurring theme in such narratives is that of the extraordinary ethos of charity and communal solidarity, the memory of which today materializes as the nostalgic appreciation of pigeon meat. Such musings always end with a lament, sometimes verging on anger, over the current inedibility of pigeons:

EB: (Eddie Becker):[7] Did you know about people's consumption of pigeons in this area?

RU: (Ruth Umbenhauer): Of course. Dead pigeons were sold for consumption after the shoots. My mother used to prepare pigeon pot pies at home on Saturday afternoons. I still remember the smell.[8]

EB: When did they stop selling them?

RU: People stopped selling them because cities where they got them started to use poison.

Another informant mourned that pigeons were no longer edible because 'they put lead in them pellets now'.[9]

Ruth above explains how pigeons turned from being edible to being inedible – that is, how in time they became 'pests' because cities began to poison them. It is as if, in such a discourse, the state of being a 'pest' has to do not just with the animal's specific and manifest qualities but also with it having crossed a certain (temporal) threshold. Pigeons are culprits but also victims of what is done to them in changing times; the nostalgic taste of pigeons is sumptuous, but equally, in the present-day, it is a reminder of what has gone rotten. The appearance of pellets in shotgun shells was one 'threshold' event. In the current inedibility of pigeons, informants seemed to see an irrevocable loss of a wholesome past, of a spirit of charity, and of a communal solidarity. In the pigeon's 'fall' to 'pest' status is condensed all that has been lost. The pigeon's 'pest' status, as a kind of commentary on the general state of things, does not depend on where they actually come from (local or urban origin), how they were fed (parasitic or non-parasitic), how they were killed (poisoned) and so forth. They are all dirty and inedible, or more correctly, they have all been made dirty and inedible.

By viewing the practice of pigeon-killing in this way, we can make sense of why the fact of their being poisoned elsewhere looms so large in local views of them. For shoot supporters often complain not just that pigeons wallow and breed in the squalor and disease of inner-city streets, but also that they are poisoned in the city and that they are 'drugged with all kinds of chemicals'. It is as if the act of poisoning itself is morally defiling, and the pigeon either a victim of – or an accomplice to – some kind of reprehensible 'drug exchange'.

Only partially understanding such comments, I was often led to ask, 'When should a pigeon shoot take place, before or after poisoning?', and became utterly confused by answers that seemed to point both ways. At times, it is said that pigeons need to be intercepted before they are exposed to the reckless poisoning of incompetent 'city bureaucrats' (who do not know how to carry out pest control properly). But at other times, it is said that they have to be eliminated *because* they have already been poisoned when they come to the (wholesome) countryside. Either way, the conclusion was the same: pigeons have to be killed.

The exaltation of the past often hides a criticism of the present; the nostalgic remembrance of the harshest times (such as the Great Depression) is a well-known tactic of the conservative. Those who complain of the pigeon's transformation seemed to be making an accusation, but of what, I could not fathom; I could not imagine the 'threshold' event. I had serious doubts about the logicality of pest discourses – to the point where there seemed to be no use in pursuing consistency in them. According to the different perspectives of past/present, locals/outsiders, or rural/urban, pigeons appear in radically different ways: victims or victimizers, pests or the inflicted, etc.

Pests and outcasts

A clue to the 'threshold event' – that which marked the birds' transition to 'dirtiness' – came to me one day in an unexpected form. The background to this is the variety of pigeon shoots practised in the region, which must be outlined briefly. Pigeons were perceived more as pets than pests in the county's heyday of industrialism. The county boasts a century-long tradition of pigeon-related diversions among its mineworkers. These recreations took the form of pigeon-fancying, pigeon-racing and trap-and-handle shooting.

Only in recent times did the latter begin co-existing with 'straight shooting', which is a recent invention practised at the Labor Day Shoot. In straight shootings, the birds used are 'barn birds'; these are ordinary, untrained birds which make relatively easy targets when used in large numbers. In trap-and-handle, the birds are 'brushed', meaning manipulated or trained to fly in particularly designed patterns unbeknown to the shooter, and are therefore extremely elusive targets. Brushing requires a long-term commitment of tender care, meticulous breeding and rigorous training, which often results in an intimate bond between trainer and birds. The birds thus bear the mark of their owners; excessive cruelty or massive slaughter of brushed birds is severely censured in the trap-and-handle arena. To this day, ex-miner trap-and-handle connoisseurs speak ill of shoots like the Labor Day Shoot.

It will be recalled that one of the prominent locals present in the Labor Day Shoot was a man named Shally. Along with his father, Shally is an avid trap-and-handle enthusiast and would not compete in a straight shoot like the Labor Day Shoot. One day, his father Steve ranted in disgust that at the Labor Day Shoot 'doctors and lawyers shot a hundred birds in a row just because they could afford them'.[10] Steve's friend, Big Bill, a legendary marksman in trap-and-handle, seconded him: 'You don't even know whose birds they are, they don't belong to anyone.'

And, cryptically, he added, 'Most of the shooters and protesters aren't even from here – until all this started, this was just a nice and quiet place.' This association between the Labor Day Shoot and outsiders is taken one stage further. Thus Steve offered another suggestion of shooter–protester alliance:

STEVE: Them Baumans only wanted straight shooting, so we gave 'em a hell.
SH: What hell?
STEVE: (*Amused*) You sneak in a flock into a shirt factory overnight and you cannot catch 'em. It ruins them machines.
BIG BILL: (*Laughing*) We sure did!

The Baumans are the family who initiated the protest of the Labor Day Shoot. They were one of the Jewish families from the Eastern metropolitan cities who came to dominate the county's garment industry that filled the vacuum left by the diminishing presence of mining since the 1960s (see Wolensky and Wolensky 1999). As more men became unemployed, the proliferating garment factories hired their wives and daughters. Intense hostilities existed from the beginning among the unemployed mineworkers against the exogenous Jewish employers, who were perceived to break up families (by hiring women). Among urban employers generally, 'pigeon gangs' (ex-miners turned bootleggers) were especially feared and detested and considered troublemakers.[11] Both Steve and Big Bill were core members of such gangs. The Baumans, in an interview with me, confirmed the occurrence of the prank Steve mentioned to their Ashland Shirt Company (plus another factory unmentionable here for bearing the true name of the family) in the mid-1960s.

Contemplating the establishment of a new garment factory, the Baumans moved to Hegins in 1961, a predominantly 'Pennsylvania German' town.[12] No sooner had they arrived in Hegins than the patriarch of the family, Samuel, divorced his wife and married his housekeeper, a young local woman of Pennsylvania German origin. This itself was scandalous, but to make matters worse, the new wife, Dorothy, conspicuously converted to Judaism. But the controversy that sparked the family's virtual expulsion from the community came, again, with the issue of pigeons. Samuel Bauman sparked a controversy surrounding pigeon-shooting at a local gun club he had recently joined. It is this incident that Steve recalled. But the Baumans remember it differently.

According to Samuel and his wife Dorothy (when interviewed in 1993), Samuel reacted negatively to his first encounter with live-pigeon shooting (or flyer shooting) at the Hegins Trap Club. Samuel immediately felt that 'something was very wrong' but, in Dorothy's words, they 'did not know about animal rights activism back then'. But still, Samuel raised his voice against the flyer shoot and tried (unsuccessfully) to organize a clay pigeon shoot in its place. He was immediately expelled from the Club. He recalled that, 'living there after that became absolutely unbearable', but did not specify how. Soon after, in 1963, the family moved to the county seat of Pottsville.

However, according to Sally's father Steve (who did not experience the incident first-hand), what Samuel opposed at the Hegins Trap Club was trap-and-handle shooting, not the flyer shoot altogether. This opposition to trap-and-handle was a class-specific statement; true to his class-origin (of 'doctors and lawyers'), Samuel refused to share the company of men like Steve and Big Bill, as it were.[13] This incident is vividly remembered by many shoot supporters, inside and outside the pigeon shoot arena. Understood in terms of this history of bad blood, the Baumans' public denunciation of the pigeon shoot in 1985 would have shocked no one.

Some two decades after the Baumans' expulsion from Hegins, Dorothy became active in the animal rights cause. She took up the pigeon shoot issue as her first mission, and with her children organized the first protest at the Labor Day Shoot. She has been successful in attracting the most powerful national animal rights organizations to the event – including People for the Ethical Treatment of Animals, Fund for Animals, and Trans-Species Unlimited (formerly Animal Rights Mobilization). To this day, Dorothy is a notorious figure in the county, especially in the Hegins area. A 'seductress', an 'animal lover' and a converted Jew, she claims that she still receives threats in the form of dead opossums and mutilated pigeons in her mailbox. Her enemies even make an effigy of her, which they hang over a cauldron of witch's brew on the float paraded down the Main Street of Hegins on every Halloween! Dorothy Bauman is particularly resented for the way she appears to bask in national media attention, and for the way she 'masquerades' as 'the local' in front of the whole world (see Barkun 1994: 116). Such an unwarranted alliance with the media has begotten a code word for those who are reluctant to name directly 'the Baumans' or to openly refer to 'the Jew': 'the media people'. The new epithet is brandished about today with considerable contempt.

The new coinage also allows some to explore extremes. I have heard many people associate the media and/or the protesters with the so-called 'New World Order' conspiracy, a supposed federal government–Zionist alliance out to destroy 'white civilization' through media distortion, trashy popular culture, the spread of drug addiction, abortion and the protection and breeding of 'disease-carrying' pigeons. Some even suggest that pigeons carry the AIDS virus, and that controversies like the anti-shoot protest are small steps towards ultimately disarming whites, and so forth (according to the National Rifle Association, 'it's traps today, guns tomorrow').

There are generational differences in conspiracy theories. Older generations, in their sixties and over, are likely to link the Baumans and the protesters with communism, but this association is almost completely absent from younger generations. The following is a comment from a 70-year-old man: 'It's like terrorism. Why don't they go to Washington DC since it wouldn't be far for them to drive, and protest in front of the Soviet Embassy about the human killings in Afghanistan? Of course, they will never do that.' This short comment links almost all major ingredients of right-wing ideology, where the federal government, terrorists/communists, and the Soviet [sic] embassy all reside in the big city.

Conclusion

One anthropological interpretation of the pestilence discourse connected with the Labor Day Shoot might be that it is a manifestation of provincial anti-Semitism, and the pigeon-killing a vicarious execution of the 'Jew' protester. According to this kind of interpretation, the animal would be a metaphor or cipher for human relations (see Leach 1964, 1971) and violence towards them a 'symbolic' displacement from the intended human target (see Stallybrass and White 1986: 53; Scott 1990). In such a symbolic reading, there is a tendency to view the route of 'displacement' as facilitated by analogous (or homologous) 'values' (of intended human target and the animal substitute) in some kind of system of differentials called cultural classification, as is lucidly exemplified in the celebrated tale of 'the Great Cat Massacre' (Darnton 1984, 1986). The problem is that the classificatory view of a culture (for example, Douglas 1966, 1975) and the descriptive impulse that it privileges (Valeri 2000), condemns a culture's 'classification' to arbitrariness and naiveté, in the name of cultural relativism, but also tacitly in the name of a certain privileged access to Nature, i.e. Western science (Latour 1993: 100–106). Thus, the classificatory view of culture is bound to be a weak form of criticism of instrumentalist reason.

What we need here is a radical critique of the instrumentalist reasoning of 'pest control', because the Labor Day Shoot's practice stands instrumentalist reason on its head: the pigeons are imported in massive numbers only to abandon them as pure exteriorities, as 'pests'. Here, a certain short-circuiting between means and ends should not escape our attention. Nor should the fact that such an economy of violence came along only after the protest and media attention began. Then, how can we relate this form of violence to the experience of a culture perceiving itself under siege by the ideology and resources of 'outsiders', vulnerably exposed to their contagious 'urban' culture/disease, and its 'true' identity distorted by their conspiratorial media?

We should begin by simply turning the problem into an inchoate form of answer: in Schuylkill County, because there are not even enough pigeons around, pest control depends on 'pests' being 'borrowed' from the dreaded urban centres. This is merely one of numerous indications that the sense of inner-directed identity or territory, in a society feeling under siege, is in desperate need of the Outsider–Other for its consistency. Take the case of conspiracy theory. A subscriber to a conspiracy theory can be called 'paranoid' when s/he detects the signs of deception and misrepresentation everywhere (see Campbell 1972; Barkun 1998). But the almighty capacity to distort can be attributed only to the one who is also presumed to hold an all-encompassing knowledge. Hence the complaint about the conspiratorial Other's distortion of myself or my community is also a protest about my exclusion from the Other's secret knowledge. The distorting Other is also an Other who is presumed to know, including the secret of my own identity; only the one who knows my secret can withhold it from me. In this sense, the conspiratorialist subjects have to 'borrow' their inner consistency from the perceived power of the Other.

The economy of pest control in Hegins repeats this logic of Outsider–Other. The expulsion of the pigeons must be repeated again and again in order to establish the boundary of the interior (see Agamben 1998: 15–29). Pigeons are 'pests' which have the power to maintain the sense of self-sufficiency and integrity of the community (Zizek 1989: 114–128). Therefore, the gesture of their banishment should continue indefinitely, even if this means importing them anew.

Notes

1 Between 1951 and 1962, the total number of employees in coal mining (anthracite and bituminous) has decreased at the average annual rate of 34 per cent and tapered to a 10–15 per cent annual decrease between 1963 and 1982. The figure began to climb again in 1983, and the year between 1984

and 1985, the year of the first protest at the Labor Day Shoot, as we shall see, saw the sharpest rate of decrease since 1962: 32 per cent (*County Business Patterns*, US Department of Commerce, Bureau of the Census, CBP-74-40).

2 This event is further explored in my dissertation in progress, 'The Great Pigeon Massacre in a Pennsylvania coal-mining region: a public event, mass mediated and locally situated' (Department of Anthropology, The University of Chicago). This research is based on three visits to the region since 1993 (totalling forty days), and three separate periods of residence, 1996–1999 (totalling seven months).

3 Despite the animal rights organizations' claims, the number of pigeons actually kept alive by their yearly rescue operations is minuscule – well under fifty.

4 Pseudonyms are used for all informants, with clues to ancestry, an important social distinction in the region, intact.

5 'Independent' here means self-employment, outside a contractual relation with big mining companies. Hence, these are small-scale coalholes, with not more than seven or eight labourers, frequently from extended families. Their work is rough and often extremely dangerous, for the government does not as rigorously monitor safety. Independent miners are staunch anti-unionists, many of them still believing that too much labour strife has cost the mining industry in Schuylkill County. Moreover, being 'independent' they incline towards the 'values' of small entrepreneurs and are militantly 'producerist', and so tend to idealize manual labour, economic self-sufficiency, and to be antagonistic towards merchants and creditors.

6 A systematic census of the feral pigeon population is reputed to be a hopelessly difficult task, and is a much-disputed issue. One study asserts that a census of visible birds would miss about 23 per cent of the true total; another calls for a minimum of one year's observation (Johnston and Janiga 1995: 229).

7 Eddie Becker is the director/producer of the documentary on the Labor Day Shoot controversy, *Gunblast: Culture Clash* (1995). This exchange was found from his unedited, discarded footage.

8 I have encountered some men who professed to have 'stolen' dead pigeons at the Labor Day Shoot during the Great Depression and sold them, by hiding in the bush behind the southern end of Hegins Community Park where 'out of bound' but injured pigeons were likely to land.

9 The informant is mistaken here, for it was only in the past that shotgun shells contained lead.

10 The majority of shooters are from out-of-state, higher-income classes. This can be readily inferred from a quick survey of the shooter's parking lot, which is separately fenced in for protection from the animal rights activists' vandalism.

11 In the region the term bootlegger designates illegal coal-extractors. For an account of an elaborate pigeon-shoot culture developed among this group especially around the time of the Great Depression, see Canfield (1993).

12 The population of those of German ancestry within Hegins Township was close to 90 per cent throughout the twentieth century. It declined a little in the 1990s. For example, in 1990, residents of German ancestry numbered 2,793 out of 3,505 (*Census of Population and Housing*). The local paper, *The Citizen Standard*, still runs a column in the 'Dutch Language'.

13 Documented evidence seems to lend credence to Steve's version. The Labor

Day Pigeon Shoot's fiftieth anniversary booklet (published in 1985, the year of the first protest) lists all the participants from the inaugural shoot in 1934 up to 1984. According to the list, Samuel Bauman participated in the Labor Day Shoot, a straight shooting, both before and after the said incident (and did quite well), up until his move to the county seat of Pottsville in 1963. It would therefore seem that his renunciation of straight shooting was less important than his expressed aversion to (lower-class) trap-and-handle shooting.

References

Agamben, G. (1998) *Homo Sacer: Sovereign Power and Bare Life*, trans. D. Heller-Roazen, Stanford: Stanford University Press.

Barkun, M. (1994) *Religion and the Racist Right: The Origins of the Christian Identity Movement*, Chapel Hill: The University of North Carolina Press.

—— (1998) Conspiracy theories as stigmatized knowledge: the basis for a New Age racism? in J. Kaplan and T. Bjorgo (eds) *Nation and Race: The Developing Euro-American Racist Subculture*, Boston: Northeastern University Press.

Blatz, P. K. (1994) *Democratic Miners: Work and Labor Relations in the Anthracite Coal Industry, 1875–1925*, Albany: State University of New York Press.

Campbell, C. (1972) The cult, the cultic milieu and secularization, in *Sociological Yearbook of Religion in Britain*, Vol. 5, London: S.C.M. Press.

Canfield, P. M. (1993) *Growing Up with Bootleggers, Gamblers and Pigeons*, Wilmington: Interlude Enterprises.

Darnton, R. (1984) *The Great Cat Massacre and Other Episodes in French Culture History*, New York: Basic Books.

—— (1986) The symbolic element in history, *Journal of Modern History* 58: 218–234.

Davis, J. M. (1975) Socially induced flight reactions in pigeons, *Animal Behaviour* 23: 567–601.

Douglas, M. (1966) *Purity and Danger: An Analysis of Concepts of Pollution and Taboo*, London: Routledge and Kegan Paul.

—— (1975) *Implicit Meanings: Essays in Anthropology*, London and Boston: Routledge and Kegan Paul.

Dyer, M. I. and Ward, P. (1977) Management of pest situations, in J. Pinowski and S. C. Kendeigh (eds) *Granivorous Birds in Ecosystems*, Cambridge: Cambridge University Press.

Glitz, M. L. (1959) The problem of bird damage to Ohio, *Proceedings of North Central Branch, Ecological Society of America* 14: 47–48.

Goodwin, D. (1983) *Pigeons and Doves of the World*, Ithaca: Cornell University Press.

Johnston, R. F. and Janiga, M. (1995) *Feral Pigeons*, New York: Oxford University Press.

Kant, I. (1992) *Critique of Pure Reason*, trans. N. K. Smith, London: Macmillan.

Latour, B. (1993) *We Have Never Been Modern*, trans. C. Porter, Cambridge, MA: Harvard University Press.

Leach, E. (1964) Anthropological aspects of language: animal categories and verbal abuse, in E. H. Lenneberg (ed.) *New Directions in the Study of Language*, Cambridge, MA: MIT Press.

—— (1971) Kimil: a category of Andamese thought, in P. and K. E. Maranda (eds) *Structural Analysis of Oral Tradition*, Philadelphia: University of Pennsylvania Press.

Marcus, I. M. (1985) The deindustrialization of America: homestead, a case study, 1959–1984, *Pennsylvania History* 52: 162–182.

McDowell, R. D. and Pillsbury, H. W. (1959) Wildlife damage to crops in the United States, *Journal of Wildlife Management* 23: 240–241.

Palladino, G. (1991) *Another Civil War: Labor, Capital, and the State in the Anthracite Regions of Pennsylvania, 1840–68*, Urbana: University of Illinois Press.

Scott, J. C. (1990) *Domination and the Arts of Resistance: Hidden Transcripts*, New Haven: Yale University Press.

Stallybrass, P. and White, A. (1986) *The Politics and Poetics of Transgression*, Ithaca: Cornell University Press.

Valeri, V. (2000) *The Forest of Taboos: Morality, Hunting, and Identity Among the Huaulu*, Madison: University of Wisconsin Press.

Wallace, A. C. (1987) *St Clair: A Nineteenth-Century Coal Town's Experience with a Disaster-Prone Industry*, New York: Alfred A. Knopf.

Wolensky, K. C. and Wolensky, R. (1999) Born to organize, *Pennsylvania Heritage* 25(3): 33–39.

Zizek, S. (1989) *The Sublime Object of Ideology*, London: Verso.

Chapter 11

Ducks out of water

Nature conservation as boundary maintenance

Kay Milton

Introduction

One of the most useful insights to emerge from structural anthropology was Douglas' definition of dirt as 'matter out of place' and of pollution as the confusion of categories (Douglas 1966). As Douglas and others have demonstrated, this idea can lead us to see many cultural norms and activities as instances of boundary maintenance. The incest taboo, for example, maintains the proper boundaries between categories of kin and prevents roles from becoming confused; the act of tidying the house or garden, of putting things in their proper place, re-establishes boundaries which, in the state of untidiness, have become blurred. For post-structuralist and post-modernist anthropologists, one of the main difficulties with this approach is its reliance on the subconscious. Unless people explicitly describe their own activities as boundary maintenance, it is difficult to argue that this is what they are 'really' doing without implying that it is, for them, a subconscious preoccupation. The analysis, as a consequence, looks more like an imposition than an interpretation.

There are some activities, however, in which the maintenance of boundaries appears to be conscious and explicit. Gardening is a good example: weeds are often described by gardeners as 'plants in the wrong place'. In this chapter I suggest that nature conservation might also be understood in these terms. My intention is not to impose this view, but to test it. I shall consider whether a campaign in which conservationists[1] are currently engaged makes sense as an effort to maintain particular boundaries and, if so, what role those boundaries play in the way conservationists think and act. My chosen case study is the campaign to reduce (and, if possible, eradicate) the population of ruddy ducks in the UK, which is part of an international effort to halt their spread across

Europe. I shall focus primarily on what this campaign can tell us about the culture of conservation in the UK, but because conservation is a global discourse, whose primary objective, the protection of biological diversity ('biodiversity'), is enshrined in international agreements, I would expect some of the observations made to be more widely applicable.

The campaign is unusual, in that it reverses the more common pattern of opposition between conservationists and land users. When wildfowl are seen as pests, it is usually by farmers who object, for instance, to their fields being grazed by geese (by barnacle geese on the island of Islay, for example, and by Greenland white-fronted geese in Co. Wexford in Ireland). In the ruddy duck campaign, it is the conservationists who see the birds as pests while land users are either indifferent to, or protective towards, them. In the following sections, I describe how and why the ruddy duck campaign is being conducted, before discussing it in relation to specific culturally defined boundaries. The material analysed is drawn from published statements by individual conservationists, NGOs (non-governmental organizations) and statutory agencies, press reports, journal articles and from my own discussions with some of the conservationists involved.

Ruddy ducks: the problem

The ruddy duck (*Oxyura jamaicensis*) is native to North America, where it is relatively common; its breeding population was estimated at around 600,000 individuals in the 1970s (UKRDWG 1995: 2). A few pairs were introduced into wildfowl collections in the UK during the 1940s. Captive wildfowl normally have their wings clipped to prevent them from flying away, but young ruddy ducks proved difficult to catch for this purpose. Some escaped from the Wildfowl Trust's collection in Gloucestershire in the 1950s, since when unknown numbers have escaped from this and other collections. A feral population became established and, over the next forty years, spread through the UK and on to the European continent. By 1994, the UK population was around 3,500, and there had been over 600 records of ruddy ducks from elsewhere in Europe, North Africa and the Middle East (UKRDWG 1995: 5).

At first, the presence of ruddy ducks in the UK appeared to pose no problem; 'it is causing no harm to anyone's interest, and is an attractive species with no close competitors among our native ducks' (Owen 1983: 18). But by the early 1980s conservationists were concerned that it might spread to Spain and compete or interbreed with the rare, native white-headed duck (*Oxyura leucocephala*) (Owen 1983; Smart 1983). By the early 1990s these fears had been realized. Ruddy ducks were first recorded breeding in Spain in 1991, and in the same year, the first ruddy duck–white-headed duck hybrid was seen (Stiles 1993). By the end of 1992, eighteen such hybrids had been shot (Green 1993).

Hybridization among ducks is not uncommon, and is considered a problem by conservationists because it can cause one or other of the parent species to lose its genetic distinctiveness and become, effectively, extinct in its original form. This is already happening to the Mexican duck, following hybridization with introduced mallards, a species which is also threatening the Hawaiian duck, the North American black duck and the New Zealand grey duck in the same way (Stiles 1993). Conservationists fear that a similar fate awaits the white-headed duck, if the spread of ruddy ducks across Europe is not reversed. Competition between the two species is an added threat. Ruddy ducks are reported to be aggressive and to dominate other wildfowl, particularly during the breeding season. If they compete successfully with white-headed ducks for territories and food, the range of the native species could be restricted even further, making it more vulnerable (UKRDWG 1995: 6).

European conservationists have put a lot of effort into saving the white-headed duck. In the early 1990s, estimates of its world population varied from 12,000 (Moser 1990: 19) to 19,000 (Hughes 1993), though by 1997 it was feared that the total might be as low as 5,000 (Hughes and Williams 1997: 15). It had once been distributed throughout the Mediterranean, Eastern Europe and Central Asia, but, as a result of hunting and the destruction of its wetland habitat, the population in Western Europe had been reduced to just 22 birds in Spain by 1977. Through the efforts of Spanish conservationists, this population had increased to 800 by 1993 and to over 1000 by 1997 (Hughes 1993; Hughes and Williams 1997). In the meantime, the Wildfowl Trust (later the Wildfowl and Wetlands Trust) in the UK had been helping to conserve the white-headed duck in Hungary (Ounsted 1985). Conservationists are afraid that the expanding ruddy duck population will not only overwhelm the white-headed duck in Spain, but will also spread east and eventually threaten the white-headed duck throughout its current range.

The campaign

Ruddy ducks and hybrids have been shot in Spain since their first appearance there in 1991, but the Spanish authorities requested that action be taken throughout Europe to halt and reverse the spread of the ruddy duck. This request is consistent with the understanding that the conservation of biodiversity is an international obligation, sanctioned by European law, in the form of the Birds Directive (and more recently the Habitats Directive), and by other international agreements, the most relevant of which is the Berne Convention.[2] The UK is seen as bearing particular responsibility in this instance, because of the understanding that ruddy ducks first entered Europe through British wildfowl collections.[3]

Within the UK, the Wildfowl and Wetlands Trust (WWT), from whose collections the ducks first escaped, acknowledged its own responsibility (Hughes and Williams 1997: 19) and took a leading role in the campaign. In 1992, after discussions with Spanish conservationists, the WWT alerted the UK government to the problem. At an international workshop in March 1993, delegates agreed to halt and reverse the population and range expansion of the ruddy duck in the Western Palearctic,[4] in order to safeguard populations of the white-headed duck (IWWRB *et al.* 1993: 1). The UK Ruddy Duck Working Group (UKRDWG), consisting of representatives from statutory conservation bodies and NGOs, was established to consider ways of halting and reversing the expansion of the ruddy duck population within the UK.

Between 1993 and 1995 the WWT, funded by the UK government, tested the feasibility of reducing the ruddy duck population on their breeding grounds and at their wintering sites, using a variety of methods (shooting, trapping and dipping eggs in liquid paraffin). This research identified shooting during the breeding season as the most successful method and indicated, to the satisfaction of the UKRDWG, that this could be done without harming or significantly disturbing any other species of bird (UKRDWG 1995: 8). The UKRDWG recommended that this approach be tested more extensively by the statutory conservation agencies in two breeding areas, one in England and one in Wales. These trials were scheduled for the 1996 and 1997 breeding seasons, but, when the time came, both conservation agencies refused to carry them out. The English agency argued that they would cost too much and expressed the view that, in any case, effective reduction of the ruddy duck population is not feasible. The Welsh conservation agency took a contrasting view, that the feasibility of reduction has already been proven by the WWT's research and that, for this reason, further work in Wales is unnecessary and pointless until there is a commitment to continue with the programme in England (Hughes and Williams 1997: 17).

Not surprisingly, this lack of action incurred the displeasure of conservationists in Europe, who saw it as a breach of the UK's international obligations. In 1997, a group of bird experts meeting under the auspices of the Berne Convention, recommended that the governments which had signed the Convention 'take actions without further delay to develop and implement control strategies to eradicate ruddy duck from their respective countries' (BirdLife International 1997). In 1998, in response to this international pressure, the UK government set up the White-headed Duck Task Force,[5] to report on the most cost-effective method of carrying out a trial cull of the ruddy duck. In the following February it was announced that this long-awaited trial would take place during the 1999 breeding season, and would be funded by the UK government.

Killing animals is always a sensitive issue in the UK. The organizations involved in the campaign have made efforts, from the start, to ensure that the public and, in the case of organizations like the WWT and the Royal Society for the Protection of Birds (RSPB), their own members, understand and, as far as possible, support their actions. These efforts appear to have been quite successful, in that by May 1999 there had been no major public outcry against the campaign. There has been some opposition, however. In 1993 a small group in Sussex started the 'Save the Ruddy Duck Campaign' (see note 3) and distributed car stickers and information sheets, but failed to win widespread support. In 1995, after the decision had been taken to attempt a trial cull, some landowners refused to allow access to their land for this purpose. Since 1995, the NGO Animal Aid has held a number of protests against the proposed cull, and its representatives have spoken out against it through the media. In addition, individual writers have, from time to time, taken a critical stance (for instance Vidal 1993; Lawson 1996; 1999). Much of this opposition comes from those who question the morality of the campaign from an animal rights perspective: whether it is right to kill large numbers of individual birds in order to conserve a species. Although there is a degree of overlap, both in aims and in personnel, between the conservation and animal rights lobbies, conservationists prefer to distance themselves from arguments about the rights of individuals.

My purpose here is not to discuss the rights and wrongs of the campaign, nor to present a fully balanced account of it, but to explore what it can tell us about the way conservationists understand the world. I have mentioned the opposition to the campaign, and briefly described its character, because it has provided a context for contesting, and thereby testing, the boundaries identified below as part of the culture of conservation.

The boundaries

I suggest that three culturally defined boundaries, of varying degrees of inclusiveness, are recognized and invoked by conservationists engaged in the ruddy duck campaign. The least inclusive is the boundary between the two species. Without the explicit recognition that white-headed ducks and ruddy ducks are distinct from one another, the campaign would simply make no sense, because it would have no purpose. The second boundary, more inclusive but no less explicit than the first, is the boundary between natives and aliens. The white-headed duck is a native of Europe while the ruddy duck is an alien from North America. In the literature that surrounds the campaign, the ruddy duck is presented as an alien twice over. From a Spanish and European continental viewpoint it is not only American but also an invader from the UK: if ruddy ducks had remained there, they would not currently pose a threat to Europe's biodiversity.

The third boundary, the most inclusive of the three but also the least explicit, is that between human and non-human processes (often referred to in the social science literature as 'culture' and 'nature' respectively). The presence of the white-headed duck in Europe is a 'natural' phenomenon; it is there because it either evolved there or arrived under its own steam or was assisted by some other non-human power. The ruddy duck was brought to the UK by human agency and permitted to colonize Europe through human carelessness. Thus its presence in Europe is not natural; as one conservationist stated during a discussion, it has 'nothing to do with nature'.

I have referred to these boundaries as 'culturally defined'. It is worth spelling out what I mean by this, given that culture is understood in several different ways both within and outside anthropology. I treat culture as having both a general and a specific meaning. In its general sense, it refers to people's understanding of the world, the sum total of human perceptions and interpretations.[6] In this sense, the boundaries identified above are culturally defined simply because they are part of human understanding. In its more specific sense, a culture is a way of understanding the world that is associated with a particular society or category of people. In this sense we can speak of 'English culture' or 'youth culture'. The boundaries identified above belong, in this sense, to a 'conservationist culture', a way of understanding that is held by conservationists and which is continually reinforced and modified through their ongoing discourse about conservation. None of this is intended to imply that the boundaries are not 'real' – I do not consider it part of an anthropologist's role to judge the truth of the ideas they analyse. But like all ideas they can be contested, as they have been in the context of the ruddy duck debate.

It is one thing to suggest that conservationists engaged in the campaign recognize and invoke the boundaries between species, between natives and aliens and between human and non-human (or 'natural') processes. It is quite a different matter to suggest, on this basis, that conservation is an activity primarily concerned with the maintenance of these boundaries. In order to test this, I need to consider the role of each boundary within the campaign and in the wider context of conservation.

Keeping the species apart

The boundary between the two species provides the campaign with its central focus. The objective of the campaign is to maintain this boundary, by reducing the opportunities for ruddy ducks and white-headed ducks to mix, and ultimately by keeping them apart altogether. This objective is rationalized as part of the commitment to conserve biodiversity, which is said to mean 'the variety of life' (HMSO 1995: 12).[7] The loss of a species amounts to a reduction in biodiversity, so a great deal of conservation effort is aimed at preventing this. Many of the species that attract the attention of conservationists are endangered because their habitat is being destroyed, or because they are the victims of human activities such as hunting. In such cases, conservationists concentrate their efforts on protecting and restoring habitat and campaigning to change the human activities that present a threat. They also try to return endangered species to areas from which they have disappeared. These are precisely the measures that have been taken over the past twenty years to conserve the white-headed duck, both in Spain and in Eastern Europe (Ounsted 1985). Thus, conservation does not always require species to be kept physically apart, but when the threat comes from another species, through predation or, as in the case of the white-headed duck, competition and hybridization, keeping them apart becomes an important objective.

Some opponents of the ruddy duck campaign have challenged this objective by questioning whether the ruddy duck and the white-headed duck really are distinct species. Lawson quoted Steve Jones, a leading geneticist, as saying, 'In the birds . . . many [species] are probably not real at all – perhaps the ruddy and the white-headed are like this' (Lawson 1996: 30). Indeed, within biology, the question of how species are distinguished is a matter of continuous debate. But this argument is less significant, in the ruddy duck context, than its advocates might think. Biodiversity is recognized as existing within, as well as between, species; in other words, diverse populations of the same species still constitute biodiversity. The important issue for conservationists is not so much, 'are the ruddy and white-headed ducks different *species*?', as simply, 'are they different?' Since they can easily be distinguished visually, and also differ genetically (Lawson 1996), the boundary between them would still constitute biodiversity, and would still be considered worth maintaining, even if they were reclassified as varieties of a single species.

A slightly different but closely related argument employed by some critics of the campaign is that the boundary is not significant outside science, and certainly not in the world outside human understanding. Lawson argued that the boundary is defined by criteria which, though important to biologists, are clearly of no significance to the ducks (ibid.: 29). The implication is that the conservationists are seeking to preserve their own categories, rather than something of significance in the 'real' world.[8] This view was echoed by Paul Evans:

> The ruddy duck is a problem created by conservationists for conservationists . . . Science still sees nature as a collection of separate things, united by causal laws, and decrees that all the bits must be maintained. The reality is that nature is in a constant state of flux.
> (Quoted in Vidal 1993)

Such arguments come close to what some anthropologists say about culture in general. An important part of Douglas' (1966) model is that cultural categories are by definition symbolic; their function is to make the world meaningful by representing reality to us. When we seek, through our actions, to protect those categories, by maintaining the boundaries that separate them, we are preserving our own understanding of the world. As I have already pointed out, the question of whether that understanding is accurate, of whether the categories are 'real', is not an anthropological issue, though it is clearly very important in the context of everyday life and in the work of scientists who set out specifically to understand the real world.

There are signs in the ruddy duck debate that some conservationists would not disagree with the view that judgements about what to conserve are, to an extent, arbitrary. Steve Jones was quoted as saying, 'Tens of thousands of bacterial "species" are probably extinguished each year – but nobody cares, although they are more distinct than any bird from any other' (in Lawson 1996: 30). And the point made by Paul Evans (above), that nature is in a constant state of flux, is fully accepted by biologists who believe that existing species have evolved from earlier ones. Chris Tydeman, of the World Wide Fund for Nature (WWF), was quoted as saying, in relation to the ruddy duck issue, 'The scientific basis is that we have reached a moment in time where we say that enough is enough and people want to keep species as they are, as opposed to letting them progress to something else' (Vidal 1993: 3). This looks like an admission that the conservation of biodiversity is, in effect, an attempt to halt the process of evolution.

Natives and aliens: ruddy ducks as 'dirt'

In virtually all the literature generated by the ruddy duck campaign, its status as an alien species is conspicuously reported. The conservation organizations, from the start, presented the duck as an import from America; its alien status within the UK was, for them, a central consideration. In the general media, and particularly in the popular press, ruddy ducks were presented initially as British and only later as American. Although much of this coverage is contradictory and inaccurate when judged against the conservation literature and official reports (such as Stiles 1993, UKRDWG 1995), it nevertheless reflects the shifting emphases in the conservationists' own presentation of the issue.

In 1993, when the first major decisions in the campaign were being taken, conservationists were concerned to stress the UK's responsibility for the threat to white-headed ducks in Spain. At that stage, it was not clear what action might be appropriate, but the important message was that, since the ducks causing the problem appeared to have spread from Britain, the UK must be prepared to act. In many of the press reports from 1993, ruddy ducks were presented as a British nuisance abroad, and inevitably compared with another famous British nuisance, the 'lager lout', a stereotyped rogue male holiday-maker who invades Spain each summer. Surprisingly, this comparison appears to have originated, not with the popular press, but with a government official, who was reported to have said, 'Ruddy ducks are the lager louts of the bird world. They have been mating their way across Europe' (*Sunday Express*, 24 January 1993).

In 1995, when the decision was taken to attempt a regional cull of ruddy ducks, conservationists had a different priority: to persuade the British public to accept the deliberate shooting of birds, during the breeding season, in the name of conservation. Part of the justification for this was the argument that the ducks did not really belong in the UK. In the resulting wave of publicity, they were described (misleadingly) as a 'US invasion'. At least one writer, who opposed the campaign, noted a comparison with American GIs stationed in the UK during the Second World War, and modified a famous descriptive phrase to suit the situation: 'Over-plumed, over-sexed and over here' (Ryder 1995).

The impression created by the ruddy duck campaign is of conservationists concerned to restore an order which has been disrupted by things getting out of place. Ruddy ducks belong in America. As a result of being brought to Europe and allowed to get out of control, they are threatening the proper order of things by confusing the boundary between themselves and another species. This image accords well with Douglas' model of dirt as 'matter out of place' (Douglas 1966). According to this model, our definition of something as 'dirt', as a polluting influence to be eliminated, depends on its location. Soil in the garden is appropriate, but soil on the carpet is dirt; food on our plates is desirable, but food on the floor should be cleaned away; dandelions in a hedgerow are wild flowers, but in a garden lawn they are weeds. A dirty world is a disordered world, one in which our understanding of what should be is challenged by what we see around us. When we tidy up our environment we re-order our world, re-establishing the proper boundaries and protecting our understanding of what should be. It would be easy to see the ruddy duck campaign as precisely this kind of activity: an attempt to restore order by eliminating a transgressor of boundaries.

But would this be a realistic characterization of the campaign or of conservation in general? Is this what conservationists are 'really' doing? There are two main points to be made in response to this question. First, there are instances of alien species whose presence, while not necessarily considered desirable by conservationists, is tolerated. These include the pheasant, introduced into Britain by the Normans (or the Romans) and now one of the most common birds in the UK, and the Egyptian goose, of which a population of around 1,000 has become established in eastern England (see Gibbons *et al.* 1993). And, of course, the ruddy duck itself was tolerated before its threat to the white-headed duck was recognized. It could be argued that the selective tolerance of certain aliens is largely a matter of resources and that conservationists might attempt to remove all alien species if they could afford to do so.[9] But this just serves to demonstrate that the elimination of aliens is not, in itself, the top priority.

Second, there are instances in which the presence of an alien species is not only tolerated, but welcomed as a contribution to its own survival. These include the golden pheasant, which is rare in its native China and has a UK population of 1,000–2,000 birds, and the Mandarin duck, also a native of the Far East, whose UK population exceeds that in any other country except Japan (Gibbons *et al.* 1993: 64–65). In 1995, when questioned in relation to the ruddy duck campaign, a representative of the RSPB said that their policy is to take each case on its merits, and pointed out that the UK might ultimately prove to be the last refuge for the Mandarin duck (Brown 1995). The implication is that, if the ruddy duck were endangered in its native land, then some other way of removing its threat to the white-headed duck would have to be found, one that did not involve eradicating the UK population.

A more detailed understanding of the values conservationists place on alien and native species can be gained by comparing their responses to problems caused by aliens with their responses to problems caused by natives. When an alien species poses a threat to biodiversity, then provided that species is not, itself, endangered, its eradication is treated as an option. This is clear in the case of the ruddy duck and also in cases where islands are cleared of introduced predators, such as cats and rats, which threaten ground-nesting birds. Attempts have been made over several years to remove ferrets from Rathlin Island, off the north coast of Ireland, and conservationists are currently discussing ways of removing hedgehogs from the Western Isles, in Scotland, where they threaten the breeding populations of wading birds. In both these instances, the total eradication of the offending predators is considered desirable, if not necessarily feasible.

When native species are seen as posing a threat, eradication is not treated as an option. If the problem species is a common one, as in the case of foxes or crows in the UK preying on rare birds, then killing the predators is considered an acceptable solution, but the objective is not to eradicate, since this would, in itself, reduce biodiversity. If the problem species is itself rare or vulnerable, conservationists seek a solution which does not involve reducing its population. For instance, when peregrines began to prey on roseate terns on the island of Anglesey a few years ago, the terns were provided with shelters under which they could keep out of sight of the peregrines.

It appears, then, that the removal of alien species is not the overriding consideration for conservationists. Their primary objective remains the conservation of biodiversity, which requires them to value species, above all, in terms of their rarity and vulnerability to extinction. Nevertheless, the distinction between aliens and natives is important in conservationists' perspective on the world, in giving them a clear understanding of which species belong where. It also provides a secondary criterion (rarity being the primary one) for valuing some species more highly than others, and therefore guides their responses to specific conservation problems. To my knowledge, no one who opposes the ruddy duck campaign has tried to argue that the ducks are not, in fact, an alien species in the UK. But the basis on which aliens are distinguished from natives is frequently contested in the wider context of conservation discourse. This leads directly to the third boundary identified above: that between human and non-human (or 'natural') processes.

The human and the natural

The distinction between natives and aliens, which is so central to the ruddy duck campaign, depends on the more fundamental distinction between human and non-human processes. Hughes (1993) states that the threat to the white-headed duck 'would not exist under completely natural circumstances since the Ruddy Duck is Native to North America'. Under natural circumstances, the ruddy duck would have remained in its native land; its presence in Europe is not 'completely natural' because it is a product of human activity. By enabling species to be identified as native or alien, the distinction between human and non-human processes guides the actions of conservationists in the manner described above. Whenever the overriding consideration, the protection of biodiversity, allows, it helps them to decide which species take priority over others.

But this is not the only use conservationists make of the distinction between human and non-human processes. For nature conservationists, as distinct from conservationists in general (see note 1), it defines the limits of their concern. Nature conservationists, by definition, conserve what is natural and without an understanding of what is natural and what is not, they would have no basis for taking decisions about which issues to become involved in. This is not to say that the products of human activity are not considered worthy of conservation. There are organizations dedicated to the protection of historic buildings and of rare varieties of domestic animals and plants. But these are not the concerns of those who regard themselves and are regarded by others, as nature conservationists. Thus the distinction defines a broad division of labour within the conservation movement.[10] But again, I would suggest that this is not the extent of its role in conservation discourse; it is not simply an instrument for allocating areas of concern and a guide for deciding how to deal with problem species.

What gives the distinction between human and non-human processes a greater importance for conservationists is the fact that 'naturalness', in the sense of freedom from human interference, is seen as a quality worth conserving in itself. For instance, in the selection of sites for designation as nature reserves, naturalness has been an important criterion (Ratcliffe 1977; Moore 1987). Ratcliffe described this concern for the natural as 'almost incidental' and essentially a practical solution to the problem of how to define the best sites for nature conservation (Ratcliffe 1997: 35). For more than a century biologists have observed that, in general, human management of the land significantly reduces the number of species able to survive on it.[11] So naturalness came to be used as a shorthand indicator of species richness. In other words, even when naturalness appears to be a primary criterion for conservation, in reality it is subordinate to biodiversity. But Ratcliffe also observed that naturalness is valued because it is rare. In the UK, conservationists have long recognized that almost the entire landscape bears the mark of human use, so it is not surprising that naturalness should, itself, have acquired rarity value. But, as Ratcliffe pointed out (1997: 37), even in countries where a much larger proportion of the land is relatively unaffected by human activity, habitats such as old-growth forest are marked out for special protection.

Once naturalness is, itself, an object of conservation concern,[12] then it becomes important to conservationists to maintain the boundary between the natural and the non-natural, between human and non-human processes, just as it is important to maintain the boundaries that separate different species. This was emphasized, for me, during a discussion about the ruddy duck campaign, when I suggested that the genetic purity of the white-headed duck might be preserved through cloning (assuming, of course, that the technique could be made sufficiently safe and reliable). One participant in the discussion said that this would be like building a replica of a cathedral while allowing the original to be destroyed. What makes the difference, the only difference, between a 'natural' white-headed duck and its clone is the human intervention involved in the production of the latter. What is implied here is that this also makes the difference between 'real' nature and 'artificial' nature, between what is authentic and a degraded and devalued copy.

There are two ways in which the boundary between the human and the non-human is contested in conservation discourse. First, the significance of the boundary is questioned by the observation that conservation is, itself, a human activity, a form of intervention in nature, and that the management of habitats for biodiversity, the captive breeding and reintroduction of species to areas from which they have disappeared, are no less artificial than techniques such as cloning. Second, the foundations of the boundary are questioned by the argument that humanity is a part of nature rather than separate from it (Evans 1996). Those who oppose the ruddy duck campaign present it, metaphorically, in human terms, as ethnic cleansing, xenophobia and genocide (see Vidal 1993; Brown 1999), challenging the morality of treating non-human nature in ways that are condemned when directed at human beings. This challenge is issued, not surprisingly, by those who seek to extend our sphere of moral concern to non-human animals. But it is also supported by the more ecocentric thinkers within the environmental lobby, who argue that, from an ecological viewpoint, humanity is just one species among many, with no special right to dictate the fate of the others.

Conclusion

What does the above analysis tell us about the culture of conservation in the UK? It appears to reinforce Ellen's observations on the multi-dimensional character of the western concept of nature, and describes one particular variant of this concept. Ellen divided our understanding of nature into three dimensions: nature as 'things', nature as 'space which is not human' and nature as inner essence (Ellen 1996: 105ff.). The first two dimensions would appear to be particularly prominent in the conservationist worldview. As Evans observed, with regard to the ruddy duck campaign, science (on which most conservationists rely for their information about nature) represents nature as a collection of separate things (see Vidal 1993 and above), which together constitute biodiversity. Nature is also seen as separate from humanity; the boundary between human and non-human processes defines the natural. The conservation of nature, as conservationists understand it, thus requires the preservation both of the separate things that constitute nature (the species, sub-species and ecosystems) and of the quality that makes them natural (their independence from human influence).

This makes conservation, inevitably, a boundary maintaining exercise. In order to conserve the things that constitute nature, the boundaries that separate them must be maintained,[13] and in order to conserve nature's 'naturalness', the boundary between the human and the non-human must be preserved. So it is not surprising if conservationists sometimes appear, when viewed through the filter of Douglas' model of symbolic classification, to be acting like nature's housekeepers, obsessively restoring order by putting things where they belong – eliminating species that are in the wrong place, returning them to where they used to be – tidying up the mess that others (sometimes, ironically, other conservationists) have created. This appearance is particularly strong in cases such as the ruddy duck campaign, in which several boundaries come into play at once. The objective is to maintain the boundary between two species. The measures required to do this are justified in terms of the boundary between the human and the natural, through the mediation of yet another boundary, between natives and aliens.

But the boundaries with which conservationists concern themselves do not always coalesce in this way. Sometimes it is necessary to tolerate an unnatural situation, such as the presence of an alien species, in order to serve the higher purpose of conserving biodiversity. Thus the Mandarin duck is accepted in the UK, where it does not naturally belong, because to eradicate it would make its global extinction more likely, and so would threaten biodiversity. And ultimately, the very project of nature conservation is contradictory, since it seeks to conserve what is natural through unnatural means (human agency). If a species can be conserved only through human intervention, in what sense can conservationists regard its continued existence as a natural phenomenon? In other words, in what sense can they claim, in such instances, to be conserving *nature*?

These observations suggest that, while conservationists in the UK are reasonably secure in their understanding of nature as a collection of things that should be preserved, they are much more ambivalent about its separation from humanity. In the practice of conservation, the boundary between the human and the natural is often obscured in the interests of conserving biodiversity. And yet, if they were to abandon this distinction (see Milton 1997), conservationists would lose an important source of value and justification for their work, and their main criterion for defining their area of concern. Indeed, without a distinction between human and non-human processes, nature conservation as we know it would become a meaningless exercise. For this reason we can expect conservationists to cling to their understanding that nature is distinct from the products of human activity, even though that understanding is continually challenged by their own activities.

Acknowledgements

For comments on this and closely related work and for information on the ruddy duck campaign, I am grateful to the following people: John Stewart, Gwyn Williams, Mike Clarke, Jeremy Greenwood, James Orr, Kim Stiles and participants in seminars at Manchester University and the University of Kent.

Notes

1 Unless otherwise indicated, when the terms 'conservation' and 'conservationist' are used in this chapter, they refer specifically to nature conservation, and not to conservation in its more general sense. This distinction is discussed later in the chapter.
2 The Berne Convention, The Convention on the Conservation of European Wildlife and Natural Habitats, was agreed by the Council of Europe in 1979 and came into force in 1982.
3 This has been questioned by some opponents of the campaign, who have asked whether ruddy ducks on the continent might have escaped from continental collections, and suggested that if other European countries effectively control their own ruddy duck populations, there is no need to 'conduct a massacre' in Britain (Information Sheet, The Save the Ruddy Duck Campaign, 1993).
4 The 'Western Palearctic' covers Europe, North Africa and parts of the Middle East (for more detail, see Beaman and Madge 1998: 9).
5 This was, effectively, the Ruddy Duck Working Group under a different name. The RDWG had 'become moribund' (Hughes and Williams 1997: 17) due to the lack of progress in implementing its recommendations. The name change emphasized the positive objective of the campaign, to conserve the endangered white-headed duck, over its more negative and more controversial aim of eradicating the ruddy duck in Britain.
6 Strictly speaking, this should be referred to as 'human culture', since I see no reason to deny the possession of culture to non-human animals, but to introduce this point into the argument would complicate it unnecessarily. (For a detailed discussion of the concept of culture see Milton 1996.)
7 For a critique of this view, see Evans (1996).
8 For a more detailed discussion of this point, see Milton (1997).
9 Conservationists who are recognized by their colleagues as purists are expected to hold this view (see Brown 1995).
10 This division of labour is not absolute. For instance, the National Trust is dedicated to the preservation of places of historic interest *and* natural beauty.
11 It is also accepted that, when looked at over a much longer period, human activity has helped to increase biodiversity by creating a patchwork of habitats through, for instance, different types of farming. Paradoxically, some of the habitats conservationists now seek to conserve, such as hedgerows, are products of human activity.
12 For a more detailed discussion of this point, see Milton (1999).
13 The preservation of the things that constitute nature is, as we have seen, selective, and not surprisingly confined to nature that is seen as relatively benign. There is no sign of support for the conservation of flu viruses, and although there was discussion, a few years ago, about whether the smallpox virus remaining in laboratories should be preserved, no one has suggested that it should be returned to areas where it once thrived.

References

Beaman, M. and Madge, S. (1998) *The Handbook of Bird Identification for Europe and the Western Palearctic*, London: Christopher Helm.

BirdLife International (1997) Ruddy duck set-back, *BirdLife in Europe* 2(2): 1.

Brown, P. (1995) Feathers fly over calls to cull alien birds, *The Guardian*, 1 July 1995.

—— (1999) Ruddy ducks threatened with genocide to save one species from being threatened by another, *The Guardian*, 2 February 1999.

Douglas, M. (1966) *Purity and Danger: An Analysis of Concepts of Pollution and Taboo*, London: Routledge & Kegan Paul.

Ellen, R. F. (1996) The cognitive geometry of nature: a contextual approach, in P. Descola and G. Pálsson (eds) *Nature and Society: Anthropological Perspectives*, London and New York: Routledge.

Evans, P. (1996) Biodiversity: nature for nerds? *Ecos: A Review of Conservation* 17(2): 7–12.

Gibbons, D. W., Reid, J. B. and Chapman, R. A. (1993) *The New Atlas of Breeding Birds in Britain and Ireland: 1988–1991*, London: T. and A. D. Poyser.

Green, A. (1993) Ruddy duck debate, *Birds Magazine*, Autumn: 82.

HMSO (1995) *Biodiversity: The UK Steering Group Report*, Vol. 1, London: Her Majesty's Stationery Office.

Hughes, B. (1993) Stiff-tail threat, *BTO News* 185: 14.

Hughes, B. and Williams, G. (1997) What future for the white-headed duck?, *Ecos: A Review of Conservation* 18(2): 15–19.

IWWRB (International Waterfowl and Wetlands Research Bureau) *et al.* (1993) *International Oxyura jamaicensis Workshop, 1–2 March 1993, Arundel, United Kingdom: Summary and Recommendations*, London: IWWRB, Department of the Environment and Joint Nature Conservation Committee.

Lawson, T. (1996) Brent duck, *Ecos: A Review of Conservation* 17(2): 27–35.

—— (1999) A shot in the foot, *The Guardian*, 10 February.

Milton, K. (1996) *Environmentalism and Cultural Theory: Exploring the Role of Anthropology in Environmental Discourse*, London and New York: Routledge.

—— (1997) Nature, culture and biodiversity, in F. Arler and I. Svennevig (eds) *Cross-cultural Protection of Nature and the Environment*, Odense: Odense University Press.

—— (1999) Nature is already sacred, *Environmental Values* 8, 4: 437–449.

Moore, N. (1987) *The Bird of Time*, Cambridge: Cambridge University Press.

Moser, M. (1990) The Trust's international partner, *Wildfowl and Wetlands: The Magazine of the Wildfowl and Wetlands Trust*, 102: 18–19.

Ounsted, M. (1985) Fragile eggs to Hungary, *Wildfowl World: the Wildfowl Trust Magazine*, 92: 16–22.

Owen, M. (1983) The aliens, *Wildfowl World: The Wildfowl Trust Magazine*, 89: 16–18.

Ratcliffe, D. A. (ed.) (1977) *A Nature Conservation Review*, Cambridge: Cambridge University Press.

—— (1997) The importance of the natural, *Ecos: A Review of Conservation* 18(3/4): 34–7.

Ryder, R. (1995) Hands off our ruddy ducks, *The Guardian*, 1 July.

Smart, M. (1983) A stiff problem of survival, *Wildfowl World: The Wildfowl Trust Magazine*, 89: 8–9.

Stiles, K. (1993) Newsdesk: those ruddy ducks, *Wildfowl and Wetlands: The Magazine of the Wildfowl and Wetlands Trust*, 108: 5–6.

UKRDWG (United Kingdom Ruddy Duck Working Group) (1995) *Information Note*, Peterborough: Joint Nature Conservation Committee.

Vidal, J. (1993) Hasta la vista ruddy duck, *The Guardian*, 28 May.

Index

affordances 105, 107, 108, 113, 114, 119, 121, 135, 142
Ainu 155, 157
Animal Aid 233
animal intelligence 69, 80, 81, 99, 180, 203
animal intentionality 73, 132, 143
animal rights 21, 74, 189, 203, 212–217, 223, 233
animals: in advertising 176; in the media 21, 147, 149, 152, 153, 155, 163, 170, 181, 209, 212, 213, 214, 216, 223, 224, 225, 233, 237
animism 171
anomalous animals 14, 15, 18, 26, 98
antelope 14, 36, 47, 64, 141
anthropocentrism 24
anthropomorphic 16, 20, 57, 161
Atlantic trade 89; and ivory 60; in southern Cameroon 60
authenticity 170, 171, 184, 185

baboons 2, 17, 39, 42, 44–48
bachelors 160
Baka (Pygmies) 18, 48–76, 155
Bantu 18, 54, 58, 60–67
Barth, F. 108, 109
Beach, H. 171, 178–180, 183
bears: attacks on livestock 1, 4, 18, 21, 23, 148; attacks on people 146, 147, 149, 150, 152, 153; bark-stripping 149, 161; crop-raiding 16, 21, 125, 126, 149, 150, 157, 162, 165; extinction of 148, 155, 156; gall of 148; hunting of 128, 145, 148, 151–154, 158, 159, 163; pity for 159, 160; sympathy for 8, 143, 146, 147, 155, 158–160, 162, 165
beasts of chase 190, 191
beasts of prey 38, 41, 190
bee-hives 149, 152
'big men' 81, 85, 87, 92, 95
biodiversity 2, 53, 70, 138, 139, 141, 142, 144, 230, 232, 234–237, 239–245
Bird-David, N. 54, 57, 68, 69, 142
Bloch, M. 108, 117, 122
Bodhisattva 146
boundaries 12, 15, 18, 22, 89, 98, 128, 214, 229, 230, 233–236, 238, 241–243
boundary maintenance 79, 229
bride shortage 157, 158, 160
buffer zones 125, 126, 142
bushidô 154

Cameroon 1, 50; Baka (Pygmies) 50, 52, 60, 68; black market for ivory 52, 53, 56
'cannibalism' 78, 81, 82, 84, 87–93, 95, 97
Cartmill, M. 196
cats 1, 15, 140, 174, 204, 224, 239
cattle 1, 4, 41, 130, 137, 148, 206
'celebrity' wildlife 187
Chaucer, G. 191, 207
chiefs 18, 19, 61, 82, 84–86, 89, 90–92, 95, 97, 134. 135, 137

children 1, 78, 39, 40, 45, 50, 52, 64, 66, 67, 80, 81, 85, 88, 93, 94–96, 98, 147, 153, 154, 160, 176, 178, 180, 216, 222
children's games 7
chimpanzee: fruit tree raids of 80; human chimpanzees 18, 95; infanticide 81; intelligence of 80, 81; sexual violence of 81; violence of 18, 19, 79, 80, 81, 84
CITES 56
civil war 19, 95, 97
cloning 241
coal-mining 213
co-existence 10, 156
co-management 12
cognition 107, 108
colonial authorities 90, 92
Comaroff, J.and J. 53
comedy 132, 136, 139
commensalism 6
commodification 98
communal hunts 38, 45
communism 224
compensation 8, 126, 128, 142, 181, 182
condors 174
conservation 1, 233, 235, 240–242; agencies 71, 124, 181, 232, 237; areas 12, 39, 42, 48; of bears 145, 155, 157, 163, 164; of biodiversity 70, 232, 233, 235, 237, 239, 240; of chimpanzees 78, 97, 98; discourse on 53, 78, 129, 230, 234, 240, 241; of ducks 229, 237, 238; of elephants 53, 56, 70, 71; incentives 13, 97; of nature 229, 241–243; of wildlife 1, 6, 12, 21, 22, 46, 47, 70, 124, 145, 155, 157, 228; of wolves 170, 174, 187
conservationism 3, 11–13, 21, 23, 155, 170, 187; exclusionary 12
conservationist culture 234
conservationists 12, 21, 46, 78, 97, 98, 129, 142, 149, 152, 155, 156, 163, 229, 230–243
conservative values 213, 214
constructivist anthropology 105, 120
crimes 93, 152, 161, 163, 207

crocodile 1, 4, 6, 17, 78, 87, 91, 93, 94
crop-raiding 2, 6, 8, 18, 21, 36, 42; baboon 2, 15, 42, 44–48; bear 2, 4, 16, 21, 125, 126, 148–152, 156, 159, 162; chimpanzee 2, 15, 18; elephant 1, 2, 18, 58, 42–45, 56, 57; monkey 1, 44, 48; pigeon 2, 38, 125, 126, 130, 140, 215–218; wild pig 1, 2, 4, 7, 13, 18, 19, 42, 44, 45, 48, 102, 110, 112, 116, 126, 127, 130, 140, 142
crows 1, 16, 239
cull 12, 13, 158, 233, 237
culling 4, 21, 142, 124, 147, 151–156, 158, 160, 200, 203, 207
cultural knowledge 108, 117, 120
cultural symbols 120
curfew 151

dairying 127, 132
deer: barking deer 128, 131; deer dances 8; musk deer 131
direct perception 104–108, 113, 114, 120, 121
dogs 1, 17, 40, 41, 45, 147, 151, 152, 159, 173, 204
dolphins 174
Douglas, M. 14, 15, 22, 79, 89 90, 105, 106, 120, 224, 229, 236, 238, 242
drums 43, 180
dualism 138
ducks: Hawaiian duck 231; Mandarin duck 239, 243; Mexican duck 231; New Zealand grey duck 231; North American black duck 231; ruddy duck 12, 21, 230–43; white-headed duck 230–35, 238–41

eagles 1, 174, 176, 181
ecological anthropology 104, 106, 114, 121, 142
ecological psychology 105
edibility 204
Egyptian goose 238
elephants: attacks of 51, 58, 64; Baka typology of 62; crop-raiding by 1, 2, 18, 58, 42–45, 56, 57; as forest

ancestors 55; hunting of 52, 54, 56–58, 61, 63, 64, 67–69; shapeshifters (*mòkìlà*) 50–54, 64–70; spirits 57
embodiment 54, 146
environment 57, 59, 62, 69, 70, 104–109, 113–115, 117–121, 129, 148, 155, 197, 206, 218, 238; culturally constructed 104, 200
environmental perception 104, 105, 117, 120
environmentalism 6, 171, 171, 184
environmentalists 141, 181
eradication 4, 13, 157, 239
ethnobiology 129
European Community 71, 187
evil 15, 65, 104, 111, 115, 116, 153, 183, 186

famine 43
fear 17, 18–20, 41, 42, 48, 67, 69, 78, 79, 93, 95, 97, 110, 114, 145, 146, 153, 156–159, 174, 175, 180, 219, 231
feld, S. 106, 114
field-guarding 7, 38
fierceness 20, 175, 176
fines 7
fires 40, 55
forestry 39, 148–150
forestry damage 2
foxes 2, 15, 174, 181, 189; attacks on livestock 189, 190, 191, 201, 202, 207, 208; control of 189, 192, 194, 195, 199, 200–203, 205, 207; as criminals 16; hunting of 8, 9, 15, 189–195, 197, 198, 200, 202–204; as noble 191; as rogue 190, 192, 202; as thieves 191; as villains 191, 192, 208, 214, 223
Fund for Animals 214, 223

Gabon 60; animal behaviour in secondary forest 57; forest dwelling cultivators 56
Geertz, C. 105, 106, 108, 111
goats 40, 41, 126, 130, 135
Golden pheasant 238

golf-courses 161
goral 131
granaries 43
graveyards 151

habitat loss 11, 148, 161
hares 190, 191, 197
Harner, M. 173
hedgehogs 6, 239
hierarchy 70, 91, 92, 137
hikers 149, 150
hippo 1, 36, 44, 47, 48
honey 6, 62, 149, 152
horses 8, 189, 192, 193, 195, 198–200
hounds 154, 163, 190–195, 197–200, 203, 205, 208, 209
hunter-gatherers 10, 18, 68, 69; metaphors 69; sharing relations 68, 69
hunting 3, 7, 37, 39, 40 45, 46, 59, 62, 64, 65, 68, 86, 93, 94, 106, 131, 132, 141, 170, 177, 179, 181, 196–199, 202, 205, 208, 209, 213, 231; of bears 128, 145, 148, 151–154, 158, 159, 163; of elephants 52, 54, 56–58, 61, 63, 64, 67–69; of foxes 8, 9, 15, 189–195, 197, 198, 200, 202–204; garden 4; magic 52, 65, 69, 94; master hunters 58; pressure 56; rituals 57, 58; spirits 57, 58, 59, 67, 106; of wolves 7, 8, 170, 175, 177, 180; of wild pigs 106, 107, 110, 113, 128, 129
hybrids 64, 231
hyenas 15, 39–41, 48, 174

identity 17, 139, 175, 177, 178, 186, 208, 225
indigenous knowledge 5, 124, 128, 129, 139, 141
Ingold, T. 68, 69, 104–107, 114, 117, 120, 121, 142, 196, 197
ivory 52–54, 56, 58, 60, 61–63, 67–69, 85

jackal 17, 132–135
jaguar 1, 7, 17, 19, 176

Index

Jones, S. 83, 235, 236

Kii Peninsula 146, 148, 160, 162
King of Nepal 128
kites 174
Kumano 146, 147, 160

landowners 192, 195, 202, 203, 207, 233
Leach, E. 7, 15, 53, 120, 204, 224
leopard 15, 36, 39, 40–42, 47, 55, 64, 69, 78, 79, 87, 89, 90, 93, 94, 97, 126, 128, 130, 131, 133, 135, 174
Lewis, J. 67
lion 1, 2, 4, 16, 17, 19, 22, 23, 36–39, 41, 42, 154, 174, 176
livestock 1, 2, 4, 6, 8, 9, 12, 13, 15, 20, 41, 124, 125, 127, 132, 140, 145, 148, 149, 170, 182, 186, 189, 201, 205–207; bear attacks on 1, 4, 18, 21, 23, 148; fox attacks on 189, 190, 191, 201, 202, 207, 208; leopard attacks on 40, 41, 126; lion attacks on 1, 4, 17, 41; wolf attacks on 179–182
local knowledge 129
lynx 170, 174, 176, 177, 179, 180

magic 4, 52, 65, 69, 78, 94, 112, 113
maize 1, 10, 38, 43, 44, 125–127, 130, 131
Malays 113, 117
Mandingo 18, 83–85, 87, 94, 95
man-eating: bears 149, 150, 153; crocodile 94; hyenas 40, 41; leopards 39, 40; lions 36, 37, 38, 39, 42; tiger 131; wolves 180
masquerades 7, 223
mauling 37, 39–41, 149, 186; bears 149; hyenas 40, 41; leopards 39, 40; lions 37; wolf 186
Mbendjelle Yaka (Pygmies) 67
media 21, 147, 149, 152, 153, 155, 163, 170, 181, 209, 212–214, 216, 223–225, 233, 237
metaphor 69, 120, 187, 224
metonym 176
migrants 18–20, 97, 104, 107, 181, 209, 212–214, 216, 223–225, 233, 237
military 67, 128, 132, 151, 153, 213
millet 4, 126, 127, 130
missionaries 36, 37, 39, 44,45, 87, 91
modernity 53, 70, 155, 187
modernization 155, 157
mòkìlà 50–54, 64–70
monkey-chasing festivals 8
monkeys 1, 38, 44, 48, 86, 125, 126, 130, 146
moral panic 79, 93, 94
morality 10, 16, 17, 81, 84, 115, 191, 233, 242
murder 16, 60, 78, 81, 84, 87, 88, 92, 93, 95, 153, 180, 191
Muslims 52, 62, 83, 110, 113
mutilations 81, 147

narratives 53, 129, 132, 133, 135, 137–140, 153, 174, 219
National Authority for Nature Conservation 181, 182
nature and culture 133
neo-shamanism 19, 20, 170–176, 183–186
New Age movement 19, 20, 171, 173, 185
New World Order 224
nostalgia 219–221

outmigration 150, 161
overkill 208
overpopulation 109
ownership of animals 206, 207

panthers 174
participatory conservation 12, 13, 71
patriotism 96, 214
People for the Ethical Treatment of Animals 223
peregrines 239
persimmons 149, 159
pest control 4, 8, 9, 16, 145, 192, 195, 199–201, 203, 205, 207, 212, 215, 216, 218–220, 225, 227
pets 15, 179, 204, 205, 221
pheasant 132, 133, 201, 206, 207, 238

pigeon: breeding 218, 219, 223, 224; fancying 221; as meat 219, 220; racing 221; shoot 212–225; training 221; trap-and-handle shooting 221, 223, 227
'pigeon gangs' 222
pigeons: damage caused by 9, 215; gassing of 217; poisoning of 217, 220; as 'rats with wings' 9, 216
plantations 9, 148, 149, 160–162
pits 95, 187
poisoning 1, 37, 38, 86, 88, 90, 110, 128, 197, 200, 216, 217, 220
police 24, 38, 87, 151, 152, 161, 163, 182
porcupines 36, 44, 48, 125, 126, 128, 131, 141
potatoes 7, 126, 127, 130, 149
poultry 190, 201, 202, 206, 207
power animals 19, 20, 173–176, 186
pumas 17, 174

rats 1, 2, 6, 9, 14, 16, 140, 208, 216, 239
rattlesnake round-ups 7
reciprocity 16, 69
regulatory predation 6
reincarnation 19, 37, 59
reindeer 12, 16, 19, 21, 23, 170, 177, 180, 181–187
reindeer-herding 12, 19, 23, 170, 177–184
rice 1, 18, 19, 80, 82, 84, 85, 109, 110, 113, 125, 126, 133, 134, 136, 137, 149
rice farming 18, 82
rifle 37, 62, 128, 180, 196, 197, 224
ritual 1, 4, 7, 8, 10, 36, 45, 46, 48, 57, 58, 59, 63, 65, 69, 111, 133, 136, 137, 171–173, 175, 180, 191, 200, 204, 205, 207
ritual associations 58, 65
ritual friendship 137
rodents 1, 6, 16, 48
Royal Society for the Protection of Birds (RSPB) 233, 239

Saami 12, 16, 18, 21, 23, 170, 171, 177–187

schema theory 104, 117–121
shaman 20, 131, 170, 174, 175, 184, 186
shamanic journeys 172
shamanism 170–173, 184, 185
shapeshifting 17–20, 50–54, 64–67, 70, 181; as a hunting technique 52, 64; power of 19, 50, 64, 65; psychological appeal of 54; secret shapeshifting society 54
sheep 1, 41, 126, 130, 133, 135, 187, 201, 206
sheep farmers 201
shepherds 1, 21, 187
slavery 18, 83–87, 95
soil fertility 110
soldiers 96
sorcery 17, 64, 65, 67, 84, 93
Souanké District 52, 56, 60, 61
spears 37, 62, 64, 130
species richness 241
spirits 10, 51, 57–59, 65, 67, 69, 106, 110–112, 114, 118, 140, 146, 153, 154, 172–174, 176
sport 46, 189, 190–192, 194, 196, 203, 205, 207, 213
sports hunting 196, 204
state 2, 21–23, 109, 127, 129, 132, 137, 173, 177, 181, 182, 185, 214
stigmatization 97
sweet potatoes 149
swidden fields 4, 7, 9, 113, 117, 121, 128

Talang Mamak 113, 115, 116, 119
terrierman 194, 195
terriers 194, 195
terror 37–39, 43, 54, 133
thief 15, 16, 90, 117, 134, 152, 180, 182, 191, 192; bear as 152; fox as 191, 192; wolf as 16, 182
tigers 1, 4, 6, 17, 19, 131, 132, 140, 145, 174, 176
timber 9, 114, 128, 132, 148–151, 160–163
tourists 124, 142, 147, 150, 157
Trans-species Unlimited Inc. 216, 223
traps 1, 45, 58, 131, 152, 213, 224
tricksters 15, 133

UK Ruddy Duck Working Group (UKRDWG) 230–232
utilitarianism 13, 216

vermin 3, 9, 14–16, 47, 189–192, 195, 202, 204, 208
victim 2, 37–39, 50, 65, 66, 81, 88, 91, 93, 153, 156, 163, 181–183, 186; bear as 160–162; duck as 235; fox as 208; pigeon as 219–221; wolf as 183
village abandonment 38, 56, 158
violence 8, 15, 17–19, 21, 59, 64, 66, 68, 70,79, 80, 81, 84, 94, 95, 163, 197, 205, 208, 224, 225
vulpicide 203

war 17, 19, 20, 39, 45, 66, 85, 86, 95, 96, 98, 151
warfare 66, 67, 70, 181; and raiding 66
weeds 4, 14
Western concept of nature 242
whales 14, 174
wheat 125–127, 130
white supremacy 213
wild pigs 1, 2,4, 7, 13, 14, 17–19, 42, 44, 48, 104, 109, 110, 114–116, 118, 120, 126, 127–131, 140, 142; hunting of 106, 107, 110, 113, 128, 129
wild yam 57; paracultivation of 57
wildebeest 47
wilderness 14, 37, 113, 141, 163, 170, 187
wildfowl 230–232
Wildfowl and Wetlands Trust (WWT) 232, 233
witchcraft 51, 54, 59, 64, 65, 67, 82, 84, 88, 90, 92, 94; accusations 82, 88, 92; associations 64, 65, 67
wolf/wolves 12, 19, 20, 22, 23, 42, 155, 170, 173–175, 170, 180–187; attacks on livestock 179–182; hunting of 7, 8, 170, 175, 177, 180; magical power of 180, 181
wolverine 170, 179, 180, 184
World Wide Fund for Nature (WWF) 237

xenophobia 21, 24, 242

youth 39, 79, 87, 92, 95–98, 160, 234

zombification 66, 67
zoophobia 24, 132, 141